MINNIJEAN BROWN-TRICKEY

DOUTZEN KROES

MINA TOLU

BLAKE MYCOSKIE

SINÉAD BURKE

EH BEE FAMILY

STEVE WAUGH

KENNY IMAFIDON

LISA BLOOM

BOB GELDOF

THULI MADONSELA

TARA HOUSKA

MARY ROBINSON

SHAHIDUL ALAM

JAZZ JENNINGS

KUMI NAIDOO

NIMCO ALI

PAUL POLMAN

TAWAKKOL KARMAN

LUKE HART

WINNIE BYANYIMA

DERAY MCKESSON

NICOLLE FAGAN

JACK SIM

DAME VIVIAN HUNT

KEVIN MENDEZ

KEVIN WATKINS

TERRY CREWS

COLIN KAEPERNICK

SIMON RODGERS

SIR KEN ROBINSON

CAROLE STONE

CAMERON KASKY

PAT QUINN

EMMA WATSON

YEONMI PARK

FATIMA BHUTTO

GINA MILLER

IF NOT YOU, WHO?
IF NOT NOW, WHEN?

KATE & ELLA ROBERTSON

To Bruce and Josh
who make all the difference in the world to us

An Hachette UK Company
www.hachette.co.uk

First published in Great Britain in 2019 by Cassell, an imprint of
Octopus Publishing Group Ltd
Carmelite House
50 Victoria Embankment
London EC4Y 0DZ
www.octopusbooks.co.uk

ISBN (Hardback): 978 1 78840 146 3
ISBN (Paperback): 978 1 78840 202 6
A CIP catalogue record for this book is available from the British Library.

Printed and bound in UK
10 9 8 7 6 5 4 3 2 1

Cover designer: James Jones
Typesetter: Jack Storey

Contents

Foreword by Kofi Annan

We feel that this book would not be complete without including some of the wisdom embodied and shared with us by Kofi Annan over the years. He was a staunch supporter of One Young World, and as such we would like to share quotes from his various speeches and question and answer sessions at our One Young World events, as he may no longer be with us but his vision and approach are more relevant today than ever before.

Activism for the young, Johannesburg, 2013

'I hope to share some of the lessons on leadership from my own experiences and career. I was fortunate to have served as UN Secretary-General soon after the Cold War, during a period of significant global change. My goal has always been to inspire people, especially young people, to step forward and take responsibility for the future of their societies and the wider, global community.

You are inheriting a rapidly changing world with problems of unprecedented scale and complexity. These challenges affect us all. Today, for example, many young people face serious obstacles to realizing their full potential because of poverty, insecurity, unemployment, environmental stress, and conflict. However, you are also blessed with unique strengths: information and communication technologies make you the most aware and interconnected generation. Social media platforms are providing you with opportunities to organize, mobilize, advocate, and create.

You have the knowledge and the tools to seize new opportunities and have an impact beyond the borders of your own countries. Unfortunately, you are inheriting a world from a generation of political leaders, my generation, who have largely failed to address the global imbalances and institutional failures that are the cause of so many of our problems today. You must never doubt your own capacity to triumph where others have failed.

You have to work and think about how we can make this world a better place for all. For I have always maintained that you are never too young to lead. Young people must take ownership and leadership of tomorrow. For that to happen, you have to strengthen your capacity and widen your horizons as global citizens. Good global citizenship begins in the community: be it a village or a school where you can team up with others to resolve problems, but you must also be aware that your activities could have an impact on people thousands of miles away. By acting locally and thinking globally you can lead the way towards a fairer more secure world.'

Peace building, Dublin, 2014

'Young people are especially vulnerable to and disproportionately affected by violence and conflict. They are caught up in and victimized by violence as child soldiers, gang members, or as refugees or migrants. Yet, you the young are also amongst the most determined peacemakers and the most effective agents of reconciliation.

Why? Because you realize that we are all in the same boat. You cannot have peace nor prosper at the expense of the other. You understand that real peace-building is conflict prevention, and that reconciling grievances is an investment in your future. You are more aware than previous generations of the complexities of conflict. You have an array of tools, in particular, social media, to help you shine light on causes of conflict whatever and wherever they may be.

You understand that genuine peace is the sum of many small actions by many individual people all across the globe. Each of us sometimes have our little bit to do. As the first truly global generations, truly global citizens, you know better than anyone that cultural, religious and ethnic diversity can be a source of strength, not only a source of division.

From my own experience in dealing with conflict, I firmly believe that young people must be empowered as agents and not simply as targets for peace and reconciliation efforts. Some of you may be focused on these challenges. Let me suggest a few questions you may ponder as you work on this issue:

The first question is, how can we ensure that underrepresented groups such as women and young people are active in political life in general and peace processes in particular?

Second, how can activists help create an understanding that peace and justice are two sides of the same coin?

Third, how can young people help build strong institutions that create trust among people, especially in societies recovering from conflict?

Fourth, how can we strengthen the institutions of global governments and make them better able to respond to threats to international peace and security?

Finally, how can activists hold leaders to account and ensure that they serve their democratic duties responsibly? These are challenging questions, but I'm confident that you will find the answers as you have done already by bringing about positive changes in your own local communities. I'm confident too that you will build on those successes to construct a more secure and fairer world for all.'

Peace building, Dublin, 2014

'Define your objectives, organize and make things happen – you have the capacity. You have to find like-minded people like you, band together, work together and decide what would be the most effective way to achieve your objective. Would it entail writing into your parliamentarians? Would it entail a mini demonstration and going to speak to your representatives in their offices? It will almost certainly entail getting other people together and saying, "Let's do something about this together and when we act, others will follow.

We should focus on the issues of tomorrow, which are your issues and you are the ones who are going to live with the consequences. Don't leave it only to the politicians, you should reach out and engage. You have the capacity to do it, so don't sit back and say, "They are not talking to us, they are not paying attention to us." Make sure they know you are there. Make sure they are paying attention to you.

Don't feel that because you are young, people will not listen to you or you cannot lead. As I've said time and time again, you are never too young to lead. If the idea is good and the objective is clear, you will be able to lead and you will get the support necessary, but of course when you say, "Where do we go for support?" You must also know what support you need to be able to articulate it and make demands.

You'll be surprised the support does not necessarily have to come from the government. Sometimes, people in your own community, some of the companies in your community will be inspired by what you are doing and support you through donations, or through offering facilities to make your work successful. There will be resistance: some may think *these young people are being uppity and jumping ahead of themselves.* You should be able to take that on the chin and continue – don't let it dissuade you.

It's extremely important that intergenerational dialogue takes place, that in committees, either on a local or on a national level, we should find ways of bringing in various generations so that the next generation is ready to take over. The difficulty we've had in our world, when you look at politics especially, is that those who achieve power hold on and hold on for too long – sometimes they don't want to move at all – so they do not create space that includes others and allows young people to come up and participate.

This is a problem that we need to do something about. I keep saying, "Let's bring in the next generation." We are all aging. Tomorrow we'll all be gone and you don't want to create a vacuum. You need to have continuity and you can only have it by bringing in young people and relying on their energy, their ideas and working with them to move forward.

A bad leader is easy to describe. You see leaders who do not listen, who believe they are always right, who are stubborn, who, in some cases, even when the decision is patently wrong, can not only not change the direction but refuses to listen to all this. You have to be open as a leader, you have to learn to listen, and a leader need not always be right. A good leader is also a good follower, you must remember that.'

Climate change, Bangkok, 2015

'Climate change is the greatest contemporary challenge facing our global community; we are rapidly approaching the tipping point beyond which climate change may become irreversible. And no other issue will have a greater impact on the well-being and security of future generations; your health, your security. It will take all of your creativity, vision and determination to find and implement effective solutions.

You will need to work together with your peers from around the world to convince today's leaders that they must act swiftly and decisively to secure the safety of our planet. Our priorities must be to secure clear and strong commitments on climate finance, a mechanism to assess collective progress, and the enabling conditions for the introduction of a global carbon price so that every country can reach a state of carbon neutrality by 2050. I am confident this can be achieved.

It is a moral outrage that 30% of food produced for human consumption is spoiled or squandered every year. Even if just one fourth of it could be saved, it would be enough to feed the 870 million hungry people in the world. Hundreds of millions of our fellow human beings also lack access to both water and energy, which are cornerstones of economic progress and poverty alleviation. The growing impact of climate change is exacerbating these challenges and risks pushing millions more into abject poverty and hunger. And as always, it is the world's poorest who are paying the highest price.

Together you can proclaim loud and clear that no target is too ambitious to reach, no obstacle too hard to overcome. Your call on climate action will make it clear to the world that the activists of today -the leaders of tomorrow- simply will not accept failure

You have an unparalleled capacity to catalyse constructive change. You must now show the world how you plan to rise to this responsibility, and show us how you will re-shape our global community, and your future, for the better.

What I will plead with all of you, is not to be afraid. I know that's easier said than done. I faced this at one time in my career, when Bin Laden put a price on my head because of my views and work on East Timor. I pushed very hard for the independence of East Timor and he claimed that this criminal, Kofi Annan was breaking apart, the largest Islamic state in the world, by taking East Timor away from Indonesia, and therefore I must be punished. There would be a certain amount of gold for whomever succeeded in killing me.

I had to decide – should I withdraw to protect myself or should I keep working? If I withdrew, what would have happened to the problems I was dealing with, to the people who were looking to me for leadership, to the people who were expecting me to stand up for the problems that they were facing?

Yes, we need to be careful, we need to be conscious of our environment and not take undue risks, but we should not be intimidated to the extent that we cease to live or give our leaders a free hand to take some of our liberties away, promising in exchange, security. I've seen many situations, where governments have promised security, where they have been repressive and things seemed very stable. In the end, repression is not stability, down the line it explodes.

Often, when governments promise security, they want trade-offs. They sometimes tell us we have to give up a bit of our freedom for security. In my judgment, it's a very slippery slope. We have to be careful. There's very little trade-off between security and liberty. If you are asked to give up your liberty for security and you do give up that liberty, do you, in the end, have security?

Terrorists and oppressors share a strategy. Their strategy is to instill fear, to intimidate and we should make sure they do not succeed. Not only should we make sure they do not succeed, we should also be consistent and uncompromising with our own values. Values of freedom, values of liberty, values of freedom of expression and association.

Let me repeat, you are never too young to lead. You must remember that and you should act and take charge where you can. I would urge you all to remember the words of Dr. Luther Martin King Jr., who reminded us that in spite of temporary victories, violence never brings peace. Put your remarkable energy, your insight, your passion in the service of reconciliation and peace. It can start at the most personal level, but small steps lead towards a better future.'

Kofi Annan (1938–2018)
Secretary-General of the United Nations (1997–2006)

Foreword by David Jones

If you are reading this book, chances are you are keen to make a difference. As the world's leaders stoop to new lows in terms of their ability to divide us and to ignore the existential threats to our planet, we are overwhelmed, firstly, by the sense that we must do something. We must act. And secondly, by the thought which quickly follows, equally powerful and concerning, Yes, but what can I do? I'm only one person. How can I make a difference?

This book is full of the stories of individuals who were just one person. But whose actions, ideas and initiatives have gone on to create major change.

Kate and Ella Robertson, the book's authors, are exceptionally talented, powerful, smart and generous leaders, both of whom I have had the pleasure of working with – in Kate's case for almost three decades and in Ella's for nearly one decade.

Two exceptional leaders

Kate's energy and drive to make a difference in the world came from growing up in Apartheid-era South Africa. And it was reinforced by one of Africa's great statesman, Kofi Annan. He was a huge influence on us and on One Young World and was in fact our first ever Counsellor. He was also one of the greatest examples of someone making a difference. And he was tireless in his pursuit of driving positive change in the world, right up until the day he sadly left us. Kate and I first met Kofi Annan back in 2008 when we helped him with his global climate campaign. He was the wisest and most impressive leader I've ever met. One of his favourite sayings was, 'You're never too old to learn nor too young to lead.' I can still hear his soft yet powerful voice saying it – he once remarked that the reason he spoke so softly was to make people listen.

Kate is the heart of One Young World. Its soul and guiding force. Someone who never stands still and who is always looking to make sure One Young World is at the absolute forefront of the issues facing the world. She has vast knowledge across so many subject areas – I personally keep abreast of what I need to know on any issue through Kate. Some people after rising to a senior level become know-it-alls. Kate is a learn-it-all. And she has imbued her teams with her attitude. She is a brilliant strategist who knows exactly what needs to be changed and who needs to be influenced in order to make something happen. And that is how she has been able to make a difference.

Ella is the irrepressible energy behind One Young World. Relentlessly driving it forward. Refusing to think that anything is impossible. She's the living embodiment of Kofi's statement that you are never too young to lead. To watch her operate and lead people who are often many years older than her, is a lesson in how to make a difference in itself. It's easy to forget that she is still in her twenties. It's perhaps fitting that such a great example of a young leader is one of the key reasons that One Young World has become such a powerful platform, or to quote Vice, 'The world's largest and most impactful youth leadership summit.'

And it's very fitting that the two of them, who form such a great team that has taken One Young World to where it is today, and who both in their lives have made a real difference, have shared their learnings and those of other great leaders young and old in this book.

How making a difference has changed

One of the key subjects this book covers and one of the great advantages that anyone wanting to make a difference today has, is technology. The industrial revolution empowered corporations, the digital and social revolution has empowered people. It allows anyone with access to technology to create a major global movement around the issues and subjects they care about changing. It has enabled a single individual to be a force for massive change. And it has mobilized communities of people to do the same. From Greta Thunberg's climate action to the #Metoo movement or Black Lives Matter.

What technology has also done is create a unique generation of young leaders. This is the first time in human history that the youngest leaders actually have a superpower that older leaders don't. Technology has created the most educated, the most knowledgeable, the most socially responsible, but above all the most powerful generation of young people we have ever seen. They understand better than anyone how to use the power of digital and social media to drive real change in the world.

Young leaders and making a difference

This was the very reason we created One Young World in 2010. To give these exceptional leaders a bigger platform to drive change in the world. And while it is easy to be despondent about the behaviour of the world's senior leaders, we can all draw hope and inspiration from some of the incredible young leaders who are stepping up to fill the giant leadership vacuum.

There are huge lessons to be learned from them: from Yeonmi Park's courage to share her experience of defecting from North Korea, to

Cameron Kasky's dedication to end gun violence, to the bravery of Loujain al-Hathloul (who has been unable to contribute to this book due to being unjustly imprisoned throughout the writing process) and her fellow activists in getting women the right to drive in Saudi Arabia.

This amazing generation is also driving major change and making a difference across the business world both directly and indirectly. Smart businesses today understand that this generation is wired differently. They know that unless they behave responsibly, unless as a business they have a genuine purpose beyond profit, then this generation will no longer buy their products and will no longer work for them.

One great example in the book of a leader who knows this is Paul Polman, the chair of the One Young World advisory board. Paul has led the way to drive businesses to be more socially responsible. In doing so he has demonstrated that doing good and doing well don't belong to different universes, but rather doing good is the new price of doing well. As proof of that, Unilever's purpose-led brands have outperformed the rest of the portfolio. And increasingly, in a world where social media has taken CSR out of the silo and put it firmly into the P&L statement, progressive businesses understand that if they are socially responsible, they will indeed perform better.

In this book there are many examples of progressive businesses and leaders who made a difference. And you will also see evidence of a new trend. In recent times, what has become very clear is that brands need to take a stand for something. That matters more and more, especially to young people.

If in this decade we've talked a lot about business moving from profit to purpose, the next decade will be about moving from purpose to activism – from marketing to consumers, to mattering to people. From Nike's incredibly powerful work with Colin Kaepernick to combat racism, to Blake Mycoskie and TOMS setting out to end gun violence, to Patagonia giving back the tax cuts they'd received to climate change charities, 21st-century brands are genuinely trying to make a difference in the world.

Reading this book will allow you to spend a few hours learning from Kate and Ella Robertson. They've both made a huge difference in the world, and to those of us they lead. And I have no doubt they will inspire you to do the same

And to quote our motto at One Young World: 'Here's to a bright future.'

David Jones,
Co-founder, One Young World

Introduction

We are living in an Age of Activism. From the Women's March to the Ice Bucket Challenge, in our increasingly connected world people are finding more and more ways to make their voice heard and make a difference. As we know more about the world around us and gain new tools to change it, flames are being lit in even the darkest of places.

Activism is making aspects of our lives which once seemed cast-iron, fluid: who would have thought a bunch of teenagers from a town of 30,000 people in Florida would be able to threaten the multi-billion-dollar gun industry in America? Or that a 15-year-old girl in Sweden would challenge the fossil fuel industry, sparking climate strikes across the globe? At the very time of writing, a new Arab spring has emerged in Algeria and Sudan. The long-time Sudanese president Omar Al Bashir has been ousted from office by thousands of protestors, as has the Algerian president Abdelaziz Bouteflika.

Many consider this fluidity to create an era of uncertainty: activism is certainly rearing its head at the polar ends of the political spectrum. From Sanders to Trump, Brexit to Momentum, Italy to Mexico… many of the most remarkable campaigns of our age have embraced the activist spirit.

There are two main reactions to uncertainty: fear and optimism. Fear tends to be felt by the establishment and the economists; which is, of course, perfectly natural. But at a time where so much of the media seems to be telling us the sky is falling in, we find tremendous hope and inspiration in knowing that brave, brilliant people are overturning the status quo and fighting to make the world a better place.

Our work at One Young World has allowed us to get to know some of the world's greatest activists who have used their voices, their networks and their abilities to change communities, companies and countries. From the historic – legalizing driving for women in Saudi Arabia – to the personal – ensuring their children had lawful access to the medication they needed – we know that every individual can make a tremendous difference to the world around them.

It was from our need to empower more and more people to believe that they could make a difference, that the idea for this book emerged: where the force of all OYW ambassadors could be combined to form a practical roadmap to making a difference at scale and with lasting results.

Along the way we have spoken to a global team of change-makers who have walked the walk – from statesmen-like President Santos and President

Mary Robinson, to protestors like Joshua Wong who have been jailed for speaking the truth. We have scoured the globe to bring together the best advice and inspiration in order to create this definitive guide to activism in the 21st century.

Anyone with a vision knows they're going to need help. In this practical book we have combined the latest thinking and current wisdom. You'll find advice on how to build the team you need to make a difference, and stories from other people who have made a huge impact. We've asked activists where they went right and also where they made mistakes. Hopefully, they'll inspire you and show that even the most daunting of tasks is possible if you set your mind to it. While there is a lot to learn from the advice within these pages, the one overriding message is: you can do it.

What is One Young World?

Every year One Young World convenes thousands of activists to work together to accelerate change. Its annual Summit brings together the most talented young leaders from across 196 countries to tackle the globe's most pressing issues, from climate change to conflict resolution.

One Young World's mission is to create the next generation of more responsible and effective leadership. Kate Robertson and David Jones founded One Young World in 2010 because they believed, at the time, that there was a leadership vacuum amongst world leaders – this picture has worsened in the last decade. One Young World finds the brightest young people with proven track records of leadership and convenes them with inspiring figures: the One Young World Counsellors.

One Young World is actively supported by a distinguished line-up of Counsellors, including Kofi Annan, Bill Clinton, Prime Minister Justin Trudeau, President Mary Robinson, Juan Manuel Santos, Bob Geldof, Archbishop Desmond Tutu, Emma Watson, Meghan Markle and Professor Muhammad Yunus. Counsellors work alongside delegates at the global Summits, sharing their collective experience in creating positive social change.

Since launching in 2010, One Young World has built a network of over 10,000 Ambassadors, whose projects have gone on to benefit more than 20 million people worldwide. After the Summit, the young leaders become One Young World Ambassadors, charged with returning to their countries and accelerating change. You'll meet many of them within these pages.

Who is in this book?

Through the One Young World network we have reached out to people we believe are making a difference in a variety of innovative and meaningful ways. We interviewed more than one hundred people in the course of writing this book and nearly seventy of them have contributed to these pages.

Activism may be having a moment but it's not a new phenomenon. That's why we've done our best to give a historic overview with contributions dating back to the Civil Rights Movement and bringing us up to date ahead of One Young World's tenth anniversary in 2019.

We have asked them for their most tangible, practical advice for people wanting to make a difference. We've tried to frame this advice in such a way as to really answer the question: 'How can I make a difference today?'

You'll find advice on simple things such as amplifying your message with social media, as well as more complicated issues such as whistleblowing and crisis management. We know that not every activist is marching in the streets or navigating the halls of Westminster or Washington – you'll hear about how you can make a difference whether at a local level or on an international scale.

We know that local activism is more interconnected than ever – that's why we've gone to great lengths to represent every continent in the accounts you will read. We have included often marginalized voices, with advocates who have disabilities and members of indigenous communities contributing their wisdom.

Our ultimate hope is that you will see yourself in this book somewhere – we've done everything we can to show off as vibrant and diverse a pageant of examples as possible. Activism is for everyone and we want all of our readers to know that they have a part to play. Young, old, left-wing, right-wing… if we are going to solve the climate crisis, balance gender inequality, end poverty…we're going to need everyone to be involved.

Is this book political?

Activism is inherently political. Political systems must be engaged with and reformed in order to bring about the change you require. We reject, however, the notion that activism belongs to the left or the right.

There are activists at all points on the political spectrum and many of them are working for the good of the planet and other people. Activism doesn't necessarily have a natural home at one particular point on the spectrum. We find conservatives who are passionately working to end the blight of female genital mutilation; we find those on the left who wish to lower regulatory levels for businesses so they can employ more people.

Some people wish to make activism exclusory – they will only welcome people of certain political beliefs to march alongside them. We understand their desire to purge their cause of hypocrites, but we fundamentally believe that a broader movement achieves more, and that greater tolerance leads to greater and wider understanding.

We have also seen unlikely alliances throughout the history of activism. In London 1984–5, the LBGT community fundraised for the miners striking in Wales, and the miners then marched at Pride.

We would encourage people to leave their political, social or cultural labels at home and take each person as you find them. If anyone is willing to support your cause, we recommend embracing them: none of us is perfect but we can all learn from each other as we grow as activists.

Making the right kind of difference

A message that we hope you'll take away from this book is that there is no wrong field of activism. However big or small your cause, what will enable you to be successful is your passion and determination. Our purpose in life isn't always logical: there is no reason why we may care more about cancer than wildlife or more about plastic pollution than HIV. Whatever you are passionate about is the cause you should pursue. Do not be shamed into thinking your cause is too small to matter or too big to take on. You shouldn't be afraid to care and campaign about a local issue because 'children are dying in Yemen'; just as you shouldn't fear becoming an activist for peace in Yemen because it feels too far away and beyond your conception.

What we warn against, however, is jumping on a bandwagon without examining the ultimate consequences of your actions. For example, orphanages have now been recognized as a major source of trafficking and exploitation, yet many well-meaning volunteers and donors continue to fund an industry that is ultimately harmful to children. Many people, similarly, organize massive recycling drives without ensuring that the refuse they diligently sort is actually recycled, as opposed to being shipped to a landfill in Malaysia.

The other warning we offer is around the concept of allyship. We believe activism is at its very best and most powerful when it is as inclusive as possible. We know that many voices are often marginalized in mainstream activism and that well-intentioned activists often try and speak up on behalf of the unheard. We've spoken to many people about what allyship means to them and they counsel all activists to ensure that they are giving a platform to the voices who need it, rather than simply being the voice themselves. Unheard voices need to be heard in their own right.

Our final word of warning that we would like to counsel against is violent protest. We know that one man's freedom fighter is another man's terrorist and we've thought long and hard about our stance on this. We have spoken to activists who have been involved in violent and non-violent protest and also read a lot of the latest research on this difficult topic. Ultimately, we believe protest and activism is more successful when it's peaceful – it is easier to justify and it usually achieves more sustainable, applicable results. We understand that civil disobedience may be a part of an effective protest but our guidance will remain that it should always be peaceful and not bring any harm to other people.

There is no right form of activism – the courage to make a difference comes from the deepest part of our souls, it cannot be prescribed. There is no rhyme or reason behind what drives us to sacrifice our time, our energy (sometimes our sanity) for a certain cause, but the human capacity to channel our efforts and ingenuity into making the world a fairer and safer place is one of the most remarkable things about our species. The prevalence of this spirit in our current era is what will make the 21st century remarkable.

What is 'effective' activism?

The people in this book are the people who we consider to be the most effective activists in the world. They are people we believe have made an effective change.

What do we mean by this? In some cases they will have succeeded in changing the law, ending a war or bringing about a revolution. Change on a massive and historic scale. In other cases, the change is humbler but no less critical – we all need to take responsibility for making our communities cleaner, our schools better, our neighbours safer.

We want this book to be a guide for those who want to change their communities as well as the people who want to change the world around them. We encourage everyone to dream as big as you dare – none of the people in this book thought they would change the world but so many of them have. Activists never begin by wanting to make history – they begin by identifying a problem and setting out to put it right.

No one says you can make a difference without putting in any effort. What they do say is that you CAN make a difference and that it is truly worth the effort.

And we know this from experience: One Young World was an idea on the back on a napkin and it now spans every single country in the world and impacts the lives of millions of people. In turn, the young leaders who have attended One Young World have left feeling empowered to go and make change themselves – some at a local level and some on a massive multi-national scale.

Chapter One
How to find a cause that matters to you

'Activism' has become a mainstream activity that our increasingly socially conscious society pushes us to engage with. At its heart, activism is seeing something wrong or unjust in the world and using the means available to you to try and do something about it, whether it is a community cause or a historic injustice.

For some people the idea of having to *find* a cause may seem incongruous. And often, causes find their activists before the activists find them – activists didn't even know they were *looking* for a cause when their day-to-day existence becomes irrevocably changed by devastation that has directly affected them or that they have witnessed.

For others the process is more circumspect: they have the time, energy or perhaps the money to make a difference, but, in a world where so many problems exist and so many causes are worthy, deciding which channel to pursue is difficult.

What matters to you and the difference you can make might be in your immediate surroundings: local community issues and injustices are often where activism begins, where change can be felt by those around you impactfully.

In fact, finding a cause that matters to you can give your life a deeper sense of purpose and fulfilment. Occupying your mind with a cause can create energy and dynamism in every aspect of your daily life. As humans we are perennially fixed on what our life's legacy will be, and finding a cause or making change often can be felt for generations after our own. Because of this, activism may be the most important thing you ever do for yourself. Indeed, many activists feel they are helping themselves even more than they are helping their cause. The sense of clarity and direction you experience allows you to achieve a higher level of performance and success. It can help reduce stress, improve emotional well-being and even benefit our physical health too.

In *How to Make a Difference* we want to debunk the notion that activism is a lofty activity or a higher calling – real change is made by ordinary folk trying to improve the world one person and one change at a time. In this chapter we want to showcase how, in a universe swirling with charity campaigns, digital demands and political dissatisfaction, you can still align your personal passions and talents with a cause which can make a big difference to this busy and often self-serving world.

The history of activism

We all have our own idea of what activism is; after all, one person's terrorist is another man's freedom fighter. Indeed, the history of activism is varied and complex, as are the protagonists involved, but certain themes and tropes keep cropping up. You can correlate recent movements like the Women's March or Black Lives Matter with earlier swells such as the French Revolution, because any injustice – the deliberate and structural degradation and disenfranchisement of various groups in society, and the inequality that creates – has historically given rise to the need for activism from the 'common' people. Be it political or be it legal, unfairness is, in its very nature, in opposition with our humanity.

There are common themes that have run through most major revolutions since written records began – across civilizations and across the globe. The convoluted processes of revolutions develop when the social order becomes strained and disrupted in several ways all at once, which leads to widespread anger at injustice. This injustice usually manifests itself in economic deprivation for some, while an elite class seems uncaring and alienated from the masses. The anger created by this injustice boils over into revolution from the public.

Successful protests have a shared message which unifies a section of society. This tends to be propagated by charismatic leaders who are able to communicate efficiently with their supporters such as Gandhi's Salt March in 1930 and Bernie Sanders's 'Feel The Bern' 2016 presidential campaign. Although many revolutions might seem to have an ephemeral trigger, it is the years of oppression which went before that gave rise to the outburst of action. For example, the fatal shooting of unarmed Michael Brown sparked the Ferguson Uprising in 2014, but the situation exploded because of decades of building tension within a system that burdens the poor and black. And added to this was the historically highly problematic relations between the police in Missouri and the African-American population. As early as Aristotle, it was noted that 'poverty is the parent of revolution' – when society and institutions preside over desolation and misery, rage flourishes. When peaceful dialogue is ignored, violence becomes inexorable.

Activism can also be contagious: United States founding father Thomas Jefferson proclaimed that France had 'been awakened by our Revolution'. What was known as the Arab Spring spread from country to country following Tunisia's Jasmine Revolution which saw the removal of dictator Zine El Abidine Ben Ali and a move to free and democratic elections. Many 21st-century movements have spread because their message or symbolism can be watched by millions – videos, posts and images can go viral across the internet in seconds – and these messages fundamentally strike a chord with people from different places: from Black Lives Matter, to the Occupy movement, to the *Gilets Jaunes* and the School Strike for Climate.

Unfortunately, most people only think about injustice when it happens to them, or in front of them, which is why many of the most powerful revolutions start quietly, in the shadows. They are treated as extremist and fanatical at the time, and later, usually, regarded as historical inevitabilities.

The overwhelming reaction that we have when we witness or experience unfairness and injustice is a universal human response and it's one of our strongest, earliest emotions. In a 2007 study, monkeys were found to invest less energy in a task if they saw other monkeys receiving better rewards for the same task. Frans de Waal at the Yerkes National Primate Research Center in Atlanta, Georgia, trained 13 capuchin monkeys to retrieve a small rock and place it in the experimenter's hands. In exchange for completing the task, the animals received a reward. When the monkeys given a cucumber saw their partners receive the preferred grape reward, they invested less effort in future repetitions of the task. This confirmed that the monkeys reacted to what they deemed to be fair and unfair treatment. This demonstrates how ingrained our reaction to fairness is; indeed, this experiment seems to suggest it is more of an instinct than an emotion.

There is a societal pride in standing up for what's right. Almost two thousand years ago, the imperial philosopher Seneca counselled that 'injustice never rules forever'. The world has more recently been seized by the fervour of *Hamilton*, which celebrates the possibility of 'the world turned upside down' – we revel in the downfall of tyrants and the rise of fairness.

Over the years, activism has become democratized and mass-disseminated. It has become easier for people to discover a cause or join the swell. The power of communicating to millions of people, which used to only be afforded to politicians, the wealthy or entertainers in the 20th century, has become available to anyone with a smartphone.

The heroes of activism have historically been the downtrodden and the underserved. Those have been traditionally the people who, through speaking out or refusing to desist, have relentlessly forced the arc of history towards progress.

There is no one way; no correct route. The key word is action.

Overcome apathy with enthusiasm

Our human psyche has evolved to avert our gaze from the homeless person on the street because we cannot give money to every homeless person we encounter. We tune out the charity campaigns because we cannot text to send £5 every time we see an advert asking for donations. We pass over 99 per cent of the news stories that we come across about Yemen or the Congo because they are overwhelming and we feel helpless when faced with them – there's seemingly nothing to be done.

Globalization has brought every world issue onto our humble doorstep. We are bombarded with more problems than ever but often feel less and less equipped to tackle them. Traditional community structures are neglected or underused: our village halls and religious institutions are often empty. This in turn has given rise to new problems: the loneliness of the elderly and the rise of mental health concerns, as people flounder without the human support networks of past generations.

People can be apathetic because of an overabundance of information and less and less time. They don't feel that they can make a difference. They feel increasingly insignificant and redundant in the face of a fast-paced world. Yet, one person is *still* enough. **If not you, who? If not now, when?** Every journey starts with a step; every big difference is made by an initial small difference: it's better to throw yourself in at some point than stay on the sidelines forever.

Just by taking the plunge into activism, you begin to make a difference and immediately gain energy from the work, as pointed out by singer, songwriter and political activist **Bob Geldof**. His activism has created widespread public anger and engagement on issues such as famine and Ebola, which had seemed previously too remote to care about:

> When you are engaged in humanitarian work, your enthusiasm (if that's the word) comes from just being able to help a little in making another person's life a bit better. With the advancements in health, technology and education, that sometimes makes it 'easier' to do.
>
> We are often focused on the obstacles and overly negative landscape, but the empirical reality is that things for the poor, dispossessed, powerless and less economically developed peoples of the world are improving. It is important to maintain that momentum and indeed that hope and optimism in your activism. However, it is also important to remember the imbecilic and terrible inequality, the vast poverty and unfairness that still exists in many, many parts of the world today. These problems are an affront and frankly stupid, and we must continue to confront and challenge them.
>
> Contrary to the cynic's excuse for doing nothing - 'What's the point, nothing changes?' - the world is in a constant state of flux. The point must be to help usher that change in the direction that benefits the poor and therefore the planet in general. It has never been easier to help guide and steer that change. What is required is the will and the commitment.

We often hear 'Me? I'm not political. I've never been on a protest before.' It doesn't matter. You don't have to care about every issue in order to be an activist. You don't have to have been on lots of protests to attend *this* rally. There's never a bad or a right time to get started and become informed.

There's something truly special about the transformative effect of joining a cause for the first time, whenever you come to it in the course of your life. It's never too soon to be an activist and it's never too late.

When it comes to picking a cause, you don't have to be personally affected by the issue but you have to personally care deeply about it. It should be a cause you feel passionately about, that you could talk about for hours, and which chimes with your own beliefs in inequality or injustice.

When all is perfect, there is no story to tell

You don't have to have something bad happen to you to be an activist. However, if something has happened to you and you feel a sense of injustice about it, or you feel that there is something you can do to prevent it from happening to other people, your experience will make you a very powerful advocate.

That power has a responsibility attached to it. Your story will be listened to and taken seriously because it happened to you. A lot of people are scared about using their personal stories and about discussing a cause that matters to them, because it's the terrible illness, it's the assault, it's the accident, it's the crime, it's the loss of someone they care about.

While it may be difficult to share some of the worst times of your life with the whole world, if you don't tell your story who else will?

Luke Hart became an activist because his mother and sister's voices were missing from the coverage of their murder:

> In every report, there was speculation that the prospect of divorce 'drove' our father to murder, implying we were responsible for our father's actions. One report stated that the murder of our sister and mother was 'understandable'. Even among close female friends of our mother, numerous rationalizations were performed on our

father's behalf. Close friends and neighbours asked if she'd had an affair, in their attempts to somehow justify his behaviour. Our murdering father was eulogized in the press despite the fact he had been abusive to our family for 25 years. We felt as if we had to listen to our father's voice through the media, even in death. This experience made us commit to raising our voices on my mother and sister's behalf and on behalf of all silenced victims, to ensure victims' stories are heard and understood.

I realized if I did not speak someone else would potentially discuss domestic abuse and violence on national and international media networks incorrectly. Our story had already received a lot of press coverage, so we decided to take action.

The power of your story shouldn't be ignored. The impact of trauma shouldn't be underestimated. A story people can empathize with and be moved by is much more impactful than a leaflet or a case study. Using your pain and applying it to a situation will bring people to your cause and create understanding, awareness, care and compassion that might otherwise be absent.

If you're going to be an advocate and you're going to use your personal story, you need to be ready. Make sure you've got a solid support system around you, whether that's the organization you are an ambassador for or your family and friends. On the whole, sharing your story will be a rewarding experience. People will rally around the cause and give you comfort. Your pain can help someone else who has gone through a similar experience, and this is really at the heart of human progress. However, you may not always get a wonderful reaction and you have to be emotionally and mentally ready to accept that. You will be sharing the most painful part of your life, so make sure you have the right support network around you before you put it out for the world to chew over.

For **Terry Crews**, telling his personal story has brought greater reward than anguish. As an NFL star turned actor, he never expected to find himself doing things like testifying for the US Congress, and classes himself as an accidental activist:

An accidental activist is someone who is thrown into their circumstances. Becoming an activist takes total sacrifice. You have to risk everything you have. However, I find solace in the Biblical phrase, 'He who loses his life shall find it.'

Two years ago at a party, the head of the motion picture department at my agency, Adam Venit, came up to me when I was with my wife and groped my genitals. I was completely shocked. Honestly, I wanted to fight him. I thought, 'I'm 240 pounds, I got a lot of muscle, I can handle it.' But then I thought, 'I am a black man in America. He is a very rich, successful white man. If I hit him, what's going to happen to me?' #MeToo is not about sex, it's about power.

There is a false belief that everybody that says #MeToo is rewarded and gets positive publicity. That couldn't be further from the truth. In fact, when you come out, you can be ostracized and it changes your life forever.

As men it is so important to be open about having been through trauma and being exploited. There are people who say, 'You are too big to be assaulted, you're too strong to have someone sexually assault you.' I always respond that even if I had beaten that guy up I still would have been assaulted. After I came out there were so many men all over the world telling me that they were molested too. Usually one predator is responsible for so much damage, yet it takes them years to get caught. This is why it's so important we come out and speak out.

One of the difficult things that happens is that everyone tends to compare and they compare their traumas. You begin to feel that you shouldn't say anything because your experience is not as bad as others. That is something I've had to unlearn. This is not the trauma Olympics. Your experience is valid and you have the right to speak out about it.

The fact that one of the #MeToo whistle-blowers wasn't a woman and that #MeToo can be valuable to men is really important. **Terry Crews** is a straight man and was sexually assaulted, which shows how widespread the issue is. Sometimes it takes us seeing the atypical to realize that it could affect us too. It shows that all of our voices can be lent to a cause in a meaningful way. There is no typical picture of what an advocate for a certain cause looks like.

The most famous activists in human history have been people who have experienced great trauma and personal suffering, people like Malala Yousafzai and Nelson Mandela. Of course, you don't have to have been to prison or have been attacked by the Taliban to have a story worth sharing. The core element that makes activism compelling is authenticity.

Activism will seep into your life in ways that you don't expect, and it will naturally change the way you look at and interact with the world because you're going to understand that issues require personal action. Meteorologist and climate change journalist Eric Holthaus made headlines when he gave up flying – he couldn't justify being an environmental advocate and maintaining a high carbon footprint. Miranda Johnson, former environment correspondent for the *Economist*, decided to give up red meat after writing a number of articles about the contribution of agriculture to greenhouse gas emissions. For many people, their activism *becomes* their story.

Know that you are capable

Everyone has the ability to do something that will make a mark, a difference to a cause. There will be charities that need a lawyer, engineer or accountant. Perhaps you have a financial background? Up to 54 per cent NGOs with a budget of $100,000–500,000 have not undergone an audit, which often makes them ineligible for grants and fundraising. Helping implement these kinds of professional measures would help charities be more effective. Do not underestimate the importance of a professional skill set to enable causes to grow and flourish.

Are you a nurse? There's going to be a need for a first aid tent at every big protest. Just because you're not the person at the front of the parade with a megaphone doesn't mean you aren't needed. All skill sets are required for activism. Everyone can help to organize the day and make sure that people show up at the correct assembly point.

If you don't have a professional qualification, you may be a great communicator or a great organizer. You may be the person who always makes sure that the bill is split properly at the end of a meal. People adept at social media and technology will be invaluable to much of the third sector. The power that evolving social media platforms put in people's hands isn't necessarily understood by the leadership of some charities, political organizations or campaigns. Younger people, who are often those that embrace these technologies, can make a tremendous amount of impact just by helping less technically confident people get to grips with it all. Everyone has a talent that will be valuable to a cause.

Combining professional skills with personal passions or hobbies can be a natural way to be an effective change agent: your professional competence will be complemented and enhanced by your zeal for your cause. Sometimes combining two seemingly opposite aspects of your life can make for a particularly innovative approach. Artist and One Young World Ambassador **Hannah Rose Thomas** has combined her academic study of Arabic with her love of art in order to help a cause that she feels strongly about: the abuses experienced by refugees.

> Ever since I was young I have wanted to be a voice for the voiceless somehow, and never imagined it could be through art. It is powerful when we can combine our compassion with our deepest passions.

> While living in Jordan as an Arabic student in 2014, I had an opportunity to organize art projects with Syrian refugees – an experience which opened my eyes to the magnitude of the refugee crisis. I began to paint the portraits of some of the refugees I had met, to show the people behind the global crisis, whose personal stories are otherwise often shrouded by statistics.

> My unusual position as an English artist who is fluent in Arabic has enabled me to cross cultural barriers, and I've been deeply moved by the refugees I've had the privilege of meeting. Each

person I have spoken to has experienced suffering and displayed a remarkable resilience. It was to share their stories that I began painting their portraits.

My portraits have been shown alongside the self-portraits that my subjects themselves paint. My most recent art projects have been with Yezidi women who escaped ISIS captivity in Iraqi Kurdistan and survivors of Boko Haram in Northern Nigeria. Teaching these women to paint their self-portraits has been a way for those who have never been to school or learned to read and write to share their stories with the rest of the world. Testimony is an important element of the recovery process post-torture and sexual violence. These paintings convey their dignity, resilience and unspeakable grief.

Assessing your own circumstances and abilities will enable you to match yourself with either open positions in campaigns, charities or causes – of which many are advertised online – or it will enable you to approach an organization with a useful offer of assistance. Acknowledging the skills you possess is key. Nothing is too simple to make a meaningful difference.

Big needn't mean impossible

The challenges of our time can feel overwhelming: climate change, economic inequality, violent extremism – even the most passionate campaigner and advocate might want to pull the covers over and look away.

Much of the time, however, it is the scale and extent of a problem that drives us to make a difference. Climate change is a prime example of something that has created a huge movement around environmentalism because people appreciate the magnitude of the issue at hand. Today's climate challenge is hard to get to grips with because it is so far beyond our collective experience. Our brains have evolved to respond reflexively to immediate threats but ignore or downplay systemic crises that creep up on us. So the best way of creating a sense of urgency about big, sometimes abstract, causes is to humanize them.

Kumi Naidoo has a long history of activism, from anti-apartheid campaigning, to becoming executive director of Greenpeace International and currently secretary-general of Amnesty International. Here he expresses how we can make environmental work personal:

> We talk about saving the planet. The planet will continue to be a rock spinning in outer space whether or not humans are on it. Actually, the extinction of the human race will probably be really good for nature. The forests will grow back. The seas will replenish. The planet will be fine, but humans won't be on it. We really need to think of climate change as saving the human race.

Former President of Ireland and UN High Commissioner for Human Rights **Mary Robinson** focuses on climate *justice* rather than climate *change*. She looks at environmental concerns through the lens of the human suffering climate change will create, as opposed to the science or the impact on nature. Mary says she thinks the face of climate change shouldn't be the polar bear but should be one of the millions of women and girls who spend hours every day travelling, waiting in line and carrying heavy loads simply to get water for drinking, bathing, cooking and other household needs.

> Environmental threats are human rights issues. Climate change is undermining people's livelihoods and development, and therefore undermining their rights to food, water, health and safety. Climate change threatens lives and is driving people from their homes.
>
> I've always been interested in justice. I grew up with four brothers, and I had to assert myself: learned to use my elbows and fight for my place. I think that later that sense of justice made me care deeply about human rights and gender equality. I studied law as an instrument for social change and took cases in Ireland to bring about greater justice. As president of Ireland, I tried to use my voice to address gender and human rights issues. I have always cared about justice. And now I am an angry granny working for climate justice!

I am lucky enough, as an Irish grandmother, to have six grandchildren from my three children. The eldest is 15 so they will be in their 30s and 40s in 2050. They will share the world with a lot more than 7 billion people, probably about 9.5 billion. When I think about the problems we face now with just over one degree of warming, I fear the problems they will encounter with the predicted three degrees of warming we are heading towards. We need to accept the warning of the scientists last October that the only safe level is to not exceed 1.5 degrees Celsius of warming, and that we need to reduce our carbon emissions by 45 per cent by 2030. What a great, transformative challenge for young people today!

It is important to remember that even problems such as climate change can be tackled and solved. The upper layer of the northern hemisphere of the ozone should be mostly repaired by 2030 and completely repaired by 2060. This is thanks to the Montreal Protocol, a global environmental agreement ratified in 1987, which paved the way for the phasing out of ozone-harming gases. When people come together, seemingly insurmountable issues can be overcome and resolved.

Big change comes from incremental steps

You don't need to dedicate your time to the biggest causes to make a difference: honing a niche area of interest and activism can be the best way to rapidly create impact. You need to strike a difference between battles big enough to matter but small enough to win. There are two types of niche causes. First there are causes that don't affect a great number of people. When HRH The Prince of Wales' letters to politicians were released in 2015, it was revealed that Prince Charles had written to ministers asking for more consideration to be given to the protection of the Patagonian toothfish. He was ridiculed for picking such a niche cause, but ultimately if someone doesn't stand up for the Patagonian toothfish, no one will. When singer and conservation advocate **Cher** decided to get involved in Animal Welfare, she received criticism about the cause she chose to back:

A lot of people don't think this is a serious enough issue to be addressing. Many people question why I'm focused on this issue when there are other disasters and human rights abuses happening to people. My answer is always that I do help people. I am engaged in those issues as well but saving elephants is my calling. It is what I want to dedicate my life to. There is no such thing as picking a 'wrong cause.' Everyone will be drawn to a different cause and that should be celebrated.

People don't always understand why the issue of elephants in captivity is such a pressing one. People grow up accustomed to zoos and circuses. It may seem normal to some that elephants are in cages. It's important to make the issue of animal captivity relatable to these people. We need everyone's support if we are going to solve this issue. I try to educate people on how social elephants are, on their intelligence, their memory and the importance of allowing them to live in open spaces. Many don't know that elephants walk an average of 25km a day. When they are informed of that fact, the enclosure elephants are kept in suddenly seem far too small and constraining.

I try to frame the issue in a way that people can relate to it. I often say 'if that was a human being, chained and isolated from their family and friends or beaten to do tricks for an audience, it would make national headlines. There would be widespread outrage. So why do we treat animals differently? Why do they not also deserve dignity and a life free from constraints?' That tends to change people's perceptions. They begin to realize how barbaric enclosures are for these animals. To see these creatures for ten minutes means they have to suffer a lifetime.

It is ridiculous we are keeping animals in captivity for human entertainment. Especially when there are plenty of other options such as virtual reality zoos. In the long run, we could have virtual reality zoos so that young children can still have the experience of seeing an animal and learning about them.

While causes like the Patagonian toothfish or a focus on elephant conservation is not something that the everyday person is going to worry about, they are still worthy of being addressed and tackled. Humble or seemingly niche causes can lead the way to bigger change. Australian cricket hero **Steve Waugh** identified the fact that while each rare disease affects only a few people, collectively rare diseases are an enormous problem. Steve argues:

> The rare-disease patient is the orphan of the health system, often without diagnosis, without treatment, without research and therefore without reason to hope. The Steve Waugh Foundation is the only standalone Foundation of its kind in Australia, there for children and young adults that would otherwise have nowhere to turn.

> So many young adults and families with children challenged by a rare disease feel so isolated and alone. A major motivation behind the Steve Waugh Foundation is that no one should have to stand alone; everyone needs a team to support them. There are up to 8,000 known rare diseases which affect up to 2 million Australians, including 400,000 children. One in ten people will be living with or affected by a rare disease in their lifetime, numbers similar to heart disease and diabetes, and they fall through the cracks in the healthcare system or charity support network. Rare diseases are rare, people with rare diseases are many.

> We want Australia to understand 'rare' diseases are actually very common and don't just affect other people…It's likely each and every Australian is connected to someone who has a rare disease, but in Australia there is still a lack of awareness of the impact they cause. They do not represent a public health priority.

By grouping lots of niche causes, Steve has created huge awareness for the problem in Australia and has managed to help people who would otherwise be left without the costly, specialist care their specific condition requires.

The second type of niche causes actually affect great swathes of people, but those people have been marginalized. The intrinsic nature of democracy and the financial impetus of the media to appeal to the mass market allows majority rule to dominate and minority voices to be ignored.

Governments don't only exist to protect the majority, they exist to protect everybody. But the nature of majority rule means that only majorities are able to speak out, or they are able to vote and conduct themselves in such a way that minorities get discriminated against.

Looking for underrepresented causes means that you will inherently stumble upon issues that are underfunded. Singaporean **Jack Sim** is the founder of the World Toilet Organization (WTO), which aims to end open defecation and strives for adequate and equitable sanitation for all. Jack was a businessman who at the age of 40 felt he had made enough money and wanted to know how he was going to help the world. He picked toilets because it was a taboo subject: he thought that a taboo usually means there is a cause that requires much closer attention than society gives it.

> I chose to dedicate my time to a problem that was neglected. I chose the one that nobody wanted to fund. When I talked about shit people scolded me and told me it was a rude subject. I was shocked by this. If it is normal to use the toilet six to eight times a day how could discussing that topic be off limits?
>
> The first step towards tackling the taboo was to approach the media and get coverage of my work. I did not want to use the professional language of the past where they referred to it as 'faecal sludge management'. It sounded very scientific but nobody understood what it meant. I call a spade a spade. I decided to make it very humorous so that the media would write about it, so I was happy when people called me Mr Toilet.

In the beginning people thought my project was a joke. I sought out mentors. I went to ask another guy who had used humour to solve a different problem – condoms. He was referred to as Mr Condom in Thailand. He taught me that if you can make people laugh, then they will listen to you. You also have to be able to laugh at yourself because if you can't laugh at yourself, you can't actually do your job properly because you'll be sensitive and will likely feel hurt and discouraged.

I started the World Toilet Organization secretly hoping that the World Trade Organization would sue me, because I used the acronym WTO. I thought if they sued me, then my work would see the light of day, and if they didn't sue me then I could use the acronym forever. The latter was what happened.

Your commitment vs your fear

What's important is not to ignore your enthusiasm, your anger, your passion, but to be realistic about your time commitment. It's better to commit a good hour a week, or a focused afternoon a week, or a full day a month, and dedicate yourself to that time completely and wholeheartedly in a driven manner, than to start and stop or risk flaking out.

A dedicated volunteer who's done half an hour a week for ten years is going to be one of an organization's most valuable and prized assets. Over time, these things add up to a meaningful difference. Being realistic with yourself and with whatever you're putting your time towards will help from an organizational perspective and allow you to prioritize in a way that will make you more effective.

You don't have to be a full-time activist, but it *can* be a career, it can be a job, and one that is financially lucrative or at least enough to get by. A lot of people find that they would rather be slightly less wealthy and much more fulfilled then incredibly financially stable and not able to make their life meaningful.

No one's ever died and wished they spent more time in the office. Everyone, of course, wants to have more time with their family and more time with their friends, but people do want to make a difference and leave a legacy. That's an important part of activism. If you were to die, people would think about your actions and what kind of life you led. What impact did you have on the planet? Did you make people's lives better? Did you make your community healthier? Did you make the planet cleaner? What was it? Those are the sorts of things that will live on after you.

Ultimately, activists will leave a legacy, and that shouldn't be underestimated in terms of its importance in human consciousness. You can't spend money once you're dead, but you can leave behind a world that is a fairer and safer place.

Change comes through influence, not authority

In some ways, activism is a full-time job: you don't always have to join or start a cause to make a difference. We all have our own spheres of power and we must assess where we hold influence. That may be in the staffroom at work or in the book club we host, or that may just be within our circle of friends, but the area we are able to influence may be bigger than we imagine. **Doutzen Kroes** is a Dutch supermodel who raised money for the Elephant Crisis Fund with the #KnotOnMyPlanet social media campaign. She points out:

> Because of my profession, I'm in a pretty unique position to reach a wide audience, and so are many of my friends in the fashion industry. With this in mind I started brainstorming to come up with a social media campaign which would rally the fashion industry into saving elephants.

Instructions like 'engage your network' or 'create a social media campaign' can seem crushingly grandiose, but ultimately they come down to asking people to help. The more people you ask, the quicker the help will come:

I asked every single person I met to join the #KnotOnMyPlanet campaign, and we garnered 1.5 billion impressions and received a lot of media attention. More importantly, we have raised over $8 million to date, 100 per cent of which goes directly to the Elephant Crisis Fund.

Of course, asking individual people to help isn't the only thing that can spur on a campaign: getting businesses, media and brands involved has an even greater amplifying effect as Doutzen discovered:

Our #KnotOnMyPlanet campaign offered companies the chance to be associated with a good cause. Social media gives brands the opportunity to reach the millennial audience in a very natural way. Of all the companies that have rallied to our cause, including Loewe, Porter Magazine and Ivory Ella, it has been Tiffany & Co, the iconic American luxury brand, whose contribution has been the most significant and whose involvement points to a new way for corporations and charities to come together for the benefit of all. Tiffany launched an entire collection of elephant brooches and necklaces called Save the Wild. Everything, all the money they raised, went to the Elephant Crisis Fund.

The Elephant Crisis Fund is operating in 36 countries, funding a total of 251 projects from 74 organizations, and has deployed over $18.5 million in the last four years. Driving the poaching is a complex international ivory trade that thrives on poverty, corruption and greed, and creates global insecurity. It was important to me to explain that this is not just elephants: by saving elephants we are alleviating poverty, preventing crime and increasing biodiversity.

It's less difficult than you'd think to be able to persuade people to care about your issue or change behaviours in order to make an impact. Simply ask questions of our friends: 'Have you thought about the impact that this might be having?' or 'Why don't you donate to this?' or 'Why didn't you use a reusable coffee cup today?' The social nudges which we are able to conduct over the course of our professional or personal lives can be hugely influential.

Team work makes the dream work

It's important to be aware of overlap. Don't do the work that someone else is already doing effectively. Instead, join them and help them. It's thinking about what's actually going to serve your cause best. Australian **Grace Forrest**, who co-founded Walk Free Foundation, one of the world's largest anti-slavery organizations, has a helpful way of placing herself within the bigger picture:

> I see myself as a means to an end. As a young activist it's important to find other individuals and groups working towards the same goal. One person can be easily silenced, but a group of us is much harder to ignore. There is knowledge and power in being a part of a collective fighting to create change. For many issues, including slavery, you must also understand the historical context and battles before you, and whether they were won or lost. We stand on the shoulders of giants in this fight.

Once you have chosen your cause, and thought about how you might make a difference, the next step is to ask: What do I need? It is likely that you're not the only person who has *ever* thought to address your issue. It may be the case in your area, city, region, country…and sometimes it is even the case in the world. But you need to find out who else is out there – you may not have to do it all alone. Who is as engaged and concerned to act as you are? What is their organization, what assets have they got, what progress have they made?

For instance, if your passion is 'prisoners of conscience', Amnesty International is the world leader on addressing that topic. Ask yourself: 'Can I do more on this particular case than Amnesty?' Perhaps the answer is 'yes', but more often than not joining an organization that is already established will be easier and more effective than casting off alone.

Egotistical drive has achieved a lot in the areas of activism. Force of personality can make effective change agents who are impossible to shake off or ignore. We have found, however, that the 'saviour complex' that sometimes accompanies socially impactful work can be an incredible hindrance.

We've witnessed over the years sad tales of people in the philanthropic sector whose desire to be the great protector or liberator – and to be *seen* as such – has destroyed what otherwise may have been terrific work. The scandal around the collapse of the UK charity Kids Company was mired in headlines about its founder, such as 'Face it, Camila, YOUR ego killed off Kids Company'. At its height Camila Batmanghelidjh was described as 'one of the most powerful advocates for children in the country'. In 2015, however, as allegations of mismanagement and the squandering of funds emerged, she was forced to stand down as chief executive. Kids Company itself, now insolvent, became a byword for financial recklessness and incompetence in the voluntary sector and raised awareness of the risks that accompany what one journalist called 'the rise of the egotistical altruist'.

The world likes to group people into two distinct categories: there are altruistic people and there are egotistical people, but actually the media attention and celebrity endorsements that sometime accompany activism can make for a very narcissistic environment. **Jack Sim** counsels:

> If you are concerned about receiving acknowledgement or getting credit, then you become the obstacle to your mission. You need to behave like a tool for your mission rather than *the mission itself*.

The most valuable player isn't always the person who scores the most goals. The people who assist and keep the strategic setup working are often those who makes something a success.

Leadership and learning are indispensable to one another

In terms of your success as an activist, finding your tribe is an important part of finding your cause. No one can change the world on their own.

Whether you find some people to follow or whether you find some people to support you, you need to surround yourself with people who also care about your cause and are dedicated to making a difference. Ideally those are people that you can work with on a regular basis. Increasingly, it is possible to connect with these people online. There are so many incredible online communities who mobilize around causes. Tapping into this online support may help your impact be scaled and replicated.

Reaching out to people who have more expertise than you is one of the most crucial parts of becoming an activist. Gaining knowledge and an understanding of your cause is never a complete job. There's always something to learn. Whether it's online or in real life, identifying and maintaining contact with people who can advise you will enable you to be a much more effective agent of change.

Academics and university professors are fantastic people to speak to because they'll be able to point you in the direction of literature and research that has already been done. Sometimes we think we've come up with something innovative and fresh, only to find out that somebody else had the same idea or similar approach 20 years ago. Many causes are so much more dense and intricate than we initially realize. **Kamolnan Chearavanont** started the Voices Organisation when she was 14 and is a senior officer at ConnextEd for educational reform in Thailand. She realized how complex issues can be when she started working in a shelter in Northern Thailand:

> I've always felt out of place in the society I grew up in. There was a lot of pressure to figure out what I wanted to do. Ever since I was a child, I've always loved being around babies. I was never traditionally good with academics or business but my parents always instilled in me that it is not the career titles that matter but what matters is that you do something you are passionate about with intent and purpose. The more time I spent with orphans and infants, the more I felt I could do something meaningful with my life.
>
> I ended up stumbling upon a women and children's shelter that welcomed me to visit them in the north of Thailand. When I got there I realized that all of the children and women under

the shelter's care were stateless and that so many of the issues of violence, abuse and lack of recourse related back to this statelessness. At that time there was not an organization that I could join that catered to stateless people, so I felt like I had to create one out of necessity.

When I started learning about the immensely complicated subject of statelessness, I often felt like a sponge trying to absorb as much information as I could. Curiosity is important when you're dealing with complex issues. It is critical to keep asking questions. When you're asking experts to help you or give you their time, genuine passion is also crucial. Nowadays it is hard to find young people who are truly genuine about their charitable or humanitarian work and it can be felt by such experts.

Your journey of discovery may lead you to find out about the root of your problem, like **Kamolnan Chearavanont,** or it may expose you to unpleasant truths about humanity. Unfortunately the development sector has some dark and depressing places. It is worth taking the time to make sure you know where your money and time is going and whether you are genuinely helping, as **Grace Forrest** found out:

When I was 15, I went on a service trip to Kathmandu, Nepal, to work with children, some as young as three, who had been rescued from child sex trafficking. That experience fundamentally shifted my perspective of the world as well as my place in it. I decided I would go back and I hoped to one day run a shelter just like the one I had worked with. At the time, that is how I thought I could create the greatest change.

Unfortunately, I learned the hard way that things are rarely how they first appear. When I returned to the shelter two years later, all the children I had met were unaccounted for. We were told by other community leaders on the ground that they had almost certainly been trafficked. A practice sadly all too common in the orphanage industry.

This experience provided many harsh but quick teachings – one of the most important was supply and demand. For every child pulled out of slavery, another one would be pulled in. This is why my father and I founded the Walk Free Foundation, to collaborate with a multitude of partners and areas of influence to address slavery where it occurs, as well as dismantle the drivers which allow it to continue. Now eight years since founding Walk Free, we know that slavery is the most profitable organized criminal industry in the world, and that there are more people living in slavery today than any other time in human history.

Learning more about your cause won't necessarily make it easier to tackle. You may well realize how little you actually know. The humbling effect of unpicking a complex problem and identifying the part you can play is helpful when it comes to the important exercise of checking your ego: it's difficult to feel like you're Mother Earth incarnate when you truly understand how far away we are from meeting the 2030 targets of the Paris Agreement (even if you are very diligent about recycling).

Even if there is an organization out there working on the issue you can't assume someone else is going to solve the problem. You can never trust the universe to put it right. The best way to make a difference is to shoulder the personal responsibility of a cause and hold yourself accountable for improving a situation.

As late as 1969 'activism' was defined as 'the policy or practice of doing things with decision and energy', without regard to a political signification or social movement. You need to be decisive: pick your cause and carry it with you, dedicate yourself and focus your skills and network. You also need to be energetic. Don't be half-hearted – winning trust and building confidence from others requires you to believe in something completely that they, in turn, can believe in you.

How to find a cause that matters to you checklist

- Find something you feel passionate about. It doesn't have to be a cause that you've been personally affected by but you do have to care deeply about it.

- Harness your enthusiasm and keep topping it up: your energy and focus are what counts.

- Recognize that no challenge is too big for you to tackle – ignore apathy in others.

- You don't need to reinvent the wheel – joining an existing movement can be the best way to take action.

- Acknowledge your own skills and be confident in your own capabilities.

- Work out the steps you need to take – every step, however small, is progress.

- Be pragmatic and realistic about the amount of time you can devote to your cause – and commit to that.

- Don't look to be able to tell others what to do; plan to persuade them and to take them with you.

- A team is always the best resource; work out who's with you and share the load and any credit.

- Be prepared to learn – you can never know what might be really useful, and really important.

Chapter Two
Who are we to tell you how to tell your story?

From cave drawing to hieroglyphics, the ancient art of storytelling has always been at the crux of the human experience. An unknown author composed the first enduring story in the history of mankind over a thousand years before the Old Testament and the *Odyssey*, it was 'The Epic of Gilgamesh' – written on clay tablets in the cuneiform writing style in ancient Mesopotamia (modern Iraq). Much has changed in our world since then, but stories haven't – telling stories and listening to them is part of human nature.

In today's digital age, our hyperconnected state can ironically make us feel isolated. Why are we on social media every day? What are we searching for on Google? The answer is we're looking for human connection and our experiences told back to us through stories. And it is stories that are remembered, that get traction and go viral, and are 'spread' in mainstream media.

Stories, and the emotions they invoke, stay in our heads much better than facts and figures. Everyone knows the Marie Antoinette saying 'Let them eat cake' (even though it's not true), but far fewer can recall the dates of the French Revolution.

A good story has the same effect on an old man as it does on a young girl. Stories are innate to the human condition: the texts of the world's religions are collections of stories from which we draw meaning and spirituality and sanctity – Christ spread his word by means of parables. It has always been apparent to the great change makers of history that the power of a story can bring people together and effect upon them the same or a similar emotional experience through which they can then direct the masses.

Sinister? Perhaps. When everyone is in a similar emotional state, they share like concerns, or become upset, or rejoice about the same thing. They can then be corralled to vote for a change maker, to follow them or to buy their products.

That's what really good storytelling can do and why we view history through the lens of stories. Famously, those written by the victors. Unfortunately, so dominant is the power of storytelling that other versions of history which may present a different or a more balanced view have almost been erased, leaving people unaware of others aspects of what happened.

But the power of the story can be used for good. For an activist, the holy grail is a story that jumps the boundary between opposing camps, and moves those on the other side from you to change their views and their actions. Having a fleshed-out, transparent story should help people relate to your cause. Everyone has had a journey that contains much more struggle and hardship than would first appear. It's only when we really understand people's stories that we can understand their motivations and grapple with what they're asking us to do.

We want you to be empowered to tell the story of your activism in the most balanced and resounding way possible. This will, of course, be entirely personal to you. Being able to bring people along on your journey and making them understand, both intellectually and emotionally, the cause you are pursuing is a critical element of successful activism.

So you're back from outer space

When we tell stories, we are trying to help people imagine walking a mile in our shoes. We are trying to help them recreate experiences that they themselves haven't seen, heard, felt or tasted. While that may be a challenge for any activist, there will usually be people we know will empathize with us: people who will nod along to things they themselves know to be true.

One group that has to work extra hard to allow others to empathize with their experience is astronauts. Only 536 people have ever been into space, 18 of whom died during space flight. Astronauts are the only people ever to have seen our home planet from the perspective of the universe – imagine how that feels? As difficult as it might be to describe your personal experience, it's probably understood by more than 518 other people on earth. That's one of the reasons why we think former NASA astronaut

Ron Garan is a good person to learn from:

> The hardest thing to communicate is simply the majesty of seeing
> the planet from space. We can do the best we can through
> video and spoken word but it doesn't do justice to what the real
> experience is like. It's a very powerful, visual experience, but it's
> much more than just a visual experience. You're floating, you're
> detached, it's a multi-sensory journey that's filled with awe and
> gratitude. It's an overwhelming emotional experience as well.
>
> I try and communicate the experience of space to others
> through as many mediums of communication as I can. The
> more people who can be exposed to the reality of the unity and
> interdependence of our planet that is clearly visible from space,
> the better off we will all be.

Powerful stories usually contain elements which the intended audience
hasn't or will never experience themselves. Ron manages to capture the
majesty and awe of the wondrous nature of space that most of us will never
come close to experiencing. There are physical, visual and sensual elements
to what he has experienced that we can't imagine on our own, but through
Ron's help we're able to imagine a glimpse of it.

> In order to return to Earth, my two Russian crewmates and I
> undocked from the space station, then did a couple of laps around
> our planet. And as we passed the south tip of South America we
> turned the spacecraft around and fired our engines in order to
> enter the upper atmosphere. We had a fiery, violent ride through
> the atmosphere at 8km per second. The parachutes opened and
> we slammed into the ground, we bounced, we rolled, we flipped
> over and landed on our side.
>
> The capsule was lying on its right side and out of the window, I saw
> a rock, a flower and a blade of grass. And I remember thinking to
> myself distinctly, 'I'm home.' But what was really interesting about

that thought was I was home...but I was in Kazakhstan. So at that moment, my home was not just Houston Texas where I lived with my family, my home was Earth. Our definition of that word home has profound implications for the way we solve problems, how we treat our planet, and how we treat each other. And broadening the definition of the word home does not come with it a requirement to forget where we came from or our national, political, cultural, or religious background. It simply means seeing those things in the context of the bigger picture. In the context of the planet through the orbital perspective.

The element of his story of coming home and seeing a stone, a piece of grass and a flower is something that everyone can relate to. It makes us all realize that this is what Earth is, rather than the parameters in which we live day-to-day. By narrating the wonder he beheld from space and relating it to something we all know, it gives the listener a new perspective – a greater sense of humanity, making us all appreciate that we're all on the same planet. Any story that's able to give us a powerful new perspective is important.

And the reason this kind of storytelling is important, is that you have to do quite a lot of work in order to allow somebody to mentally or emotionally walk a mile in your shoes. It can be frustrating because, in some ways, people should be able to imagine what it's like to be a person of colour or use a wheelchair...emotionally and intellectually we expect people to be able to make that leap, but the reality is people can't unless you hold their hand and you take them there with you through your words and experiences.

When it comes to getting people to understand your experience, no matter how extreme or unrelatable it might be, **Ron Garan** advises:

Don't go after the low hanging fruit. It is easy to fall into the trap of trying to explain the experience that you had in a superficial way because it's easier for people to understand. If you want them to understand it on a deeper level, and any worthwhile experience should be understood on that level, you have to really dig deeper in yourself. You need to get beyond platitudes and buzzwords. You

really need to dive in on what is the core of that experience.
Try to discuss the meaning of it, and the importance of it.

Creating a deep connection with your audience is no easy feat but it is what you must strive for as an activist. No one will give you money or time because they have a vague stirring – they will only help you because they were profoundly moved.

One of the issues many activists have is the fear of vulnerability, but vulnerability is the birthplace of change. If we are being truly honest, then we are naturally making ourselves vulnerable because we are portraying an image of ourselves that is far from perfect – something that is increasingly hard to do in the age of Facetune and flattering Instagram filters. Many people don't want to share their stories because they don't like the idea of people feeling sorry for them.

Pity is powerful and it's something that people are very afraid of. No one wants to be pitied because it implies inferiority to the person who is pitying you. But by making yourself vulnerable you are breaking the boundary of curation and allowing people to connect with you on an intimate and deeply personal level. Rather than seeing that as a shameful thing, we need to embrace pity as part and parcel of people's humanity and compassion and appreciate that people are trying to reach out to us. This can be channelled in a really positive way.

Directing people's compassion can enable you to encourage others to take up the mantle of your cause, even if it's something that is far removed from their personal experience, as disability activist and self-identified little person **Sinéad Burke** demonstrates:

> I want to leave people with empathy and not sympathy. We have this inspiration porn problem in how the disabled community are framed and discussed. There is this notion that if you are disabled, you solely exist to inspire and educate the rest of the world.
>
> It's a personal choice, but I have never found anger to be constructive. I try to encourage my audience to look for a creative solution. I've learned that if it's just little people trying to fight

for solutions, it will take us an eternity to construct them and implement them. We need to bring everybody with us. I also make myself publicly vulnerable, creating an emotional connection with people that they can invest in. I use stories as a way for people to engage, build empathy and relate to what I'm discussing.

Whether it is talking about a toilet or an ATM machine, you're talking about things that people know and experience. I ask people of average height to imagine what it would be like if they had to live in a world designed for people who were three foot five...lots of bending.

Your story may make people uncomfortable – which is, in fact, a good thing. A certain level of discomfort is important because it makes people see that something needs to be done: it makes them feel unable to return to their lives unaffected or just sit back and be an onlooker. You need to balance the right amount of discomfort without alienating or horrifying your audience to the extent that they feel that there's nothing to be done – that they can't do anything, or that the situation is too depressing to bear. If people are too uncomfortable, they won't help because they feel totally incapable. Equally, if people are completely comfortable, they don't think help is needed. It's treading the fine line between the two. Sinéad continues:

Humour for me is a particular mechanism that I use to relate to people. When you're talking about subjects such as exclusion, or you're talking about discrimination or bias, if you are part of the majority that conversation can be incredibly uncomfortable. I think humour has an amazing ability to relieve tension but it also gives people a way to relate to me. Humour transcends culture, it transcends language, it transcends class. I think a level of discomfort is important in order for people to be conscious of the worlds they are blinkered to, but it should be used in a productive way where people are encouraged to do something and be part of the solution, not simply made to feel bad.

Humour is an incredibly important tool in helping us address uncomfortable issues. It is one of the great, unifying storytelling tropes that has crossed cultures and centuries. Sometimes dark humour is really helpful; the very fact that we're able to laugh at something appalling while also confronting it reduces its power. For those who suffer, if they are able to make light of their experience with humour it is a potent way to ease the listener into the narrative. The shared emotional connection forged through universal humour allows for a difficult story to be told and heard.

Nimco Ali is a survivor of female genital mutilation (FGM) and the cofounder of Daughters of Eve organization and The Five Foundation. She uses humour and satire to highlight the serious and often uncomfortable topic of FGM:

> We've got these vagina suits that we wear in order to have conversations about the female genitalia. We wear them because we don't want girls to feel ashamed. People never talked to me, they talked to and about my vagina so I thought I may as well wear a vagina suit.
>
> There's a public conversation going on about our bodies but not necessarily with us so we though we'd take it to parliament and the streets. We started making c*nt cakes, wearing vagina outfits, etc. FGM is one of the most ridiculous forms of violence against women and children. People want to sit around and talk about it. I thought: if you really want to talk about vaginas let's have one in the room.

Nimco also discusses her personal experience alongside using humour, in order to capture the public's attention whilst informing them of the sombre reality of FGM.

> My family and I were in Djibouti on holiday, and it was just a normal day. The cutter, who came into the room, looked a little bit scary. I didn't know what she was going to be doing. To me, she looked like an African interpretation of what a witch would look

like. She was all dressed in black, and she wasn't exactly the most cheerful person. I remember waking up after I had FGM, and I was confused. I didn't understand what this was about. And nobody really talked about it after that.

When I was back in the UK I talked to my teacher in order to get some kind of explanation: What was it? Why had it happened? But she just gave me a very flippant answer. She said, 'This is what happens to girls like you.' I didn't even know what 'girls like me' meant.

I never spoke out because I thought, 'I'm not a poor African girl, I don't want people to be thinking of me as this victim.' In that moment, my silence was complicit, because everyone was thinking it didn't happen in the UK, and it was all to do with culture. But these are misconceptions.

It was only many years after, in 2006, that I went to a local high school in the UK, and I met these 13-year-old girls. Thirteen out of fourteen of them had had FGM, and I was completely horrified. So I started to work on child protection and tried to get more guidelines on what legislation should be passed. It was only in 2010 that I started to talk about my own experience as a survivor. I had educated myself and understood why I had FGM –because I was a girl and I was unvalued within that society. I assumed that the mothers of these daughters had figured that out as well. But they hadn't.

I sat in board rooms and discussions where people were talking about eradicating FGM as though it was some kind of virus. Through my own experience I knew that FGM was organized and that a lot of people benefitted from it, so I started Daughters of Eve along with other survivors so that we could start recognising FGM as a form of violence against women and girls and as a form of gender genocide. Grassroots funding has always been an issue so more recently I co-founded The Five Foundation with Brendan Wynne to raise funding for frontline groups working to end FGM in Africa.

Trying to find that right balance of urgency, while encouraging people to question their assumptions and challenge their preconceptions, is incredibly important. Think strategically about which elements of your story people *need* to hear and which may end up being gratuitous and lose you supporters. The more concise and authentic you are the more compelling your story will be. That will help you capture the public's imagination and support.

Good advocacy is empathy

Being a good storyteller requires you to innately understand other people's stories and challenge yourself to discover empathy and compassion in every tale. Our media landscape often doesn't offer us a variety of perspectives – frequently we only hear one side of conflict, political disagreement or uprising. Pakistani poet and writer **Fatima Bhutto** highlights this in a really good way. When talking about the film *American Sniper*, she said, 'Can you imagine if there was a film called *Iraqi Sniper*?'

Laura Ulloa, a political scientist at the University of the Andes, was able to use her own story of being kidnapped as a child by the FARC (Revolutionary Armed Forces of Colombia – People's Army) and her ability to find forgiveness in order to start a broader conversation about reconciliation in Colombia:

> Fourteen years after my kidnapping, during the peace process, people started to think about forgiveness and Colombians became interested in learning about how to forgive when they heard about my experience. They became fascinated by the story of a little girl who, after being kidnapped twice by two separate guerrilla groups, decided not only to forgive her captors in order to live a happier life but also to work with them to create a better future.

During my kidnapping, instead of questioning why I was in captivity, I wanted to understand why my captors were there, in the mountains, far away from their families, just as I was. I began to ask about their stories and their pasts, and soon they asked about mine. The results surprised me, opposite worlds came face to face. Mine, one full of opportunity and love, and theirs marked by abandonment, poverty and lack of opportunity. Our common denominator was up there, far from civilization, we all had been deprived of our freedom.

While kidnapped, I forgave my captors because I wanted to look at this episode without hate or resentment. I couldn't hate people who had suffered so much. On the day of my release I promised them that I would work so they could have a second chance in life, and I have dedicated my life to this promise.

You need to dig deeper once you become a storyteller of activism. It involves a resolution to overcome negative responses such as anger, hate and resentment. This heroic triumph of the human spirit inspires people: it changes them, it changes the world. All the most admired activists manage this feat – from Martin Luther King to Malala. They have more to do than nurse their own feelings. They write their stories, not the people or forces ranged against them.

We often think that individual accountability trumps a person's backstory. That might be the case if it's one person, but when it's a whole movement of people, like the FARC in Colombia, it's important to examine why all these young men were mobilized and forced to sell drugs and take up arms in the mountains away from their families. If you refuse to look at the backstories of those militants, how can you tackle the root causes of the conflict? In truth, we need to think beyond our limits, we need to interrogate the truths we are presented with and cross-examine why things happen.

Today, we are uncovering a lot more about the relationship between the number of traumatic instances in someone's childhood and their capacity for violence as an adult. But there is still an inherent problem in our politics: the political right wants to put individual accountability for people's actions at the top of the agenda, and the left wants to blame solely systemic failures, both failing to look at the combination of individual choice *and* societal conditioning. Nuanced analysis is so grossly absent from our politics that it is no wonder that empathy for others is dwindling and our discourse is becoming more and more brutal.

Humility is a fundamental component of listening. Understanding and being able to say, 'I understand that this is horrible but I'm not able to imagine the experience myself' is very important. For instance, most men don't know what it's like to walk home at night and feel the need to get out their keys and hold them between their fingers in case the person coming up behind attacks them. They can empathize, they can show concern, but they will likely never undergo that universal female experience. If you're not a person of colour you don't fully understand the emotionally lived experience of being racially abused. These are experiences that belong to somebody else – you can empathize and you can be affected by it, but you can't understand it. Appreciating that other people have distinct experiences from your own is an important part of listening to a story. You can empathize with someone without trying to falsely claim your life experiences match or resemble theirs.

You have the right to remain silent

Not everyone wants to tell their own story and sometimes we want to be activists on other people's behalves. Speaking out on someone else's behalf is not always a sign of being a good ally: we need to carefully examine what right our voice has to tell someone else's narrative, especially if we have no lived experience of what we claim to be advocating for.

We asked **Fatima Bhutto** how she approaches telling other people's stories:

> I suppose, I believe fundamentally, that the only responsibility of the writer is to truthfully observe the world around them. I don't think it's necessarily the writer's job to advocate for things or to provide solutions. The writer's responsibility really is observation,

and when you're observing the world around you truthfully you can't not report or say what you find.

The basic principle is to follow the pain. To be in a place, to try and understand where the pain is, and to go and follow it. That's how you come to the causes that you want to raise awareness about. It's about something much larger than yourself. You think, 'Where is the pain?' and then you get to, 'What can be done to alleviate it?'

You may find out things you are not supposed to find, these may be things that the people around you wish for you not to point out, but that's your duty. You're duty-bound to raise questions, to ask uncomfortable questions and speak of what you see. That has been the guide which has helped me most, and also helped me decide what exactly I want to write about, and to maintain the freedom of what it means to be a writer.

You do not want to be a parachute writer. You don't want to pop into someone's life or pop into someone's country for a week and then go off and write a book about it as though you know everything. In that sense, if you're interested about other parts of the world, about a story, I think that you owe it to yourself to sustain focus.

One of the issues activists come up against is that some of our world's biggest problems are the ones that are the most hidden. You need to spend a lot of time getting to grips with an issue and familiarizing yourself with the communities that it affects before you speak out about it. Sometimes we think we know what a community needs and we donate or try and provide this rather than what would actually be intrinsically helpful to them – asking affected people rather than making assumptions is one of the most fundamental tenets of successful activism.

Unfortunately, people experiencing hardship and oppression are often the least able to advocate for themselves. Structural barriers can prevent access to media and discrimination can lead to people not being listened to. Poverty is immensely time consuming: if you're standing in line all day trying to get your application for social security or a welfare package sorted you don't have time to go on a rally, let alone pay for public transport to get you into the city for a march.

People undergoing hardship are also more likely to be suffering from mental health issues. The stigma of their situation may make them feel ashamed and, in turn, prevent them from speaking out on issues that people desperately need to hear about. Food writer and poverty campaigner **Jack Monroe** thinks that this means that key voices are missing from today's activism:

> People aren't going to come out the woodwork and say, 'Excuse me, can I talk to you about my shit and depressing life?' You need to actually approach people sensitively and say, 'I want to listen to you. I want to hear what you have to say. I'm going to make time and space for you in which you can tell your story. I'm not going to judge it, and I'm going to try to help if you'd like me to help you.' That's what seems to be missing from discourse around poverty. A lot of people, with an awful lot of privilege, in positions of power, are making decisions on behalf of people for who they know absolutely nothing about.
>
> Even audiences who care enough about poverty to turn up at talks I give still don't understand because it's not their lived experience. I've seen the penny drop at the hundreds of talks I've given big and small – I can see it in the audience's faces – the point at which people realized, 'Oh God. She's got to choose between feeding her son and feeding herself. You've got to choose between taking that half-eaten McDonald's cheeseburger that's poking out of the bin or not eating at all. Oh my God, I can't believe this happened.' Then I go, 'Yes, but that's just me. There's 4.2 million people a year in the UK living like this. What are we going to do about that?'
>
> That's the combination of a really powerful story, quite an emotive one, and then backing it up with unimaginable statistics that really

hammer home to people the scale of need and that, for so many people, the system is well and truly broken.

Don't ever be ashamed of your story. Chances are it affects other people too and by speaking out you are able to let them know that they are not alone and get others to take up the challenge of making a difference.

The loneliness and humiliation we feel when our life hits rock bottom can seem crushing – it may be impossible to realize at the time that these are among the strongest human emotions and, therefore, the most powerful. As Canadian swimmer **Mark Tewksbury** says about his homosexuality and the effect it had on his mindset at the Olympics, 'What had been used against me my entire life became my differentiator and became my strength.'

The fact that your story is so painful is going to be what makes other people act. Even the most humble, straightforward account will add important, real, needed colour to facts and figures that would otherwise fail to inspire. Sometimes there is nothing more powerful than a completely ordinary person who is just there to tell their story. **Jack Monroe** described being part of an inquiry into the rise in food banks use. The woman who spoke with her was a food bank user. She was a cleaner with four children. Everyone was moved by hearing how cuts and delays to benefits had essentially destroyed her life and self-esteem. No one else could have spoken for her. It had to be her.

Never underestimate the clout your story may have. Your job as a storyteller is to help your audience understand what you feel, hear and see so that you can recreate it for your audience and they can picture your experience as vividly as possible. Real detail and vivid language are your best tools. When it comes to helping people be deeply understanding of your cause, sometimes granular detail can be the most relevant because this is what goes beyond the platitudes and gives true texture to your tale.

The catharsis of sharing your experiences will benefit you. The validity that comes with being heard will reap benefits beyond activism. Telling your story well should help your cause and help you as an activist. **Jack Monroe** described the self-actualizing effect of her story being heard:

One of the things about living in poverty that I think gets overlooked is that it's really isolating. You end up staying in all the time because you can't afford to go out. You lock yourself away. You decline social invitations. That's when I started to write. When I was first invited to Parliament to speak about a year later, it was almost like I had faded into a complete obscurity from my friends, from my family, from my own life. I was just a shadow, I'd been erased, like a non-existent face. It was almost as if somebody had started colouring me in around the edges again when I was asked to speak.

I was starting to be seen, and I was emerging from this real lonely, isolated depressed place, because somebody actually thought that what I had to say had value. I felt I had value as a human being with experiences. I can't even begin to describe how that felt, that somebody had taken an interest in me as a person again.

Unfold the petals, don't rip the flower

Nobody should rush you or overstate the urgency with which you should tell your story. Sometimes timing can align so that an optimal moment appears for your story to be told. That could be a wonderful thing as it can provide a perfect platform and a real sense of momentum, but it can also create a lot of pressure because it may feel like it's now or never.

You also need to prepare yourself, and that involves forming and grouping the right support network around you: your family, your friends, necessary medical support, emotional or financial support from your colleagues… whatever it is that you need, have it in place. This framework of support and allies will give you strength to find your voice, speak louder and ensure the right people are hearing your cry.

A lot of people feel as though they are only able to tell their story a piece at a time, which is very understandable, especially in cases of trauma. However, when you can, we think it's better to tell your whole story:

1. If there are experiences that are so traumatic you're not ready to talk about them yet, then you probably still need to seek help and support from those around you or perhaps from a counsellor or therapist.

2. When you tell a story a piece at a time, there are inevitably bits that are missing. This can open you up to unjustified but potent criticism about inconsistencies and falsifying facts.

3. There is something really beautiful about telling the whole truth. It is a great antidote to fake news and false headlines. If you are able to contribute to that as an activist, it's a service to society.

Yeonmi Park, a human rights advocate for North Koreans, encountered these issues after her famous speech at One Young World 2014 Dublin:

> Personally, I was trying to tell the world my story gradually. But people cared, second by second, about the details. I was criticized for saying someone was killed for watching 'a James Bond film' in one speech and then 'a Hollywood film' in another. I was referring to the same film, but people picked up on these details and tried to discredit me. People are always looking for the flaws in a story. It's so hard to remember what happened when I was five years old. Was my father arrested when I was eight or nine? It was hard to be sure.
>
> My advice is to pay attention to the useful feedback but make sure you're blocking out the noise. One of the things I didn't anticipate was how intensely people would examine my story. I had to recall my experiences perfectly, because if I didn't people would use that as an opportunity to use my mistakes as ammunition to criticize the validity of my story. It was a really valuable lesson to learn that every detail matters to the outside world.

> Evidence shows that a traumatized brain cannot recollect events or memories in the right order, therefore, a true testimony is always a gradual process for the survivors to tell. However, the general public refuses to accept this scientific fact and instead wants a black and white simple version of a story. Even though it is impossible for the survivors to be sure of every detail in their lives, it is good to be mindful of the public's tendency to want them to.

> Sometimes, people have a hard time believing survivors' stories because the experiences of survivors are beyond their world experience, therefore, their imagination can't reach that far. However, it is still worth telling the truth no matter the resistance.

Yeonmi was later able to rectify her comments in a book, *In Order To Live*, which gave a fuller picture of what she experienced. There is a terrible but real risk that your story may be disbelieved. A lot of victims of rape and sexual assault and sexual harassment experience disbelief. Similarly, victims of racism or discrimination are often met with statements like, 'Why didn't you report it?'

People disbelieving your story can be a renewed trauma. The demoralizing effects of that shouldn't be underestimated. If you're putting yourself out there, there's a chance your story may go viral, or may be on the front covers of a newspaper. In those circumstances the nature of our society, where everyone can be an investigative journalist, is that people will dig and deliberately seek to unearth facts about you not publicly available.

At the point at which you tell your story, try to have an entirely consistent narrative that can be fact checked. Simply put, stick to your story. You may feel as though your experience is not the most exciting one out there, but don't embellish it. Your story, in and of itself, has brought you to this point and that is enough. No one else owns it.

That is the reason politicians use stump speeches – a speech they repeat time and again during election time – because they are highly aware that consistency in messaging isn't only about getting people to remember your message it's about protecting yourself from people who want to find contradictions.

We knew a young activist who got carried away with embellishing her story – her life had been blighted by knife crime but not to the extent that she portrayed. Her activism was gaining momentum – she even got a standing ovation at a political conference. Of course, journalists started investigating and found that parts of her story weren't true – cue front-page headlines about her 'shame of misleading politicians'. This poor girl had lost friends to knife violence and she was a good campaigner with a good message, but her need to make her story more dramatic undid all of her good work and cost her worthy cause a lot of credibility.

The moral of the activism tale is never be tempted to stray from the truth when telling your story, even if it's a small exaggeration. In our digital age, everything is traceable. Keep your story clean: it will speak for itself.

Backlash doesn't just come from tabloids and trolls – haters come in all shapes and sizes. Many activists find that the communities they expect to have their back end up abandoning them, as Yeonmi did:

> In my naivety, I never thought anyone would question the facts I presented about North Korea. But, as we know, there are people who deny the Holocaust. There are people who think the earth is flat. People believe conspiracy theories. I suppose it should come as no surprise then that there are people who claim there are no executions inside North Korea.
>
> I was only 13 years old when I escaped. When I spoke out I figured everyone already knew about the situation in North Korea. I didn't see myself as a threat to the government in any way. I didn't expose any state secrets like a nuclear programme...There is satellite footage of the concentration camps and the UN has witnessed the mass starvation in the country! Yet the regime targeted me for speaking out. Anyone who was left in North Korea that was related to me was made to contribute to a propaganda film against me. When I was writing my book I received threats from the North Korean government over the publishing of my book.

It wasn't just Kim Jong-un's propaganda team who took me on: many North Korean defectors talk about North Korea but don't talk about their experiences being human trafficked in China. There are victims who resent the fact that I talked about my story because they want to be able to keep telling themselves that it didn't happen to them. They want to be able to deny their lived experiences so they can have what they consider to be a second chance at life. As a society, we punish and shame the victims instead of the perpetrators. The research shows us nine out of ten women who defect from North Korea end up being trafficked at some point.

Backlash of any kind can be disheartening but it can also be informative: it can tell us a lot about where we are as a society. The fact that people have a problem with what you are saying or what you stand for often indicates that it's high time the conversation started.

If you need to tell your story, there may be somebody who is desperate to listen to it. If you feel that you are able to stick your head above the parapet then know that there will be other people, just like you, who are grateful for you speaking out – even if they don't have the courage to do so themselves. Coming out in 1993 meant that Olympic champion **Mark Tewksbury** became a figurehead for LGBT sportspeople, even though relatively few athletes are out of the closet even today:

There's never a right moment for activism. I got to a point where I knew that I had to share my story because it became such a weight. I felt I had been lying about who I was for as long as I could remember. Sharing my story gave me my integrity back. I no longer felt torn inside, I felt solid. It brought me my power back.

My advice to anyone who wants to open up about their experiences is to find somebody that you know you can trust, somebody that will accept you no matter what. You think when you're ready to share your story and start your journey, everyone's going to be excited for you. But for a lot of people it's often the first time they have heard of this issue, or talked about it, so it takes them time to get to where you are.

I was an Olympic champion, my country loved me. I was on the front cover of *Time* magazine, and everyone kept saying, 'Oh, you're so great.' I thought, 'Okay, let's test this.' I decided to use that enormous amount of goodwill to shake people up, to put in people's faces: 'I know you don't think gay looks like this but, baby, THIS is gay.' Some people might call that brave. I was desperate to be myself, longing to be a whole human being. It came across as brave but it was just an act of survival.

Discrimination is an insidious thing because often you don't see it. I had one big contract that I lost as a result of me publicly coming out but who knows how many more organizations didn't partner with me as a result. When you're brave enough to move forward, you might lose stuff, but it will be replaced with more interesting things.

The most important thing is to tell your story for YOU. You may receive backlash, you may receive adoration…it is possible that no one will even listen. The act of speaking your truth is a service first and foremost to yourself. Keeping a purity of mind about the reasons you are telling your story will help drown out the noise and the naysayers. You never know what road your activism will take you down; focus on the truth and your cause, rather than your audience. You don't need to go into the lion's den straight away – start with people you trust and care about and build your confidence from there onwards.

Method is more important than strength

Truthfully, knowing that you want to share your story is half the equation. Finding the medium that works best for doing so is fundamental to successful activism. Not everyone is a writer and many people hate public speaking. Finding a way of communicating that chimes with you and your message may be a challenge.

Try and find what feels natural and right for you. It might be public speaking. It might be writing. But it might be music. It might be through your YouTube channel. Just because you haven't seen it done before doesn't mean it won't be effective in conveying your message.

Any medium can be effective for storytelling. When you've found the one that's comfortable for you, you should then look at what tools complement that platform. If you're a writer, that might be Medium, Tumblr or Twitter.

It also depends on the age of your audience. If you're connecting with Gen Z, you almost certainly should be using Instagram or Snapchat. Younger people put visual communication and photography at the heart of how they see the world and record events. Finding a technology which enhances your storytelling is optimal. And keep a lookout – you can do well as an early adopter of the next big channel or streaming service. In terms of preparing to tell your story to the press, you need to be proactively curious about the ways in which different news sources will handle issues. It's all very well to regularly watch CNN, but if you don't know how Fox is interpreting the same event you won't know how your story may be picked up and dealt with. You need to register the spin that different media outlets will add to further their agenda.

The more you can inform yourself about the types of news that different people are consuming, the better. We're not saying read the *Daily Mail* or the *Sun* every day, but it's important to know what a big chunk of the population are reading about Brexit, if you want to understand what views people are taking with them to the ballot box. Public libraries are good places to access a range of publications. You should read different qualities of journalism from different sources so you can understand the broader discourse. Remember that when you convince your naysayers you are more than halfway to your goal.

The medium that inspires you may be something close to home. **Jack Monroe**'s success as a poverty campaigner is rooted in her food blog which became a huge hit. Food is something that is very personal and, like **Ron Garan**'s flower (page 29), something everyone can relate to:

I started off my writing with a politics blog. I had about 17 followers. When I started to write about food, that's when it really took off. Food is political but also everybody needs it. I think the blog really brought home the reality that some people don't have three meals a day. Some people don't have anything to eat. Some people watch their children eat tiny little snacks that they can't eat together. My post in 2012 really touched a nerve - I wrote that: 'Poverty is the sinking feeling when your small boy finishes his one Weetabix and says "more Mummy, bread and jam please, Mummy" as you're wondering whether to take the TV or the guitar to the pawn shop first, and how to tell him that there is no bread or jam.' People were shocked that in Britain, the sixth richest economy in the world, people live in absolute desperate poverty.

Picking a medium that people can relate to, whether it's food, or photography, enables others to personally respond to experiences they may not have encountered. The subjective responses that people may have can create a deeper emotional resonance with your cause.

We are visual creatures

We all know the maxim 'a picture speaks a thousand words'. We are biologically hardwired to give a lot of credence to images – the visual is, fundamentally, how we perceive the world around us. Photography is often thought of as an objective, and therefore unbiased, medium for documenting historic moments. However, photographers make choices on composition, cropping and subject inclusion. They introduce a point of view into the work which influences the way we see and understand the image.

We're bombarded with so much imagery on a minute-by-minute basis these days that our most common response to photography is indifference. But if you're able to move people with a photograph you will have succeeded in partly telling a story.

A good photo can place you at an exact moment in time or history. A photographer is able, through artistic licence, to show not just what they were seeing but *how* they were viewing it. This is why activist photography can be so potent.

Fifty years ago, the national police chief of South Vietnam calmly approached a prisoner in the middle of a Saigon street and fired a bullet into his head. A few feet away stood **Eddie Adams**, an Associated Press photographer, who captured the exact moment of the gunshot. The photograph won a Pulitzer Prize and became one of the most powerful pictures of the Vietnam War, or any war, ever taken. The picture ran on the front pages of many US newspapers. Its frozen portrait of agony fuelled the anti-war movement and helped end US involvement.

However, Adams later warned against the limitations of activist photography – for the same reason that they are impactful, the eloquence of an image can be dangerous:

> The general killed the Viet Cong; I killed the general with my camera. Still photographs are the most powerful weapon in the world. People believe them, but photographs do lie, even without manipulation. They are only half-truths. What the photograph didn't say was, 'What would you do if you were the general at that time and place on that hot day, and you caught the so-called bad guy after he blew away one, two or three American soldiers?'

Like **Fatima Bhutto** (see page 35), Bangladeshi photographer and media activist **Shahidul Alam** warns that 'parachute' activists can have a negative impact on the places you are trying to help. You give people a literal 'snap' of a community which has more complexities to it than can be captured in a single image:

> Photography is one of the most powerful ways we tell stories. Perceptions of countries like mine have largely been created by visiting photographers. Their take on our culture, our country and our society has been very narrow and very blinkered, and blatantly following a particular stereotype. The Drik Picture Library

was aimed at challenging that. In countries where textual literacy is relatively low, images have a greater reach. The power of photography is immense. It's used by corporations in marketing, it is used as propaganda. Our minds are influenced by a language that we have never been trained to understand or decipher.

There is an unjust power dynamic in mainstream photography. In order to truly share someone's story you have to recognize the systemic inequalities that exist in this industry. *The Times* editor, the person who is farthest removed from a situation, has the most power over a story, whereas the villager who is being photographed and knows the most about the situation is in the position of weakness. That villager has zero input on how the story is told. We felt we needed to change this. We wanted to turn that model on its head and use local photographers and tell peoples' authentic stories. We set up our own gallery and started to teach photography.

Shahidul Alam's dedication to the truth has long caused intense friction with the Bangladeshi government, culminating in his arrest in 2018. He was released on bail and named as one of the *Time* People of the Year in 2018 which honoured '"The Guardians" in the War on Truth' – journalists who have been targeted for their work, including Jamal Khashoggi.

Use photography to enhance your activism – it will help others see your case with their own eyes.

Art takes courage

Photography is such a powerful storytelling tool because it can be both an accurate record and artistic. Injecting creativity into your activism will help make it more effective. When it comes to telling your story, you will combine the creative power of the arts to move people emotionally with the strategic planning required to bring about social change.

Art moves the heart and the soul, whereas activism is about making change in people's minds. Ultimately, to be a successful activist you have to win hearts AND minds and art can help evoke the emotional responses you need to urge real action.

You may not feel that you are the most creative person or it might feel uncomfortable to put your artistic side out for all to see. Courage starts with showing up and being seen. If you don't know where to start in terms of making your activism more creative, try taking up a creative hobby and using it as a private outlet for your emotions. Over time, this might develop into an artistic skill you're able to share with the world, as mental health campaigner and poet **Hussain Manawer** found:

> I have always been a writer; it started as bars (raps) then moved on to stories and then poems. I believe it is so important to invest in your mind, and using poetry is a way to do this in order to convey emotions through written words. I write poetry to help get people through life. I like to see it as a daily dose of realness, and a daily dose of depth. I talk about issues that actually really affect people, and aren't really spoken about.
>
> Experiences such as depression and anxiety can affect us all in different ways and to varying degrees. When you're dealing with such subjective occurrences, art such as poetry, painting and music can offer the opportunity to share those crippling emotions in a form devoid of any stigma. If you speak to people in a language they can interpret in their own personal way, you reach deep into their hearts.

When you are being your authentic self you are more concerned with truth than other people's opinions. Your testimony and ability to hold a mirror up to society is your most basic but powerful way to create change and make a difference. When you tell your story, your honesty can become your legacy.

It's not the words or the means that matter – it's the story. The great storytellers in history are often not the best writers or the best singers, but their story will stay with you. Telling your story, in whatever way you can, will educate and empower your audience. You can shift responsibility away from victims onto society as a whole – when we tell stories they become collectively owned by everyone who has heard them. You will be able to bring a unique human element to your cause and make abstract issues like corruption or censorship less about mechanisms and more about morality.

Hearing other people tell their stories lets us know that we're not alone – storytelling in itself is a service to society and enriches our understanding and future generations' understanding of the human experience. If you have a story, get it out there. Someone is waiting to hear it.

Who are we to tell you how to tell your story checklist

- Use your story to create empathy – even among people who have not had your experience. Find the part of your experience that will enable people to empathize with you.

- Be bold with your storytelling – don't dilute your message.

- Don't be afraid of making people feel uncomfortable – it can make them see that something needs to change.

- Think about using humour – even dark humour – to address uncomfortable issues. It can be an incredibly useful tool.

- Make sure you're certain that you have the right to tell another person's story before you tell it.

- Remember that the most humble stories are often the most affecting.

- Don't be in a rush to tell a story – it can be told bit by bit – but be sure that you are ready for the consequences of how you might feel and how it might be received by others.

- Look carefully at the various mediums with which you can tell a story and choose one that suits your abilities and that is accessible to you.

- Don't ignore pictures – remember 'show and tell' is one of the most memorable ways of telling a story.

- Make sure you stick to your story; be consistent and don't embellish it.

Chapter Three
How to use social media effectively

Technology has always shaped significant social movements. The tactics and communication systems of activist movements have always adapted to the technology of the day. During the civil rights movement, the Wide Area Telephone Service was crucial to communicating issues from the Jim Crow Deep South across the United States, enabling activists to report local civil rights abuses to the national media and the FBI.

Internet activism existed before social media was even a phrase. In the 1990s, Mexican rebel group the Zapatista Army of National Liberation (EZLN) started a grassroots uprising against the government in response to the North American Free Trade Agreement. They organized gatherings and protests primarily through emails, eventually forming the anti-globalization group called Peoples' Global Action with other world activists in 1998. Together they focused on protesting against the World Trade Organization.

Activism on social media has become a global version of Speakers' Corner in Hyde Park, where people once got up on soapboxes to declaim about the issues of the day. Social media allows us to reach inconceivable sizes of audience with our message online, potentially creating real action offline. Before social media, no one individual outside the very highest levels of power could individually reach millions of people. It just couldn't be done. Television, and sometimes radio, could do it, but that was about it – and mainstream media was way beyond the access of most activists. Then, suddenly, the world woke up to viral campaigns that reached millions across the globe.

The internet has provided a space where people can express their views on any issue at any time, which is a fundamental shift in the power dynamic of communications. We can amplify sentiments and experiences faster than ever before, pitting Davids against Goliaths for the first time ever in the mass communications industry.

Being able to share messages and forge connections with people on the other side of the planet has made the world seem smaller, brought remote voices closer and allowed us to find commonalities which, until 15 years ago, may have been confined to our local communities or passed on by word of mouth, magazines or newsletters. People have been experiencing things for their whole lives, for generations or even centuries, and may have thought they were the only ones who felt a certain way. Social media has allowed us to understand we are not alone in our experiences and that some of these are even universally felt.

In terms of activism social media is important because individual outrage is where activism starts, but it can only take you so far. You need mass outrage to spark a movement and drive change, and social media has become the forum for mass outrage or mass empathy. In many countries, the combination of radical transparency and shared experience helps shine a light on corruption. For example, in 2012 Sabina Essa, a South African model, bragged via Twitter that she had got out of paying a traffic penalty by bribing a police officer. The tweet went viral because so many people related to it – South Africans recognized it as a frustrating everyday incident. It provoked such an enormous outpouring because many people were angry with her bragging about the event but also were infuriated by the corruption in the police. Since then, the ability for citizens to express dissatisfaction with corruption has transitioned from online outrage to political consequences: in the past two years, we have seen corruption issues upset governments (and, in some cases, even lead to the imprisonment of senior political figures) in Romania, South Africa, Argentina, Brazil, Moldova, Guatemala and South Korea, among others.

Social media is increasingly becoming an important tool in political campaigns. Elections are usually won by the candidate with the best grasp of the technology of the day: from Kennedy to Obama, to the Brexit Leave campaign – even though most of the world might wish that Donald Trump had never discovered Twitter, his ability to use the medium to dominate mass communication with instant engagement and reactive updates undeniably contributed to his success in the 2016 election.

The phenomenon of social media has created multiple easy entry points to activism – memorable movements like #BringBackOurGirls, #MeToo and #BlackLivesMatter have seen wide international coverage in recent years. There is no doubt that social media has led to breaking records in awareness – millions of likes is a great accomplishment. It's wonderful that someone's actually bothered to press a button to say 'I'm on your side', but if that is as far as that goes you will not be able to make real change. Activism must go beyond hashtags and filling empty hearts with your finger to make a real difference. Social media is a weapon in awareness raising. It is a weapon that allows you to contact and potentially talk to the powerful. It can make them listen but can it make them act?

Growing and rallying an audience

Building an audience can seem like the biggest challenge on social media – if only your grandma and your friends from college are liking your posts, how are you ever going to make a difference? Audiences grow when you have a strong profile and consistent, quality content. Posting regular, original content will guarantee audience growth as long as you keep up to date with the current trends regarding captions, links and cross-referencing content. Beyond the simple truth of dedication leading to success, you can increase your audience by having engaged, lively accounts which interact with other users and groups – social media is more like a conversation in the pub than you might imagine: being responsive and reactive creates more connections than simply shouting without listening.

Because of the way the algorithms on these platforms work, social media campaigns often preach to the choir, to those already on your side. The challenge is how you can get your message to jump over the barrier into either the opposition camp or to the sea of indifference and motivate the apathetic and your adversaries to support your cause. For example, in 2019, the Trump campaign and its supporters are a closed circle – they're people who support one another's views. It doesn't matter what comments Trump makes or what he does, his supporters are absolutely immovable. Reaching out to those people on social media by an opposition camp has not been done before in a meaningful and consistent way. If you're trying to have real influence over these people, the way they make their decisions and where they get their information from, you have to engage with these communities online. This will ensure that your base support is diverse and widespread which will enable you to have a powerful support system offline.

Consistency of message and commitment to the cause are also really important in social media. There are so many blogs that last for a few weeks before the blogger/writer gives up. If you want to use social media for activism, discipline and dedication are really important. Social media is so ephemeral that if you're not providing constant updates and the freshest, most accurate information, there will be fresher and more accurate information elsewhere. Consistent messaging and regular updates are fundamental.

Kenny Imafidon is the 23-year-old managing director of ClearView Research and director of Bite The Ballot, a campaign to increase young voter turnout ahead of the Brexit referendum. He discovered that an audience can be built through strategic partnerships:

> The #TurnUp campaign had over 50 partners providing support in different capacities. By working with a variety of partners, such as UK Youth, Tinder, Uber, Deliveroo, Ben & Jerry's, Starbucks UK, Unilad (and many more), the #TurnUp campaign was able to spread its message to a wider audience in creative ways. For example, in 2016, Tinder launched Swipe the Vote in the US to help US users learn more about the presidential candidates. As part of the #TurnUp campaign Tinder partnered with Bite The Ballot to provide UK users with Swipe the Vote: UK Edition to help users learn more about the European Union ahead of the EU referendum.
>
> Tinder's third largest market was the UK and more than 20 per cent of Tinder users in the UK swiped right to learn more about the referendum. After completing the survey, 90 per cent of participants, who were millennials between the ages of 18 and 34, had more clarity on the issues surrounding the UK referendum. They also had the option to learn more about the issues and – most importantly – easily register to vote through a direct link.
>
> By collaborating with the partners we worked with, we were able to ensure that the #TurnUp campaign stood out. We focused on working with brands who already could reach millions of millennial voters and were willing to use their brand influence for social

good. We had to make sure the campaign was as exciting as possible, and involved brands and influencers who were not the usual suspects in the conversation around politics.

Campaigns such as these obviously require detailed planning and a coordinated team before you start engaging with the public – but, as Kenny points out, just because you aren't a major player on a certain issue doesn't mean you won't add significant value to it – people know what to expect from the 'usual suspects' but your voice may add something fresh and unique.

If you don't have an audience yourself, consider partnering with an influencer who does. This can be challenging if they are not known for their activist work – creators and influencers can be complicated partners – but it can be worth putting in the effort in order to elevate your message. The **Eh Bee Family** have over 8 million YouTube subscribers and 11 million Facebook followers who love their family-friendly comedy. They appreciate the complexities of asking an influencer to use their platform for something new, and offer the following advice:

There are a lot of creators who are worried about advocating for something that they believe in because it's off-brand. They're worried that they would normally get 4 million views per video but, if they speak out about a social cause, they are afraid that they're going to get a 100,000 views and it will look like their channel's dying. Many creators fear becoming irrelevant.

It's very hard to convince a creator who has been creating one type of content for so long to step out of their comfort zone and say, 'You know what? I'm going to make a video about inequality on my channel.' It hurts a lot of these creators when their views drop because of their advocacy. If you're partnering with an influencer, we would advise to give them freedom. Make sure that they're on point with the messaging but do allow them to use their platform freely. They know how best to speak to their audience, so giving them complete flexibility will make the influencers feel empowered and will probably lead to better engagement with the content.

Whether your audience is 100 people or a million people, you can use your following to amplify your activism. The **Eh Bee Family** have been able to work with their millions of subscribers to tackle social causes that matter to them:

> We try to keep our content funny and family oriented. When it comes to activism we know that we can't advocate for everything, because if you advocate for everything, then what do you stand for? When you can't home in and specialize in one cause, everything gets watered down. We feel most connected to issues that protect women and children so that is what we choose to discuss.

> We try to create content that keeps with the Eh Bee Family tone; we still try to make our messages light-hearted and not too judgemental. We are careful not to make people feel like we're preaching at them. We've always lived with strong family values, strong morals and integrity. We can still have fun and laugh while changing the world. You can use whatever it is that you're passionate about, whether it's animal rights, or poverty alleviation, and use all of your efforts to advocate for these causes while still doing so in a light-hearted manner.

You may not be a great comedian or storyteller, and indeed your issue may be serious, but it's worth recognizing that the internet is awash with issues and people have shorter and shorter attention spans – presenting your content in an entertaining and easy-to-consume, digestible way can help create an engaging entry point to activism for your audience. Remember, most people won't be looking for a hard-hitting campaign when they log on to check their social media accounts. You need to get people on side.

While building an audience is important, don't get preoccupied with numbers. Someone may have thousands more followers, but those followers may be bots. A smaller but more focused audience can sometimes be more impactful. Egyptian activist **Wael Ghonim** organized mass demonstrations through the Facebook page We Are All Khaled Said, which ultimately resulted in the resignation of President Hosni Mubarak. He explains:

Don't be disheartened if reality doesn't meet your expectations. The timing of a change, it's nature and how it manifest itself is out of our control. The unexpected collapse of the Ben Ali regime in Tunisia made it possible for Egyptians to imagine a better future for themselves, something that wouldn't have ever been imagined by any activists pre-revolution.

When the page was created, in the first three days 100,000 people joined. People initially liked the page, then interacted with the content, shared their own ideas, and eventually participated in decentralized street activities. Members of the page were deepening their engagement in collective actions.

In the attention economy there is a lot of weight on numbers as a proxy for value which can be deceiving. Our Facebook page was more active and effective when it had 250,000 members than when it had more than 1.6 million. Optimizing for numbers is a game with diminishing values. It's about who are these people, what do they stand for, and what are they willing to do. I'd advise activists to focus on those who are committed to advance their cause, not those who are providing them with attention.

The Arab Spring was a particularly historic movement within the rise and power of dissemination social media activism. A series of anti-government uprisings started in Tunisia and then spread like wildfire across the Middle East. Social media enabled protests to occur in societies where press censorship was very prominent. Activists were able to broadcast a call to action and announce logistical things like meeting points and times to large numbers of people.

It was a global awakening of the power of this tool. Social media exposed people living under authoritarian systems to information about democracy. The hope and possibility for the rise of democracies manifested in places which previously would have been perceived as authoritarian strongholds. What was particularly interesting about the Arab Spring was that all of the Arab countries speak Arabic so there was much more understanding between the parallel movements. It created a sense of unity which made revolution seem possible for others when protests began to spread.

Social media – while having no magic in its own right – was a powerful organizing and rallying tool, so powerful as to draw enough people to the streets to overthrow multiple dictators.

You also need to organize protests or engage mainstream media alongside your social media campaign. Greta Thunberg stood outside of parliament during a school day with a sign to campaign for greater action to combat climate change when she was just fifteen. Social media has amplified her campaign and allowed for it to thrive and spread, but it is important to remember that her campaign exists in the real world and engages people face to face. The same is true of the #BringBackOurGirls campaign. They went and protested at parliament every week. The international pressure created because of the viral hashtag made people in power pay attention and allowed the #BringBackOurGirls campaigners to keep up the fight in the real world. If **Wael Ghonim**'s campaign had only been about social awareness, it would not have toppled governments. It was the gathering of people in public places that did that. It was the engagement and transition into offline action that made it so significant, as Wael explains:

> The goal of the page was to align the interests of its members. We would poll people about our next plans. What is our next collective action? Who is doing what? When are we doing? etc. We encouraged people to submit photos, videos, and written content. In return, we got many people involved in enriching the members' knowledge and creativity. Engagement is critical. It allows people to collaborate on exchanging knowledge. It liberates the human imagination, and creates endless opportunities for what can't be created individually. True leaders inspire not direct.

> The more a cause is attached to an ego, the less it survives. It's important to evolve our understanding of our causes collectively and find a role for all of us to play in nurturing them. January 25th started by an anonymous call on Facebook, I'd imagine that contributed to its success. No one represented 25th of January, so 25th of January represented everyone.

Building a community online

Despite the common trope that social media is making us antisocial, it does allow us to connect with people about causes that matter to us. If you're experiencing something and it is causing you problems, the chances are that somewhere in the world someone else is experiencing it too. Even in the case of rare illnesses. What was previously a feeling of 'being alone' can now be a shared discovery of global belonging. If there are only six of you in the world with a certain illness, before social media you would never have known each other. Now you can connect with those people online.

The disabled community has been able to do this successfully. Some people with disabilities aren't able to leave their house alone and may have previously struggled to connect with others, but social media has enabled them to create meaningful connections with other people – they can share their issues openly, or share photos or artwork if they prefer. Ultimately, these relationships are fundamental to individual well-being as well as to activism.

The trans community's activism and solidarity has also been amplified by the internet. Trans and gender non-binary people are able to find other people with whom they share similar experiences. **Jazz Jennings** is a LGBT rights activist and YouTuber, who cofounded TransKids Purple Rainbow in 2007, an organization which assists transgender youth. She also has a TLC television series called *I Am Jazz* which documents her experience transitioning from male to female. Jazz sees the building and maintaining of a community as being the core tenet of activism:

I never look at it as a responsibility. This isn't just about me, it's about the entire trans community. I try not to put that pressure on myself because even though I am trying to speak out for all trans voices, I'm still just Jazz and I can only be the best representation of myself that I can be. My favourite part of being an activist is being able to speak to kids and families, and seeing how our family and story has been able to positively influence their lives, it's just really incredible.

The most important thing for activists is building a community. A lot of people don't know there are other people out there who feel the same way or are suffering in the same way that they are. Every single year we throw a party at the Philadelphia Trans-Wellness Conference for transgender and gender non-conforming kids and their families. It's really incredible because all these kids get to gather together for the first time and meet others like themselves with their families present.

When it comes to my advocacy, my main focus is trying to build a community to help out kids and families who are looking for support. It's also important to speak out to those who haven't been introduced to someone who's transgender before and don't know what it means, or maybe are transphobic. I try to ask people to have an open mind. If you listen to me or another transgender person speak and you hear our stories, then you'll realize that we're human beings too, just trying to find our happiness in this world. I try to tell people to step into our shoes - I know that they don't have gender dysphoria, but I try to get them to imagine what life would be like if they did. I tell them to imagine that they felt they were another gender while the whole world was telling them that they had a mental illness or that they should be locked away or that they're crazy. I try to make them feel empathy for transgender people which is easier to do when I have a community behind me.

Once a sizeable community is formed around a cause, it's sometimes difficult to agree on what your demands and actions should be. Defining them and getting agreement on them is crucial. A lot of movements fail because they have too many demands, or indeed their demands are too vague or not enough people agree on the steps needed to be taken. The more unity and shared ownership you can forge, the more successful your community can be, as you are united by one finite message.

Building a community is always going to be complex because you might all care about a social cause, but you may disagree about everything else in the world. It's important that your community stays fairly focused, otherwise there will be too many lines along which you can splinter.

Broadening your audience's horizons

Community building goes hand in hand with creating more awareness about a campaign or a cause. The emergence of a community online can, in itself, become a story, because it is a manifestation of the extent to which people are affected by an issue. During the early days of the #MeToo Twitter storm, many men expressed surprise at the sheer number of women using the hashtag to identify themselves as someone who had been abused or harassed. Collectiveness, previously under wraps, exploded into public awareness.

Black Lives Matter also showed how universal certain experiences were. #BlackLivesMatter proved that police brutality was something experienced by African-Americans in many cities at the hands of many different police forces and numerous justice departments. It proved that this wasn't something that was only experienced in Cleveland or Ferguson; that the historic degradation and disenfranchisement of African-Americans in America was still very much alive and that the American establishment hadn't progressed. The world would have never known about the 276 Chibok girls who were kidnapped by Boko Haram if not for the hashtag BringBackOurGirls. **Edith Yassin**, the Chairperson of the Strategic Team told us how social media shine a light on the emergency:

> In February 2014 in Buni Yadi, the Yobe State, 59 boys had been murdered. The pictures were out in traditional media. They had been murdered and there was an attempt to set their school alight. Some of them were partially burnt after they had been murdered. Nigeria just seemed to have moved on from that event. It just went by like nothing had happened. I was furious. Then in April, Boko Haram kidnapped the girls for attending school. This time I felt outraged but other people did as well.
>
> The angst about the Chibok girls started on Twitter. Women were tweeting about it and demanding a march. The government was still in denial and was not telling us the truth about the situation. So on the 30th of April we marched. We marched to the National Assembly. We marched to parliament in the pouring rain.

A member of the Chibok community had said, 'If you leave now, the issue will be forgotten.' In light of that truth, we agreed we would meet again the next day and the day after that. From there, it just snowballed, and we marched every single day. We were just putting everything out there on social media in real time. We used Facebook and Twitter especially. That always gave traction to the story and that was how come the whole world learned about the issue. We just didn't relent.

Soon we were hosting meetings and deciding on a strategy to pursue. We formed a media group, a security group and a strategy group. We had to break into groups to deal with every element of our campaign efficiently. In the first 40 days we were constantly harassed by government agencies. We had to keep changing venues just to evade government security forces. Of course, we did not know that our movement was going to go on for over four years.

The Chibok girls did not belong to the so-called privileged class of Nigeria. Things would have been very different if the child of a minister was in that school. However, social media did not discriminate based on class. People heard about the fact that young girls who had been attending school were kidnapped. Their class didn't matter to people online.

Social media has made it easier for people to be 'aware'. Raising awareness is something that's fairly straightforward to do if you have an audience, but also requires intelligent consumption of the news and intelligent redistribution of key information. Articles that are on the BBC or CNN are widely read pieces of journalism. But as a social media activist you can go beyond the mainstream and provide your audience with more depth. The BBC and CNN are catering for the general public. They stop the analysis of issues at the point where the general public loses interest. Your community – say, a community that is interested in Syria – has a deeper level of interest. You can provide them with more information. Broadcasting niche and specific information on your issue will enable people to engage with the issues at a deeper and more intellectual level.

DeRay Mckesson is one of the most prominent figures of the Black Lives Matter movement and uses his Twitter feed to help his followers (over one million of them) gain access to a deeper understanding when it comes to issues of race and justice:

> I try and use the platform now to make sure that anybody who follows me is seeing news that they otherwise might not see or a perspective that I think is really important. I do think people have gotten much smarter on Twitter than they were before. I think that is a net positive. I think that people have more language than they had before and have been more exposed to a range of issues. That's really powerful.

The more that you're able to share nuanced, sophisticated analysis of issues with an audience who genuinely cares about them, the better you can contribute to solving a problem and forcing change to happen.

As well as building your own audience and sharing your opinions, consider the role that social media can play in empowering the communities you want to help. Social media puts cameras and reporters on the ground and in the hands of people whose voices may not otherwise be catalogued. Everyone now has the ability to document their lives and tell their stories. For the first time ever history is being recorded and written at the same time, is made, and it is accessible to almost everyone who has internet access.

For so long, tragedies have been narrated by external (mainly Western) news organizations, often only at the point that the suffering is so extreme they have to make time for it. Social media redresses this power imbalance. As we've said before – as good as our intentions may be, often the best type of activism is getting out of the way and letting people tell their own stories in their own way. Social media allows many communities to do this for the first time in history – this raises awareness in a whole new sense: people can now be truly aware of what life is like for the people who need their help.

Beware slacktivism

Slacktivism is when people become engaged with causes for fairly brief periods of time on social media. They may like something, retweet it, use a hashtag … at the very most donate a fiver or sign an online petition. None of these actions are bad. But none of them are solving problems either. They spike quickly but can equally quickly dissipate and be forgotten for the next trend.

To an extent, slacktivism has an important role to play in the sense that it raises the general level of public consciousness of social issues and creates a sense of caring and concern and global solidarity, all of which are good things and a sign of an increasingly healthy society. The danger of slacktivism is that people think they've done something. They become complacent and feel a false sense of accomplishment. They're not quite averting their gaze but they aren't fully engaging with the issue either.

The combination of the general exhaustion with social causes and the sense of self-congratulation that accompanies slacktivism can mean that problems don't actually get addressed. The depth of the issues is brushed under the carpet because nobody really has the attention span to engage with it for long enough. Their attention is diverted and they move on.

Activism has to go beyond hashtags, gifs, memes, shared images, posts. It's not good enough to be passionate about a cause and just retweet something occasionally. Social media has much more power than that, and it can be used very successfully for campaigns.

The Occupy movement was born in September 2011, and is an interesting example of online activism meeting physical activism. The hashtag #Occupy enabled people to mobilize and gather, but it was the image of people physically occupying spaces such as Wall Street that made headlines and caused genuine inconvenience to bankers. While its aims of reforming big banking and campaign finance were unsuccessful, the movement brought the concept of the 1 per cent and the 99 per cent into the mainstream – a fundamental lesson about inequality which we didn't have before.

Kony 2012 was a very creative and impressive social media campaign, but has become a poster child for the hazards of slacktivism. The campaign promised to capture Joseph Kony, a Ugandan warlord who is responsible for kidnapping children to make them soldiers. The 30-minute campaign video reached 100 million views in six days. It was important in showing that you can get people to care about someone they've never heard of in a country far away. Success on the internet is binary. We aim to raise a certain amount of money through crowdfunding or hit a certain number of retweets – you either accomplish your goal or you don't. We either find Kony or we don't.

No one in Uganda necessarily thought that finding Kony would solve the deep entrenched problems in Uganda resulting from many, many years of conflict. So why was a 'solution' proposed which was so far removed from what would actually help people on the ground? In part, this is because the people running the campaign were not the ones who had been on the ground for years in Uganda. Kony 2012 showed how excitable and also how naive people can be. It's not clear what kids in Wisconsin or Tokyo were supposed to do about locating Kony, but the campaign wasn't entirely pointless: *Time* magazine called it the most viral video ever, and the US Senate ended up sending troops to the African Union.

Both #Occupy and Kony 2012 achieved certain things, but neither of them came close to solving the problems they set out to fix. Perhaps they were too ambitious or their goals intangible. However, their main problem was their lack of a plan to achieve their goal. If you get vast numbers of online supporters, the chances are you will get the mainstream media knocking on the door. What are you going to do about that when it happens?

The Kony 2012 campaign could have had millions of people rally to their cause. But their supporters just endorsed the message. It didn't translate to substantial offline action in part because the creators were not expecting the reach they had, and had not strategically plotted their desired outcome. They did not have a plan to take the social media campaign to the next stage. This was in many ways a wasted opportunity – it is critical to have an end goal in mind, but also to plan the steps that you will take to reach that end.

What we can learn from these examples is that creating mass participation on the internet is far from impossible, but directing that mass participation to making a difference requires a strategic plan behind the catchy hashtag or a funny challenge. **Kenny Imafidon** offers the following advice to make your campaign go the distance:

1. Do not launch your campaign until you have a clear plan and strategy. Make sure you think carefully about the key stakeholders you need to have on board, identify who you are trying to influence and, crucially, what actions you want them to make. Also, think carefully about when the best time is to launch your campaign, as timing can be everything.

2. Ensure you have effective communication with your team. Make it clear from the beginning in what ways you will communicate. In the middle of a campaign, things might get crazy and you cannot afford to have ineffective or problematic communication.

3. Raise enough capital to finance the online campaign team or make sure you have enough volunteers - you do not want members of your team to burnout in the heat of the campaign.

Steps that may seem like common sense are too often overlooked, especially the element of setting clear objectives. Remember that the internet is much more black and white than real life and your demands need to reflect that. You can't solve every single problem with one campaign so double down on simple messaging in a way that allows your audience to get to grips with it. If you want to deal with police brutality hone in on one change you'd like to see first, whether it be a racially diverse force or disarming officers, and hammer that message home. There has to be structure to your objectives and you have to maintain your focus on what you want.

Turning slactivism into meaningful activism

Humour and entertainment are important aspects of internet activism – most people surf the web for enjoyment, so making your activism accessible and amusing will help grow and engage your audience. You don't have to be a comedian or a creative person yourself to bring the key ingredients for successful social media activism together. The ALS Ice Bucket Challenge used a fun challenge to raise money for a motor neurone disease, leading to research breakthroughs such as identifying a third gene which causes the disease and developing new gene therapy and drugs for treatment. **Pat Quinn** was diagnosed with ALS, a neurodegenerative disease that affects the nerve cells in the brain and spinal cord, in 2013, when he was 30 years old. He was one of the founders of the challenge, and explains how social media was critical to its success:

> Social media is powerful and connects us with one another faster than ever before. I didn't truly understand the power of social media until the summer of 2014. The Ice Bucket Challenge wasn't originally for ALS. It was going around for a number of different causes until one golfer in Florida took the challenge for his cousin's husband who had ALS. It caught on in this patient's town and the power of social media brought it to my attention. I will never forget the day I saw a friend from grade school take the challenge as he said he was doing it in my honour. No one could have imagined what was about to happen.

> All of the local events, community outreach, speaking, networking, and everything else I did in that first year-and-a-half following my diagnosis, led me right to the ALS Ice Bucket Challenge. I was lucky enough to be in the right place and time to make the Ice Bucket Challenge grow. I built a strong supportive network and connected with the right people. I reached out to another young patient shortly after diagnosis, Pete Frates, and our friendship we built would be the key to the challenge.

> A worldwide movement like the Ice Bucket Challenge doesn't just happen. It's not like I was sitting in a dark room drawing up blueprints to orchestrate the biggest movement in the history of philanthropy either. We live in a world that revolves around likes, shares and hashtags. We pushed everyone we knew to get out there and post their Ice Bucket Challenge video. And, without hesitation, they did! Once our family and friends took the challenge, friends of

friends did as well, and it spread from there. The multiplier effect of social media is unparalleled in any other medium.

The Ice Bucket Challenge raised $115 million for The ALS Association, but raised $220 million globally. You can reach so many people in a very quick period of time. Online activism is vital to reach the masses. There is no faster way to get your message out than online but do not undervalue your offline action. Offline action is where you develop more personal relationships. It's where you put a face to what you preach. The offline action I get involved in is talking directly to schools, colleges or universities, companies, sports teams, etc. Other offline action that's important is hosting events to rally the local community. You need a strong central support network right around you to get your message out quickly, but more importantly with passion. Anyone can tell you a story. However, if someone tells you a story with their heart, you will be more inclined to tell someone else.

Once you build your audience, you are in a position to ask your audience to do things offline. Creating a bridge between online awareness or discussion and offline action is very difficult but really important. Ultimately that is what social media activists should be striving to do.

For example, many people have tweeted #RefugeesWelcome. Let's unpack the sentiment and cross-examine what it means. What about asking ourselves questions such as 'How welcome are they? Are they welcome in your home?' There are many organizations which will allow you to put up a refugee for a couple of weeks or a couple of months in your spare room when they arrive in the country. Making sure that the options to get involved are available and visible to an audience who has expressed solidarity with an issue is relatively straight forward, but it's still done too rarely. A lot of people will stop at the hashtag and then will not try and address the concrete steps. Getting people online to take offline action is the biggest step in social media activism.

The aim is to lead people by the hand out of the whimsy, projection, self-promotion of social media and into *active* activism. Social media is a great place to reach out to people and stimulate conversation. While simply having these conversations may inspire some to become activists, to get mass involvement in a campaign activism must be made accessible. Providing links to fundraising pages during these discussions can help break the barrier between the digital and the real world. Sharing information about grassroots events that people may join will help attendance and engagement. The Climate Strikes that occurred around the world attracted millions of followers and were predominantly organized online.

The trolls who lurk under the bridge

Even non-activists are aware that social media is a fairly brutal environment. People don't go on Twitter to have a nuanced conversation. They get on to shout about issues and shout at each other.

Unfortunately, the safety of a computer screen brings out the 'brave' side in a lot of racist, sexist and mean people, who might not say something racist to somebody on the bus but are very happy to say it on Twitter.

There's another element of trolling that's just to do with success. For female activists this is a particularly worrying one. There are female politicians in the UK who have received threats of rape and death once appearing on news channels during primetime. The violence and vitriol that's targeted at women who speak out on issues is terrifying. Online hate speeches turn into hate crimes, such as the tragic murder of MP Jo Cox in June 2016.

That trolling and threats of violence online can manifest themselves in real life is an unfortunate aspect of the reality of activism today. Mandela was willing to die for the right to vote; the suffragettes were willing to be arrested and force fed ... often activists have to be willing to put themselves at risk to defend what they believe in.

Our recommendations to deal with trolling are as follows:

1. Prepare yourself for the fact that online abuse is too often a part and parcel of activist life.

2. Don't read hateful information. Feel free to disable comments

and be really disciplined about not reading responses and comments – reading vitriolic things is not going to make your activism more efficient. The reality is, most trolls are people you will never encounter in real life. The less you can engage with them, the better it will be for your mental health.

3. If someone in your community is being trolled, consider standing up for them. Being part of the fight can be important. The internet loves smackdowns. If you don't have a confrontational personality it can be really uncomfortable, but defending others is important. The fact that an activist receives solidarity from their supporters when they are being trolled can provide a lot of heart and comfort.

Ultimately, solidarity is one of the best aspects of online activism – movements such as #IStandWithAhmed, which expressed camaraderie with 14-year-old Ahmed Mohamed when he was arrested on suspicion of terrorism for bringing in a homemade clock to school, and #WhyIStayed, through which domestic violence victims shared the many complex reasons why they didn't leave their abusers, demonstrate the extent to which people are yearning for connection and support online.

As with any aspect of activism, the hard times are usually outweighed by the positives. Trolls and haters will be drowned out by the waves of support you get from your fellow activists. **Jazz Jennings** receives far too much abuse as an openly transgender teenager, but acknowledges that the encouragement she receives and help she is able to offer is far more important:

> It's definitely hard. My life is really out there for everyone to see and I made that decision consciously. I knew what I was getting into. I would consider myself a somewhat reserved and quiet person – a little introverted – I think it's truly important that I share my story, including all those personal details even if it opens it up to haters. I don't really care because I focus on the positive comments. Seeing all those people who I've been able to impact in a positive way just completely outweighs the negative 1000 per cent.

It's a crazy feeling to know that you have that profound effect on someone else. People have messaged me, saying that they were contemplating suicide, but then saw the show, and understood what it means to be trans. It's insane knowing that, not only have I changed lives, but my family has been able to save lives as well.

Bringing the fight online

Social media is not only used by activists for good. Extremist groups across the political spectrum have great success online, sometimes even greater than they do offline because their radical messages resonate well in the echo chamber of the internet and they are able to use analytics to find their target audience very effectively. In tackling extremism, we need to understand why extremist groups succeed online and how we can be even more successful than them in our online activism.

We all witnessed the rise of ISIS whose black flags tore through Iraq in 2014. This was the first time that we saw the danger of social media. The bad guys were suddenly using the same tool that we were using to try and find Kony and to occupy Wall Street. ISIS was using it to take children from their beds and bring them to Iraq to marry ISIS soldiers. The calibre of the technologists and social media people working for ISIS at its height in 2014 was remarkable. They understood how social media was able to replace a state broadcaster.

They also really understood that dreadful content, like beheadings and people being burned in cages, is content people want to watch. In the same way that people rubberneck on the highway when there's a car crash, people are drawn to the chaos and carnage of our human experience, the true mortality of us all.

The sensationalism of the ISIS 'brand' was certainly a potent use of social media. When someone liked or commented on a video it enabled ISIS to become aware of who might be a potential recruitment target. Social media was essentially used as a means to build a global army.

Fatima Zaman works with Extremely Together, an initiative backed by the Kofi Annan Foundation and the European Commission to counter violent extremism such as ISIS propaganda and promote peace. She recognizes the role that online networks can play in peace-building as well as radicalization:

> ISIS was an extremist organization which coordinated itself through social media. Its social media was prolific in engaging people. It used 38 different languages across multiple platforms. It published information 24/7 to ensure it would reach people in every time zone. In the past, terrorist organizations would radicalize people in the local communities they existed in. Few organizations had the reach that ISIS had. It was a very calculated approach. There were two levels of engagement with all potential targets. The first level of engagement was on more public platforms such as Facebook and Tumblr. The second level was on more private and personal apps, such as WhatsApp and Telegram, where the process continued.

> ISIS was successful in normalizing violence in social media behaviours. ISIS created sexy Hollywood-style videos of beheadings which were shared across channels and retweeted thousands of times. Videos of people being shot were modelled after Call of Duty. ISIS used hashtags to fit into the algorithms in order to spread their information and their visuals. When people searched the #CallofDuty they could easily be exposed to ISIS propaganda. This is one of the ways ISIS manipulates social media.

> Extremely Together recognized the propaganda was dynamic so our counter narrative needed to be equally dynamic. We had to take the fight to them online. Regardless of whether you are vulnerable or not, if you are only exposed to a violent narrative without pushback it will win and prevail. Having a counter narrative is the antidote to a violent ideology. I witnessed this in my community in east London. People became radicalized when they lost faith in society. Renewing that faith is key.

We taught people how to discern extremist content online and built their resilience to extreme ideology. We taught them how to become young peace-builders. If young people build a moral and spiritual resilience, and critical thinking, then when they are faced with extremism they will be able to reject it.

Combating misinformation in the era of fake news

An important aspect of countering extremist narratives is differentiating between real information and fiction. Fake news is an ongoing threat to a healthy press and a healthy civil society. For as long as there's been communication there has been propaganda and there's been the massaging of facts. Fake news has been a growing menace since Stalin began erasing purged political figures from photographs.

Its reach can now be accelerated by bots and often in sufficient volume to obscure or call into question the veracity of other, potentially factual, news.

While it's not a new occurrence, fake news can now be disseminated at a much greater rate than we could ever have imagined. The viral meme of Donald Trump calling Republican voters 'dumb' in *People* magazine was believed by millions of people, despite being completely false. One of the reasons why fake news has become so popular has to do with our willingness to consume it and to further confirm our prejudices. With this in mind, we too have a responsibility to break free from our echo chambers. We have to be aware of our perceptions and biases and actively seek to be informed by different news outlets and media platforms.

Fact check as much as you can. Being vocal about fact-checking things and providing alternative sources of information is really important. Use tools like Factcheck.org and PolitiFact.com and do your best to call out fake news whenever you see it.

Some fake news is obvious and some is very sophisticated. Educate yourself about the tools you can use to spot and report 'deepfakes'. Deepfakes are a type of video created by picking up one person's facial features and movements and grafting them onto another person's. This process requires a substantial amount of video and speaking material from a subject in order for them to be replicated. This means people in the public eye are more likely to be targeted than those who aren't.

One of the most common ways to detect whether a video is a deepfake is blinking. People in deepfake videos often blink far less than those in real life. Blurring in the face but not in the rest of the video, a partially obscured face or blurred edges may also point to a deepfake. The more research you do on these topics, the easier it will be to identify these misleading videos and information.

The AI Foundation is developing a tool called Reality Defender, because people's ability to fake video through artificial intelligence and sophisticated rendering is developing at a terrifying rate. Numerous elections have been affected by videos or recordings of politicians caught off guard; new technology is enabling people to fake these videos more convincingly than we would ever have believed possible.

Truth is a fundamental cornerstone of activism and fake news and 'alternative facts' will only stand to get in the way of your progress. Ensure that all aspects of your campaigns are entirely honest and call out fake news whenever you see it. The more photos and evidence you can provide, the less likely you are to fall victim to a campaign of misinformation. As with all aspects of social media, combating fake news requires diligence and determination.

The convenience of social media platforms can lull us into thinking that social media campaigns can be successful with limited effort on our parts – this is far from the case. Even if your campaign goes viral, you may not achieve your aims. Success in social media activism requires dedicated action offline as well as online – the world is yet to be changed by a hashtag alone. Be as energetic and committed on Twitter or Facebook as you would be at a protest or in person and always try to convert likes to offline action.

How to use social media effectively checklist

- Know who your audience is likely to be and know where they gather on social media.

- Build a community of people who support your clearly stated demands and actions – they are the core.

- Find out where the audience is that you need to convert to your cause – the people who don't share your view right now or who are potentially in agreement but are inactive.

- Be ruthlessly disciplined in consistency and constant attention – an audience on social media can disappear very quickly otherwise.

- Be ready for the moment when your message suddenly gets traction. Be patient.

- Keep it simple. Simplicity is a driver of awareness – so present your online content in an easy-to-consume, engaging way.

- Numbers on social media are not enough – engagement and commitment are what drive change. Put engagement and commitment before numbers of 'likes'.

- Know exactly what you want online followers to do – real-world action as opposed to clicks.

- The trolls will always be there – beware them and ignore them unless you have a great retort that will deliver you more followers and more action.

- Learn from your opponents' positions online and counter them proactively – call out fake news or disinformation. Fact-check and be vocal about it.

Chapter Four
How to protest

Protest is the noisy, angry, impassioned side of activism. It's about ordinary people showing their power – it's a movement from the 'bottom' up.

It can make the procedure of the courtroom or the process of parliament seem sterile and uncompassionate. Protest is the physical manifestation of discontent – anger, unhappiness and frustration are no longer theoretical when you see people protest; it is politics at its most raw.

Protests can take many forms – from solo hunger strikes to mass demonstrations; from peaceful to violent resistance. Sometimes people just want to feel heard; other times they may have a specific call to action. They are important because they are physical activism: they provide the images of activism that we remember – from the Vietnam veterans throwing their medals at the US Capitol to the Tank Man in Tiananmen Square, protests create iconic moments and lasting images that make movements become historic.

When protest exists solely in the digital world it evokes a different response to when it happens in the physical world. With an offline protest the emotions appear stronger and the sense of common purpose more obvious – it's like the difference between streaming music and a live concert.

One of the most important aspects of protest is that it encourages dialogue around an issue, especially in the media. Media exposure and public attention are so important to push causes up the political agenda, but making your protest stand out among the plethora of protests that happen every day is a challenge. Most marches and protests don't work. Most demonstrations are ignored. Every day, in front of nearly every parliament and government in the world, there are protests that don't make a difference. They may enable a sense of solidarity and a cathartic outpouring of sentiment, but they don't necessarily enter public consciousness, and it is far from certain that they affect public conscience whether through mainstream or social media.

Some of the biggest marches that have ever happened have not led to a meaningful legislative change or policy alteration. One of the largest marches in the UK was against the war in Iraq in February 2003, when

750,000 to 1 million British people demonstrated their opposition. When Prime Minister Tony Blair took British forces into Iraq a few weeks later, it was clear that he was not representing the will of his people.

Yet coming together as a collective and physically communing as one homogeneous movement gives you a sense of momentum and solidarity, which is critical in activism. If your support is dispersed throughout the country, you may feel isolated and alone, not a part of a whole, and this can dishearten many activists. The physical manifestation of people being in the streets together in good heart and good voice can give your movement a significant boost, as you feel the power of your collective belief and argument. Together, unified, we are stronger and can find strength from one another.

Protests have always signified an absence of apathy on an issue: people have to get off their sofas and physically go somewhere (unless they are striking, in which case they may stay at home). Now more than ever, when most of our interactions happen online, people physically coming together and taking time and energy to protest gives a cause a significant weight and meaning that an online petition can't.

Why bother protesting?

Protests on their own don't change the world. Like all aspects of this book, they are just part of an activist's toolkit – and employed well they can raise awareness, change attitudes and clear the way to change the law. They require a lot of work and organization, and getting people to turn up (on time, in the right location) to a rally is an accomplishment in itself. It asks more from people then a click or a like, it asks for active participation. However, numbers shouldn't be the end goal. So much energy can be expended on a protest that it's critical it is channelled into something meaningful which will drive your message forward and further into the public eye.

Leading mobilizer of the Black Lives Matter movement **DeRay Mckesson** reflects on the role that physically protesting and occupying a space still plays within the breadth of actions that make activism successful:

Protest is about telling the truth in public. We were telling the truth with our bodies and with our voices and with our hearts. That is what protest is. I'm mindful that protest isn't the answer, but protest creates space for the answer.

We knew that just the act of standing in the street was not going to wholesale change the criminal justice system. We also knew that there would be no change to come if we didn't stand out in the street. The protest forced the issue and forced the conversations that then allowed people to strategize. It then allowed people to refine demands and make more demands, and to bring things to the light that people were trying to hide. I think that's strategy.

We tried everything from emails, calls, meetings to voting. But it wasn't until we stood in the street and disrupted people's sense of normalcy that things changed. It shouldn't be that we live in a legal and political system where you have to literally and physically disrupt the sense of normalcy to get people to respond.

Those sorts of protests, like shutdowns, are always about awareness. They are about bringing attention to an issue. With Michael Brown's murder in St Louis in 2014, if we hadn't shut down things, people wouldn't have paid attention. Awareness isn't enough, but you need awareness to create real understanding and to engage people.

Disruption forces people outside of your movement to pay attention to what you are doing. Being subversive and against the system raises awareness for the cause to which you are trying to draw people's attention. When there's no disruption at all, it's very difficult to persuade people to engage with your message as their attention is diverted to so many other attention-grabbing news stories, issues and medias. Politicians and the media are confronted with so many requests every day that, if your cause is presented in a way that's easy for them to brush off, the chances are they will. They need to a reason to filter your cause from the mass of issues raised. A bold radical disruption will require them to stop and think about your message. Ideally, the disruption that you instigated is linked with your message.

For example, in 2016 there was a British Black Lives Matter group who caused disruption at London City Airport. It eventually transpired that they were disrupting flights to protest against climate change, and their message was that climate change ultimately affects people of colour the most. Although this caught people's attention it was too convoluted a way of drawing attention to racial injustice. The protest and message weren't synced – the disruption was not clearly related to the movement behind it and as a result there was very little sympathy garnered as people focused on the disruption rather than the cause.

However, a more successful demonstration took place in 2017, when 15 activists protested the deportation of immigrants, which caused disruptions to flights at London Stansted Airport that were specifically deporting immigrants. People immediately understood the relationship between the issue and the protest, which led to much more attention across the media and also to public sympathy and support. When the protestors ended up being sentenced, there was an outcry from the general public, which again resulted in an increased level of awareness about forced deportations.

Aim to create a crystalline link between what you are protesting about and the means of protest taken, as it will make the message more compelling. You need to make sure there are as few obstacles as possible in understanding what you want to convey. It must be immediately impactful.

However, the work doesn't stop after the protest. The follow through is very important: the delivery of the petition, the engagement and support in the mainstream media, the raising of questions again and, if necessary, the repeating of the protest are necessary strategic steps that need to be planned out, as the prominent environmental activist and founder of 350.org, **Bill McKibben,** explains:

> The number of people who are engaged in the climate fight keeps increasing. We started by doing very small distributed actions around the world. In 2009, on a single day we had 5,200 demonstrations in 181 countries. Some of them were pretty big but most of them had around 100 to 300 people. Over time, as people

began to believe that a movement was possible, it became easier
to get larger numbers of people.

It helps other people understand the moral urgency of the
situation. If we don't win quickly, we don't win. Which makes this
different from other campaigns in the past. Normally, you fight
for something and you get some part of it and come back the
next year and so on and so forth. That's not the case with climate
change. We need action now.

Protest is great but it's not enough. We need a Green-New-Deal-like
commitment to renewable energy across the world. There are few
issues that are as global and as vast as climate change. Equality is
another such issue. What you're really aiming for is not some new
piece of legislation but rather a change in the zeitgeist. Until you
achieve that, you can't win and once you've got it, you can't lose.
The question is, 'Can we change people's sense of what's normal?
Can we change that fast enough or not?' That's why a focus on
policies as well as protest is key.

My house is covered with solar panels and I'm proud of them.
I drove the first electric Ford in the state of Vermont but I don't try
to fool myself that that's how we're going to solve this problem.
If we're going to solve the problem, it'll be when individuals decide
to be a little less individual and come together in movements
to counterbalance the fossil fuel industry. Travelling by plane
someplace warmer for a week is probably not such a good idea.
Stay put and trust me it'll get warmer there soon.

Physically assembling people not only demonstrates and showcases
support by head count for your cause, but it helps build a community
that can work together beyond the day of the march, or period of protest,
to keep the ball rolling. It creates connections and bonds through shared
experiences which strengthens folks' relationship with the movement
and their commitment to it. Through the solidarity of protest can come

friendships and memories, which will help cultivate the collective action needed to create long-term change.

The other advantage of a physical protest is that you are able to achieve more when you are on the ground. **Tara Houska** is a tribal nations advocate and attorney. She is national campaigns director of Honor the Earth, which funds Native environmental groups, and a former advisor on Native American affairs to Bernie Sanders. She has been protesting the controversial Enbridge Inc. Line 3 oil pipeline replacement that runs from Alberta, Canada into northern US states. The presence of protestors on the ground has enabled them to observe the practices of the oil company and hold it accountable. She argues that physically being present is an important aspect of protest:

> Clearly, the legislative processes are not enough. They're not working, they haven't worked for a very long time. We're in a very serious situation with climate change globally. Sticking to the process that oil corporations have heavily influenced and corrupted won't get us very far. More people need to be out there disrupting the status quo, and more people need to be engaged, because the status quo is literally killing the planet.

> When I look at the full spectrum of what activists can do and how they can engage, there is nothing more direct than actually physically putting yourself into a space and disrupting the status quo. Just yesterday, we went out and exposed an illegal drilling operation on the banks of the Mississippi River. These things are incredibly important moments because they have ripple effects on the chain of events.

> If you go out and expose illegal activity by a pipeline or fossil fuel company, that in turn may lead to a whole other series of events, which may involve lawyers and potential penalties for the perpetrator. That in turn leads to legislative bodies hearing about what's actually happening on the ground. This can reach the investors who are looking at the project and saying, 'Wow,

the resistance on the ground is very intense.' It may also influence the public if it reaches the media. This might change the social, political capital of the people. They may push their elected officials to delay this project or cancel it altogether.

Keep going, keep growing

Protest is often a numbers game, about being able to turn people out. The size of the crowd can add to a sense of mounting public pressure and there is a safety and solidarity in large numbers. Having more police than marchers makes a cause look paltry, and poorly supported, but a large crowd lends credence and power. Small numbers of activists shouldn't, however, be a reason not to protest – from Greta Thunberg to Gandhi, one person can spark a whole movement.

Minnijean Brown-Trickey was one of the nine African-American high school students who were the first to attend a previously white-only school in Little Rock, Arkansas. Despite being few in numbers, the teenagers stood down the most virulent opposition and racism to get their education, becoming symbols of heroism. Her experience was that even if your numbers are small, sometimes especially *because* they are small, you can stand for something much bigger:

Ordinary people can do extraordinary things. We didn't intend to stick our heads above the parapet - we were just plain, ordinary teenagers. There was strength in us being teenagers because we had the pure rebellion and defiance in us that's only really found in the young.

They [the white students at Little Rock Central High School] wanted us out so bad and they did so many things to make us want to go home that we just didn't. Students would spit on us, boys would walk on our heels until they bled. Girls would call us awful names all day. I thought to myself, 'You don't want me here, well I'm not going anywhere.'

People said, 'Did you know you were living history?' We did,
because every night we got home to letters from around the world.
People sent gifts, cards and whole classes of kids wrote letters – it
helped us feel supported and we really understood the importance
of what we were doing. The nine of us became the darlings of civil
rights at the time. It's the first time black kids had ever been on
television or in newspapers and we captured the imagination of
the world.

Within a small group solidarity is especially important. There aren't enough
of you to allow yourselves to be divided or splinter off. A united front is
important in communicating your strength but can also ensure that you
have the mental resolve to keep going. **Cameron Kasky** is cofounder of
the March for Our Lives movement against gun violence, a campaign that
inspired over 450 demonstrations across the United States on 24 March
2018, with hundreds and thousands of attendees turning out in Washington
DC. He reflects on the importance of sticking together in the aftermath
of the deadly mass shooting at Marjory Stoneman Douglas High School:

I think that the first thing we did right was, we stayed together as
a group. Since then, everybody's branched off a bit and are doing
their own thing. Some people are no longer involved, but for that
one month in the spotlight, we were each other's rock. If it weren't
for the team, nothing would have been done. I'd like to think that's
really the buoy that kept us floating.

Starting small is fine – you need to start somewhere. But staying small is
limiting. Over time you need to grow the number of people supporting
your cause, whether that is through advertising on social media, passing
out fliers in your neighbourhood or simply from word of mouth. Usually,
there will be many others who share your concerns who you can draw in.

However, you won't become truly significant if you're just talking to
people who are already in agreement with you. If your numbers are going
to be significant, you need to bring in a plethora of organizations and
groups. Reaching out to unlikely allies may mean you need to re-examine

some of your current methods – consider, for example, what changes the women's march might make if it were to have the objective of making Conservative women feel welcome? Would a broader base put more pressure on governments?

Kumi Naidoo has done this successfully while leading both Greenpeace and Amnesty International, and has clear advice about where the value in alliances lies:

> You shouldn't be dissuaded from activism because your numbers are initially small. If you want to broaden your cause and gain more people you need to communicate your ideas proudly. Be willing to try new creative ways of mobilizing people. Reach out to unlikely allies. Find ways to broaden the movement. Don't just find ways to talk to the same people. Movements can only become truly broad when you form unlikely alliances. This is where you should invest your time because the diversity will give you the broad base on which to build.

> In activism, we can spend a lot of time establishing communications with governments or institutions like the UN or the World Bank – people say, 'the President then met with the protestors' and class it as a victory. A meeting by itself won't have changed anything – that's access to power, not influence over power.

> We made a big mistake and we confused access for influence. I am not saying we should never speak to government or never speak to people with power but look at it on a case by case basis, ask yourself whether you have achieved your goals or whether you have just made a politician look good by being photographed meeting protestors.

The key to unlocking diversity is allyship. The word 'ally' has a variety of meanings to different groups, but essentially in becoming an ally you have to be prepared to take someone else's problem as seriously as you would take you own. You have to stand in true solidarity with people who are marginalized, even if you are not. A marginalized individual cannot easily cast away the weight of oppression. They cannot become straight or white or naturalized if they feel like it. Being an ally doesn't necessarily mean that you completely understand what it feels like to be oppressed, but it does mean taking on the struggle as your own. Your movement can embrace allyship by creating a culture of true inclusion and lifting others up with your advocacy.

We can all be allies. Men can be the allies of women, the well-off can be allies to those who are in poverty, straight people can be allies to the LGBT community, etc. An ally recognizes that although they are not a member of a marginalized group(s) they can make a concerted effort to better understand and support the struggle. An ally might have more privileged access, they are powerful voices *alongside* marginalized ones.

Allyship clearly has a role to play in all aspects of activism, including online and in policy, but the physical risks that accompany protest make it even more crucial, as **Tara Houska** points out:

> I would say to allies that are looking to support a fight – for example, in my work, looking to help Indigenous groups defend their land – that you should recognize that your privilege is very real when it comes to a frontline situation, such as interaction with law enforcement or a militarized response.

> When we were protesting the Enbridge sand tar line, a group of white valve turners, who were part of the Catholic Workers Group, shut down the pipeline and were released or charged with misdemeanours. In another similar situation, there were three Indigenous people who were alleged to have been engaged with tampering with equipment. Those three Indigenous people are currently facing felonies, they're facing massive tens of thousands of dollars of restitution to the companies and have had very high bonds set on each of them. The treatment could not be more different.

It really is a matter of life and death in certain cases. Native
people are more likely to be killed by the police than any other
racial demographic in the United States. I hope that more people
understand that they have privilege, and they should use that
to support and take some of the risks off Native people when
possible.

Once you recognize you have privilege or a platform, you need to work
out how you are going to use it. This may come with a cost   from schools
suspending students who have skipped school to attend protests, to the
long history of athletes who have been penalized for their role in protest:
Muhammad Ali refused to be conscripted into the military on religious
grounds in 1967. As a result, he was arrested, stripped of his championship
title and banned from boxing in the US for three years. After being part
of the NBA-title-winning Chicago Bulls team in 1992, Craig Hodges
brought a letter to the White House celebratory visit strongly requesting
that President George H. W. Bush take steps to address issues affecting
African-Americans. Hodges was cut by the Bulls that year and never played
in the NBA again.

One of the most famous protestors of our era, former football quarterback
for the San Francisco 49ers **Colin Kaepernick**, has not played in the
NFL since the spread of the 2016 #TakeAKnee movement, where he
started kneeling during the US national anthem prior to games, rather
than standing. He says:

It is my right as an American to protest. We protest because we
love ourselves and because we love our people and because we
love our country. While taking a knee is a physical representation
of who is excluded from the notions of freedom, liberty and justice,
my protest is rooted in my love for people.

Love is at the root of our resistance. It is our love for 12-year-old
Tamir Rice who was gunned down by the police that will not allow
us to bury our anger, our love for Philando Castile who was killed
in front of his partner and his daughter, our love for Stephon Clark

who was shot in his backyard that will not allow us to stop until we liberate our people. We've gone from Jim Crow to New Jim Crow, from mass plantations to mass incarceration.

I recognize that I have a position of relative power and a platform. I now have a voice and I feel I need to use it for those who don't have that privilege. One of my roommates was moving out of our house in college, and because we were the only black people in that neighbourhood the cops were called and we had guns drawn on us. This isn't something that's a one-off case. This kind of injustice is a daily occurrence for black and brown people in the US. It needs to be addressed.

I decided to kneel to make people aware of what's going on in this country. There are a lot of things happening that are unjust that people aren't being held accountable for and that's something that needs to change. America stands for freedom, equality and justice for all and that's not happening for all of its citizens right now.

While many of us may never play for the NFL or collect an Oscar, each of us has our own unique platform and circle of influence. We can all use our platforms to promote issues that matter most to us. If you have a platform at church, at your job or in your neighbourhood, you are able to spread messages of importance. We can leverage our own power and authority and use our voice to create change for the greater good.

While individual action is important and can be very powerful, long-term sustained protest requires the participation of others. Part of your power is being able to empower others to protest. If you're going to march, make a point of inviting others to come with you. If you've already invited people to come with you, try to add someone who has never come to a protest or march before. See what you can do to make their first experience as straightforward and enjoyable as possible – be prepared to offer help and explain what's happening. Do they need a ride? Do they need lunch or snacks? Can you introduce them to other members? Facilitating access to movements and being welcoming to new participants is critical to growth, and sometimes it's the plain old practical things that really matter.

If you want something, you'd better make some noise

If you don't have a significant platform or number of supporters, you need to think of other ways to engage people with your message. A lack of funding and a lack of support can help increase your resourcefulness and make you more creative about how you can approach things. If you don't have general mass support then you need mass media support, so that you can broadcast your message to a bigger audience. A surprise or shock factor combined with celebrity involvement or with humour is going to get media attention.

A protest is a form of mass communication. The easier it is for people to relate to a cause the more likely it is that they engage – so engagement requires comprehension and memorability. People need to understand what a movement is about, and your mantra should be: the simpler the better.

A simple short slogan is the hallmark of movements that have been successful in terms of awareness and number of supporters. There are lots of current examples – #MeToo, #BlackLivesMatter, #Strike4Climate.

Creative, witty protests will be picked up by the media, whether it's pussy-cat hats or EU dairy farmer protestors using a milk cannon against police in Brussels. These are the kind of things that the public can latch on to. One protestor who has managed to turn a small movement into a big splash is **Matt O'Connor** with the Fathers4Justice campaign:

> There are about 3,500 protests a year in London alone. If you want to stand out you have to be creative and determined. Personally, I think most forms of protests are justifiable so long as they are peaceful protests and don't hurt anyone.

> When I started the campaign, we had no money and we were a small group. We had to do something that was ironic and iconic.

Scaling Buckingham Palace dressed as Batman was both. That stunt was inspired by the fact that every father's a superhero to his children. There was a lot humour in it as well. I found it amusing that a bunch of overweight guys in Lycra could breach national security. We saw that stunt as a custard pie in the face of the establishment. It was obviously risky – dangerous even. We were all banking on the fact that the police wouldn't actually shoot Batman.

Fortunately or unfortunately, the more outrageous you are, the more coverage you're going to get. That's just a simple fact. That's how the media works. I think we're constrained by that in some ways. I would love us to have a more intellectual, more intelligent media that covered the issues. We don't because the media itself is under huge commercial pressure. If you do something outrageous you are going to get coverage, but if you try to talk about issues in a deep and meaningful way, the press, the media aren't interested.

I had a very clear ambition for what we wanted to do. My ambition was to get on the front page of every newspaper, to be on the cover of *Time* magazine, to get a book deal and a film deal within 18 months – and we did it all in 18 months! It just shows that with tenacity and sheer brute determination you can achieve these things. What protest does is it creates its own centre of gravity – we had more dads come to us and report unfair treatment once they read about us in the press, the more cases we were aware of the more we could prove the scale of the problem.

We can't and don't wish to compel people to break the law. However, it would be remiss not to acknowledge the role that civil disobedience has played in activism, from Rosa Parks to the ANC. One man's terrorist is another man's freedom fighter. Just because something is illegal doesn't mean that it's wrong, and just because something is legal doesn't mean that it's right.

It is up to the individual to decide the extent to which they hold the law in high esteem. The reality is that you can be legally and civilly protesting and still get arrested. In most countries in the world people get arrested for peaceful protest at some time or another. In 2018 Jazmine Headley sat down on the floor in a public benefits unit in New York, with her baby boy, in protest at them stopping his day care assistance. She ended up getting arrested and having her son forcibly taken from her arms after refusing to stand up. At the G20 protests in 2009, peaceful protestors chanted 'This is not a riot' – making the heavy riot gear that the police were wearing seem disproportionate.

Just because you don't break the law doesn't mean that you won't end up with a criminal record for your activism. It is undeniable that law-breaking and the causing of inconvenience and disruption creates news. The suffragettes attacked golf courses attended by government ministers in protest at the force feeding of imprisoned fellow protestors. That was newsworthy. And made history.

Non-violence is the weapon of the strong

Sometimes it is right to criticize the government. Sometimes in order to be on the right side of history, you have to break the law. The notion that all laws are fair and correct is a fallacy, but breaking the law has serious consequences. If you get a criminal record, you may not be able to run for public office, you may not have access to certain places or fly to some countries, which will inhibit your personal capacity as an activist. It will also affect other areas of your life – for example, it may reduce your employment potential.

Breaking the law and causing damage or enacting violence can also lose you public sympathy, and can create significant public frustration. In the eyes of the public, protestors might be seen as criminals, and losing public support can kill a movement.

David Riveros García is the founder of reAcción Paraguay, a grassroots anti-corruption non-profit organization that uses education to empower and engage students from high school to university. He is also a founding member of the Global Youth Anti-Corruption Network and is the network development director for the International Youth Ambassadors Network. David has found that even when frontline situations get heated, rational peaceful voices can still be heard:

> People mistake peaceful resistance and strategy with cowardice. So I try to convince them by asking the following question: 'Who has more courage? Is it the young man with his face covered and a rock in his hand going to protest or the mother that walks in the frontline of the group with her face uncovered and no weapons or protection?' Moreover, who is likely to bring more people to the movement the next day? Protests are about numbers, too. And violence seldom gets more numbers, especially in the long run.

> It must be noted that context truly matters. It is a completely different thing to protest an authoritarian leader than a democratically elected one. And yet, historical evidence shows that, even in brutal regimes, the most successful protests and demonstrations were those that were peaceful, steady and strategically coordinated. In the right contexts, non-violent resistance can bring parents, the elderly and children to the movement, not only the youth. Police forces are also less likely to repress families or children.

> The anti-corruption NGO that I founded decided to join the protests against the former president of Paraguay, Horacio Cartes, who was trying to illegally amend the constitution to allow for his re-election in 2017. We invited our volunteers to join us. This was risky because the day before the police had shot rubber bullets on peaceful demonstrators who blocked the only international bridge that connects us with Brazil. People were angry and there was chaos on the streets.

> When we arrived, the idea floating around was to burn down a senator's house. I needed to get people's attention so I asked all our volunteers to sit down in a circle and I started an improvised workshop on civil resistance and non-violent conflict. People around us started to notice the simple act of sitting and talking,

and after a while a bunch of people had congregated around us
and were listening to what I was saying. This allowed for debate to
take place. It did not take coercion to make people listen, just an
act of organization.

History is filled, after all, with coups, rebellions and civil wars – many angry protestors don't see how a peaceful protest could possibly upend a powerful, authoritarian regime. But David is right in that peaceful protests are most likely to succeed. From 1900 to 2006, campaigns of non-violent resistance were more than twice as effective as their violent counterparts in achieving their stated goals.

Researchers used to say that no government could survive if just 5 per cent of the population rose up against it. Recent data compiled and analysed by Erica Chenoweth and Maria J. Stephan for their book *Why Civil Resistance Works* shows the number may be lower than that. A successful protest requires the active and sustained participation of just 3.5 per cent of the population. However, the only campaigns that have achieved this level of support from 1940 to 2006 were non-violent ones.

Other research, by the *Washington Post*'s Max Fisher, shows that protests become about 50 per cent more likely to fail if they turn violent. It seems to be the case that once protesters pick up guns the state's use of violence in response is legitimized, even if it is a disproportionate use of force. Security forces are much more likely to open fire – and individual police or soldiers are much more likely to follow that order – if the opposition is shooting at them. Uprisings can often cause a crisis of legitimacy within the government, particularly if the relationship breaks down between the head of state and the military or security forces, which can, in turn, cause that government to fall. Violent uprisings are more likely to unify those in power.

Violent uprisings risk increasing support of the government, whereas a government crackdown against a non-violent uprising can reduce public support for the regime. Violent resistance movements, even if they do succeed, can create a lot of long-term problems: countries with non-violent uprisings 'were way more likely to emerge with democratic institutions'. They were also 15 per cent less likely to 'relapse' into civil war. After all, a non-violent movement may be inherently democratic, a sort of expression of mass public opinion outside of the ballot box.

Not every activist is trying to overthrow a government, of course, but these findings can provide lessons for every movement: public support and sympathy are best engendered through peaceful resistance. **Kumi Naidoo** sees a clear distinction in the value of non-violent civil disobedience compared to violent protest:

> Change comes when people show moral courage. I've been seeing lots of civil disobedience emerging from young people which I would encourage. However, there is a danger that this legitimate frustration and anger at current leadership might lead some young people to embrace violence. Civil disobedience is best when it's about peaceful action. When violence is embraced as part of one's strategy, it gives the authorities the opportunity to present a legitimate protest as a dangerous mob. Once the media hones in on this characterization, the message of the protest will be lost. We need to be very disciplined, creative, innovative, but ultimately peaceful in whatever we do. Civil disobedience done creatively and innovatively opens up the possibility for our leaders finally being forced to listen to what we are saying.
>
> The movements for justice need a diversity of skills and experience. When I climbed the oil rig in the Arctic with Greenpeace, it was important that not everybody climbed the rig with me because somebody needed to capture the story. We needed good videographers, we needed people to take the boat back with the footage, so we could show it to the world. Not everybody needs to be willing to get arrested. Some people are willing to make those sacrifices, some people find the idea of going to prison unimaginable. People who are anxious about breaking the law should not be dissuaded from participating in other ways. We should combat the narrative that only if you're willing to get arrested are you a full activist. It's much better if you can use your skillset to see how far you can progress your cause rather than only sitting in a jail cell, however tough that sacrifice might be.

Every action has consequences, every silence, too

Of course, the notion that going to prison as part of your activism is a choice is foreign to many in nations where freedom of speech and assembly is limited. Sometimes even the most peaceful civil disobedience carries heavy penalties. In 2014 people in Hong Kong took to the streets to protest for their right to have the chief executive of the territory democratically elected as opposed to appointed directly by the Chinese government in Beijing. The Umbrella protests in Hong Kong were, overall, a diligently clean, exceedingly polite and scrupulously peaceful insurgency. People were seen distributing food and water as well as cleaning up after themselves in the famously orderly city. The umbrella, used initially to protect against tear gas and pepper spray, became an eloquent symbol of the protest: non-violent but, when times were difficult, the protestors all came out together, just like the umbrellas all come out at the same time when it rains. At the main protest site at the city's government headquarters, students sorted plastic bottles for recycling while donning goggles and plastic sheets to protect against pepper spray. A polite note was also seen left on a vandalized police van, apologizing for the damage: 'Sorry, I don't know who did this but we are not anarchists – we want democracy.'

Despite this, and despite the fact that the movement had no official leaders, central figure **Joshua Wong**, secretary-general of the pro-democracy party Demosistom and originally the founder of the student activism group Scholarism, was imprisoned (he was released in June 2019):

I was locked up in prison last year, and was also banned from running for office. However, we have no regrets at all because we realize that compared to the price dissidents around the world pay, our sacrifice is a small piece of cake.

I deferred my studies last year because of my jail term. I'm now a year five university student. I have a court case scheduled, and I'll possibly have to serve time again. I'm not sure how many times I will be prosecuted in the next three, five or ten years. I'm 22 now and I may be in prison until I'm 29.

I think the 1989 Tiananmen Square uprising really showed us the power students could have. You cannot suppress people forever. There are more of us than there are people in power. With the passion and the commitment of this generation, we believe we can fight for a better future. At times it feels like the battle between David and Goliath but we must persevere and be certain that we can make a difference.

No one becomes an activist and wants to serve a jail sentence, but we just hope to show that we'll keep on with our fight. I think our faith, courage and passion has come from how the local and international community keeps supporting us.

The international community has numerous motivations for supporting the Umbrella protests. Many countries cynically view any challenge to the authority of Beijing as being a positive. However, one of the reasons the movement continues to maintain support is precisely because of the appealing peaceful images of protestors thoughtfully cleaning the streets and helping each other with homework. Contrast that with the intense criticism the #StrikeForClimate marchers faced in the UK in March 2019 after the amount of litter that was left, which severely served to undermine their environmental message.

When we spoke to **Cameron Kasky** for this book, he asked us to include his admiration for Joshua and the students of the Umbrella movement. He is, after all, the survivor of a mass shooting and has faced intense pressure as a result of standing up to the NRA. He said, 'People should know that what they are doing is true activism.'

The symbol of the umbrella movement was resurrected in 2019 when protests in Hong Kong erupted at the introduction of a bill in June that would enable the Chinese authorities to extradite people from Hong Kong to mainland China. Over one million people marched in protest of the bill. Shortly after being released from prison, Joshua Wong lent his support to the protestors.

Threats to liberty and safety do, however, occur frequently in supposedly liberal democracies, as **DeRay Mckesson** points out:

I'm mindful that the people that want us not to do this work will do anything to try and scare us to not do it. I've had a movie evacuated because somebody said they were going to kill me. I've been held by police officers in two different states. My phone was hacked. The first person ever permanently banned from Twitter was banned for raising money to try and get me killed. There's been a host of different things. I try to stay focused and remember that there are people that came before me that faced far greater consequences, far greater issues, and they figured out a way of doing the work.

There are a lot of people who forget that the everyday person will always be the foundation of a movement. The people with money, the people with visibility, they'll come, they'll certainly come once they know they won't lose anything, but it's actually everyday people who have lost so much already who will always be the people who will fight the hardest, and you've got to stay close to that.

Of course, the arrest or abuse of activists often thrusts the cause into the media spotlight and generates public outcry. Often other activists, journalists and sometimes international forces jump to the defence of the detained. **Tawakkol Karman** cofounded the Women Journalists Without Chains group in 2005, which aims to promote civil rights, freedom of opinion and expression, and democratic rights within Yemen. She also was awarded the Nobel Peace Prize in 2011 in recognition for her work in non-violent struggle for the safety of women as well as for women's rights to full participation in peace-building work across Yemen. Tawakkol was the organizer of the student protests during the Arab Spring uprisings in Yemen in 2011, and after a week of protests she was detained by security forces in the middle of the night. This became a defining moment in the Yemeni revolution: media outlets reported her detention and more demonstrations erupted across the country. The protests were organized by students, civil society activists and politicians, and Tawakkol became known as the Iron Woman and Mother of the Revolution:

I think of myself as an advocate for freedom and anti-tyranny, but perhaps I was called the mother of the revolution as a result of my activities against the overthrown regime before the 2011 revolution and because of my call for the regime to end. When the revolution took place, I strongly expressed its objectives, which led to my arrest by the regime. This led to the anger of my fellow revolutionaries. Subsequently, I was released. I was ready to die for the revolution, and I was often close to death. When I won the Nobel Prize, I considered it a recognition of the greatness of the Yemeni revolution and the Arab Spring youth.

Early on, I realized that Yemen needed real political change. I wrote articles calling for the rejection of the then existing regime, i.e. the regime of the deposed President Ali Abdullah Saleh. After that, I went to establish Women Journalists Without Chains through which we prepared periodic reports on freedoms and corruption. Additionally, the organization focused on training journalists and human rights activists of both sexes. We took to the streets and staged sit-ins to support the freedom of the press.

My decision to take to the streets and talk to people directly via a loudspeaker was due to the fact that not all people could read newspapers. We had to do this in order to reach various people if we wanted to create a broader awareness and achieve the desired change. Moreover, I was also driven by the desire to stand up to strict restrictions on the people's right to demonstrate.

Communication is the language of leadership

You must be able to communicate your message. Awareness should always be an early and ongoing priority. While it's true that sometimes punishment meted out to the leader of a protest delivers instant mass attention, the punishment itself should never be an aim. It is much more preferable that you are free to make your voice heard than to be in prison or physically incapacitated!

Tawakkol Karman's leadership led to such large protests because she communicated with people beyond the politically engaged, out into the general public, going so far as to help illiterate people get involved. This commitment to inclusion and awareness-raising among all people is something that all activists should be inspired by: if we truly believe that everyone can make a difference, we have to raise awareness so that everyone *can* make a difference.

DeRay Mckesson also endorses the view of keeping messaging straightforward and accessible in order to maximize your support:

> I always say to myself, 'If I can't explain it to my aunt then it doesn't matter.' My aunt is a very smart lady but she has a life that is busy and complicated – she is not watching CNN all day.

> So I don't talk about judicial reform theory – I show people. I show them that there are clauses in laws and contracts across the country that say things like, 'An officer has to be disciplined in the least embarrassing way possible.' Showing people is always more effective than telling them. No one likes preaching.

> I want to get the other person I'm talking to to do more work intellectually and come up with their own ideas so that they participate. People ask me, 'Are you saying the police should never kill somebody?' I respond, 'When should the police kill your child? You tell me. What can your kid do to make you be okay with an officer putting a bullet through their forehead?' Then, people say, 'I don't know.'

> When I'm talking about welfare programmes, I don't give a lofty speech about human rights and dignity of people. I'm saying, 'What does a four-year-old have to do to earn dinner? What does a seven-year-old have to do to be worthy of shelter? You tell me.'

The success of a protest depends on whether the articulated demands have been met. If you are striking because you want your pay to increase and the pay increases, the strike ends. However, many protests don't have specific asks and aims — many people want different outcomes or have different demands. A lack of a clearly articulated goal eventually causes the movement to lose steam as there is nowhere for it to summit. Often the aims become numerous and the message becomes diluted.

Of course, aims and demands may evolve over time, but this can mean that the ultimate messaging is weakened. It's important to balance a broad, easy-to-access demand with specific practicalities on how that demand can be met. 'No justice, no peace' might be a catchy chant, but what does justice mean in that particular situation? What policy and steps do you actually want to be taken in order for your protest to have been deemed successful?

Agreeing on aims and policies can be really difficult. People can come to a protest with incredibly strong and divergent opinions. The level of education and expertise on the issue is going to vary hugely among the number of people protesting. People with the loudest voices aren't always going to be the most informed. Working within the movement to try and engage all of the members to agree on a definitive set of demands is critical to ensuring your aims and demands are strongly supported and so can be articulated strongly. Unity as a movement ensures that critical mass is sustained – sub-groups quickly begin to lessen your critical mass; in-fighting proves to detractors that the cause itself is divisive.

Part of communicating your aims is to impel the media to stay on message. This can be difficult when there are dramatic or controversial elements to your protest, but message discipline is critical to landing your points and achieving your aims. **Cameron Kasky** reflects on the complexity of achieving this in the wake of the Parkland shooting:

> It was very important that we ignored the shooter's name. I think that one of the biggest aspects of school shootings right now is that a lot of people want to go into a school with a gun, and they want the whole country to see them. The shooter at my school released a video where he said that the world will know his name,

and you know what, he was right. People all over the world know that guy's name.

We said, 'I know you all want to focus on the blood, the gore and the sensationalist aspect of this tragedy, but we dare all of the country to focus on how we can change.' I'd be going on the local news or national news, or whatever it may be, and people would ask about the blood and gore of it. People would ask about the grisly details and what it was like to be locked in the room as a student. Many of those perspectives were important just to understand really what a mass school shooting is and how it affects people, but the country doesn't need to know about the hundreds of kids locked in a room. They need to know about how we can stop that from ever happening again.

The media will often seek to sensationalize, which is why you have to ensure that your crowd behaviour and mentality is immaculate – you have to hold the moral high ground. It's also important to use whatever technology you have available to you to film, photograph and then disseminate as much evidence as possible, so that you can prevent your movement from being mischaracterized. **Tara Houska** has learned this the hard way:

The importance of independent media cannot be stressed enough. According to some of the media coverage, we were attacking police officers and were violent. There were allegations that we were killing cattle locally with bows and arrows. This is an example of ridiculous over-the-top racial stereotypes being used to depict us as criminals.

We had our own media outlets and frankly that kept us able to continue what we were doing. It allowed us to show the rest of the world that we were not violent. We were actually peaceful. We had video footage of all of our protests and livestreams so we could prove we were not violent. Making sure that you can control your own narrative is very important because, even in the face of evidence, media can't always be relied on to tell the truth.

For example, we recently went to a sit-in that was directly in the pipeline route and I made very certain that we live-streamed everything, that nobody went anywhere near any equipment, that we didn't talk to anybody – we were just showing what was happening. The story that they ran in the media the next day was that we caused $100,000 worth of damage. That's such a falsehood but that's how we were portrayed by the press.

So not only are we facing this historic gold standard of how people of colour in particular need to behave, but the treatment of protestors by the media leads to anti-protester sentiment and the othering of protestors. When protesters are in fact just composed of your fellow citizens. They're people that are concerned. They're youths that are saying, 'I want to have a world.'

Perseverance is power

Momentum and energy are hard to maintain. Knee-jerk responses to issues and the buzz, adrenaline and excitement of the day of an actual occupation or march can only last for so long. The extent to which the interest in your protest lasts is always going to be slightly ephemeral because not everyone can protest every day.

If you have a one-off march, having a clear communications campaign among your community is key to ensuring their continued involvement. Your community needs to know about progress so that they are aware of what additional steps need to be taken. If the protest is successful, you need to share that news among your community so they can celebrate the victory with you. If you are still encountering the same problems you set out to tackle, you probably need to protest again. Being organized about gathering contact information of people who attend the march and keeping in touch with them, as well as thanking them for taking part, is very important. **David Riveros García** reminds us that all of these practical actions are what add up to successful protests, and that patience has to be part of your mantra:

> A protest is a long walk, not a sprint. Do not think it is about one mass demonstration. You need to manage your expectations first, so then you can manage the expectations of the people you lead. Read about civil resistance and non-violent conflict. History shows that the most successful victories of civil resistance were the products of a long and patient sequence of actions. We often crystalize protests in speeches, key demonstrations and moments. But in reality, most of them took months or even years of preparation and coordination. If all you want is a quick fix, ask yourself: is what you want civic therapy in the public square for a few days or is it real change in the long term?

If you're part of an ongoing protest, like Tahrir Square in Egypt, #BlackLivesMatter and Ferguson, Missouri, the nature of the community that forms on the ground will create its own momentum. There is a certain tunnel vision that people have once they decide that they're going to protest by occupying a public space. That organic energy and determination is critical but it won't last forever. The role of leadership in keeping movements going beyond the early days of kindling passion is critical. One Young World Ambassador **Farai Mubaiwa** founded the Africa Matters Initiative, an organization dedicated to empowering young Africans to embrace African identity, while changing youth narratives. She argues that strong but responsive leadership, combined with sticking to your objectives, is the best way to retain energy:

> Alternating leadership, kindness and remembering the WHY.

> First, a single person cannot lead a protest alone, nor can they uphold the momentum and morale on their own. The most successful protests I have seen have alternating leaders – all of

whom understand their privilege. The alternating leaders maintain the momentum and morale of the protest as they bring different energy levels, different personalities, and a unique personal story and connection to the protest.

Secondly, I have seen protesters become unfriendly and even violent towards one another when morale was down. It is essential to remember that your fellow protesters are there because they too believe in the cause and strive for change as well. Be kind to them and recognize that they too have their own story which connects them to the theme or message of the protest.

Thirdly, remember the WHY. Why are you protesting? Why does this matter to you? Remembering the WHY will keep your morale and momentum up throughout the protest, even when it seems that you are unlikely to achieve your outcomes.

Staying true to your intentions is critical: set your intentions and live and protest very deliberately. Good intentions do not always lead to good outcomes, but coming back to your *why* will help you calibrate your compass. Intention will shape the nature of your action – being constantly mindful of your intention will help keep you on track.

Because protests often spring up overnight, it's not always possible to build from the manifesto up. You can, however, develop written goals and aims in the early stages of protest and it's important that you keep coming back to them and letting them be your 'true north'. These are the foundations from which you can build a successful protest but you need to keep these secure otherwise your whole cause can crumble. Stay tethered to your building blocks, these are the central tenets of your protest. You came to the streets or blocked a bridge for a reason – try not to let the noise of the media or law enforcement or internal divisions distract you from your purpose.

Movements do fall apart, it's often inevitable. Sometimes people's aims are too diverse – a protest movement can't be all things to all people. This is an ongoing issue with Pride, because some believe it hasn't been inclusive enough of certain groups. The question about whether dividing a movement is the right thing to do or whether it's better to try and reform from within is a perennial issue in activism. The outcome will depend on whether you think you can stay and make change from the inside or whether you think that the problem is too far gone. Similarly, you yourself may no longer be useful to the protest – your presence may at some point be a roadblock to its success. Don't let your own saviour complex get in the way of the movement's success.

As your movement grows, you may achieve successes or travel to places which take you away from your community and the people you are trying to help – your *why* can feel very distant when you're in Washington or London. Keeping one image or face in your mind can help maintain the tunnel vision you need to see your protest through to the end. For **Tara Houska**, that image is the wild rice that is so integral to the Ojibwe people:

> I hope that when people engage in these spaces and are willing to take on these risks and fight for the future, that they sit with themselves and really take the time to think about what they are fighting for. Developing your intent behind your resistance and action is very important. In some instances, like in North Dakota or where I'm at currently in northern Minnesota, this is about the cultural survival of the people. There is a tar sand line I'm currently fighting. If it breaks it will wipe out the wild rice which is part of our history, our culture and our livelihood. Wild rice is the heart of our people. Being mindful of this threat helps ground us and keep our intentions authentic.

Successful protesting is some of the hardest work in the activist realm. Done right, it's a productive use of our time and attention, but so often it can be a bit of theatre that makes us feel virtuous but brings an issue to the fore just for a 24-hour media cycle. You can't predict your success at the start, and your execution and consistency will end up mattering more than your intentions. Being committed and optimistic are critical – a protest that sprang up in a matter of hours may turn into a decades-long campaign. Do the work you feel like you were called to do, and be prepared to do it every single day as hard as you can. And, as **Minnijean Brown-Trickey** reminds us, don't let your struggles interfere with your joy:

> If you don't do it with joy, you're going to become depressed and stop. When you look at those now famous photographs of us leaving the school building, someone was always laughing. Even against the backdrop of people screaming abuse and spitting in our faces. There were a couple of comedians and someone was always cracking a joke. You can take your work really seriously without taking yourself seriously. Being an activist is hard, but it can be done with joy. It must be done with joy.

How to protest checklist

- Don't underestimate the power of physically occupying a space – being on the ground will always have value.

- Don't be put off by low numbers. A small number of protesters isn't a reason for you not to do it; eventually your protest will grow as long as you start somewhere.

- Communicate your idea with pride, humour and joy.

- Remember that access to those in power does not equal influence over them.

- Protest can come with a personal cost – assess what you might lose and be prepared for that to happen.

- If you believe you will have to break a law, be aware of the consequences for you personally and for your freedom.

- Violence will make your protest less effective – peaceful resistence is the most effective method.

- As with online activism – simplest is always best for your message.

- Try to see the big picture for your protest – if you see that you really can change the world, your vision will give you immense strength and staying power.

- Plan your execution and be prepared to take the time to achieve what you want.

Chapter Five
How to change the law

Charlie Brown says to Lucy, 'People can't just go around doing whatever they like.' Lucy answers, 'They can if no one stops them.' And at its simplest that is why there are laws: so that people can't just do whatever they like. That's one angle. From another perspective though, laws can make people do whatever it is that the lawmaker wants.

These definitions and all the arguments that surround them are the subject of the study of jurisprudence. The 17th-century philosopher Thomas Hobbes believed that we are inherently selfish beings and defined contract as 'the mutual transferring of right'. He believed there are no limits to the right of natural liberty, and that the social contract is an agreement where individuals mutually transfer their natural rights, so creating laws. Another way to look at this comes from another 17th-century philosopher John Locke. For Locke, all men are free 'to order their actions, and dispose of their possessions and persons, as they think fit, within the bounds of the law of Nature. The state of Nature has a law of Nature to govern it', and that law is reason. Putting this simply – although we are selfish, we are reasonable, and we see that in order to live together in harmony we give up some of our rights to do as we please by creating laws.

Depending on where you live, the law to one extent may protect you – for example, human rights legislation that bans discrimination on the basis of race – or it may entrench injustice, like the laws of the South African apartheid regime.

Sometimes the law is used maliciously, and sometimes the law fails to protect people, but if the law supports your aims you may have access to the many instruments of the state. Whether it's anti-discrimination law, or work protection, or the franchise, with the law on your side you have recourse to something that is essential to the pursuit of your cause and you can argue that your cause is a just one.

There's something symbolic about rights being protected or upheld by the law. It legitimizes your cause and lends it credence. You can state with confidence that the highest authority in the land has got your back.

But the law is not a permanently engraved legislature, it is can shift and change in order to represent new and emerging issues. If the law does not support your conviction you can actually get it changed. It's not easy, but it can be done. The law belongs to you. As the 17th-century philosophers told us: we give up some freedoms by mutual consent. The laws that govern our lives together are ours – they should be what we want them to be.

Until recently, stalking was not explicitly against the law in the UK. This meant that if someone reported a stalker to the police, nothing would be done as it was not a crime, despite the fact that stalking can be devastating and has strong links with violence and homicide. Movements such as the National Stalking Awareness Week and the Suzy Lamplugh Trust had to convince Members of Parliament, police, magistrates and probation officers that new legislation was necessary.

Without the law on your side, it's very difficult to enforce the types of protection that you may need. Some of the most significant moments in activism have been the ones which instigated changes in the law, whether it's women's right to vote, the civil rights movement or the abolition of slavery. All of these efforts required legal instruments and in some cases even constitutional change in order to be successful. Once changed, a law still has to be implemented or enforced.

Legality and morality are not the same thing. History has showed us again and again that the law isn't always on the side of the righteous. It was legal to have slaves. It was legal to rape your wife within marriage. Stalking was not illegal but homosexuality was. The law doesn't change by happenstance. In theory the law supports the ideal of the society in which we live, but often there's a time delay between current thinking and the implementation of legislation that supports it. The law changes because enough people campaign and encourage lawmakers to change their minds.

William Wilberforce was the man we can thank for the abolition of slavery in the UK, and the housewives he convinced to avoid using sugar because it was made by slaves were as much a part of that movement as he was. Together they created the groundswell of support that was required for the law to change. This generated a huge economic shift, which eventually brought about the Slavery Abolition Act 1833.

The fight for equal rights for women would seem pretty well advanced in the UK – at least in terms of changes to law. Women have had the vote since 1918, and it has been illegal to discriminate against women in employment since 1976. Upskirting, the act of taking a photograph up a women's skirt, only recently became illegal in the UK. Although it is clearly an assault on another person, which is in itself illegal, prosecuting someone for taking such a picture couldn't be done because it had to be spelt out as a specific crime. Historically, laws have been made by men, and we didn't have camera phones. As technological and societal changes occur, we need new laws to keep up with them. Laws won't just change organically. They need a person to challenge them and people to change them. Laws are made by people.

Campaigning to change the law is very important because the law does not naturally or necessarily cover subject matter that we need it to. The most obvious example of this is the almost total failure of governments everywhere to make and enforce laws which regulate the digital world. As we've said, the law – the legislative, executive and judicial bodies of every country – moves only after social change. Certainly the making of law usually follows rather than leads society. In the digital age this looks to be a chronic problem. The digital world is developing and effecting change faster than any one set of actors – be they tech titans in Silicon Valley or governments anywhere – can control.

Today, you are technically able to act online in a way that many countries do not permit you to do in person, because the laws have not caught up with technology. For example, you are able to spew hatespeech online to millions of people in a way that you wouldn't be able to do in a public square without being arrested. This area is even more complex, as the laws that should govern the digital world appear to need mutual agreement by many if not all governments!

If a government is like a machine it is a big, unwieldy thing, made of many parts which are not always running in harmony; supranational bodies are even bigger, and slower to adapt and change due to the countless competing interests of national governments which make up their members. We need campaigners to continue to hold lawmakers to account so that the law stays as up-to-date as our smartphones.

Just because something is legal doesn't make it right. There are plenty of things that are legal but immoral, and it's the role of activists to try and keep the law in line with morality, current morality, as much as possible. Many took issue with some of the practices that led up to the 2008 financial crisis, even though the bankers were actually well within the realms of the law. There are lawmakers who campaign to reform banking laws so that that kind of crisis doesn't happen again, but the financial industry is incredibly difficult to regulate. The speed of contagion in the 2008 crash took governments by surprise – they could and should have moved earlier than they did to ensure the capitalization of the major banks. But this is an instance where rules in one country can't save a situation – all governments had to act in concert because the digital world of finance is borderless.

As much as individual citizens might be trying to bring legal practices in line with what benefits citizens, there are a lot of people who don't believe the law should change. Even the Upskirting Bill was delayed because one out-of-touch MP believed that it should be debated further on a point of principle as he opposes legislation being brought to Parliament on a Friday, despite later admitting that he hadn't done enough research and did not actually understand what upskirting was. There will always be lobby groups and corporations with an army of lawyers who have a lot more money than individual activists and who will do their best to obstruct changes to the status quo. Why? Because they aren't on the frontiers of the new world, and they are fuelled by the echo chambers they surround themselves with.

If you identify an area of activism that requires the law be changed, it is difficult to know where to begin. The law can be alarmingly complex and difficult to understand. The legalese sometimes make it feel as if the law is designed to be inaccessible to everyday citizens.

We asked **Gina Miller** – who successfully challenged the right of the British government to invoke Article 50 after the EU referendum, arguing that only Parliament can take away rights that Parliament has granted – to explain when to use the law as a means of activism, as opposed to other methods such as advocacy or protest:

When faced with a complex issue especially in a febrile
environment, debate is often shut down and we witness bullying

and abuse in media and across institutions. At these times, the dry letter of the law can take out the emotion from the situation and can be the best way to bring back objectivity to deal with emerging problems. The law serves as a shield and balancing scales at these times of social unrest.

The law and independence of the courts should also be used when a matter is urgent. Informing the public and funnelling civil society pressure on governments attempting to put themselves above the law is a vital tool for our democracy; such as in the Brexit related case I brought against the UK Government.

Don't think of the challenge or a campaign ahead as one big fight. Think about it as one step at a time in the journey to your desired destination. Enjoy taking the first step and the next because when you look back, suddenly, before you know it, you'll realize you've actually journeyed quite a long way. My advice is don't be afraid to take that first step but try to gather people along the way as collaboration, teamworking and assembling people with different talents is much more effective than you holding all the risk, responsibility and resilience.

Taking on a legal establishment, be it through government bills or through the courts, is daunting, but you don't need to be a lawyer yourself to be successful. Rather, you need to have a clear idea of what you want to achieve. Feel confident that your passion for your cause and your innovative perspective can bring clarity and fresh thinking which may be sorely needed. You may not succeed on your first attempt, but as you learn to navigate the corridors of legal power, you will come across different means of making a difference.

Bill Browder is the founder and CEO of Hermitage Capital Management, an investment fund that was the largest foreign investor in Russia. Due to Bill's advocacy against corporate corruption, the Russian government denied his entry to Russia in 2005, seizing Hermitage Capital Management's funds. He lobbied for US Congress to pass the Magnitsky

Act, a law which would punish human rights violators by freezing their assets and bank accounts. The Magnitsky Act was signed into law in 2012 by President Barack Obama. Bill found that it was his background as a financier that helped him pass one of the most effective human rights laws in recent history:

> You have to constantly course correct in your pursuit of justice. Initially I went to the state department in an attempt to get them to impose a sanction on the Russians who killed Sergei Magnitsky. They have an executive order which allows them to ban visas of corrupt foreign officials. Once my request was rejected I decided to change my tactics. Instead of trying to work with the state department I tried to go through the legislative branch of the US government rather than the executive board.
>
> Part of the success of this campaign is that I come from such an unconventional background. Most people who go into human rights work start out as being interested in human rights and politics. I come from the business world. I know what kind of people violate human rights and I know they're obsessed with money. The bad guys in Russia are ready to kill for money. Money is the only thing that matters to them.
>
> I said to myself, 'If money is the only thing that matters to them, why not go after the thing that matters to them most?' This makes perfect sense to everyone I know in finance; but politicians, who come at it from a different perspective, were less sure of the Act's efficacy. They didn't understand the power of this concept until the Magnitsky Act actually came into place. When the first Act came into effect and they saw these tectonic reactions of the Putin regime, they started to realize that we were on to something big. Governments have gravitated to the Magnitsky Act and it has been rolled out again and again - not just for Russians, but for many others, including Nicaraguans, the Khashoggi murderers and many more.

Build a team that can win

There are two main ways that activists can change the law: one is creating enough groundswell that legislators feel that they need to take responsibility to change the law, and the other way is through litigation – fighting your case in the courts. We recommend that activists only litigate when they feel that campaigning won't create meaningful change. The legal system tends to be inaccessible to non-lawyers, and litigation is costly, time consuming, exhausting and usually designed for you to fail.

However, many things do need to be litigated, and if that is the case then you shouldn't be afraid to take on the work. But your first port of call shouldn't be to jump into a courtroom. There are many steps that need to be taken before you get there.

Often, a campaign for a law change can be very effective. A good campaign will emotionally and logically appeal to legislators, encouraging them to take the correct steps on your behalf.

Depending on your system of government, you may be able to change the law by getting your elected representatives to bring a bill on your behalf. This can sometimes be more straightforward than challenging something in court. You may be involved in the drafting of that bill or you may be able to provide the expertise that goes into informing what's in that bill.

If you do end up going to court, it is essential to have the right team around you. Many people get lured into representing themselves and we strongly advise against this. Your own lack of knowledge can be a real danger. Many people elect to represent themselves because they are put off by legal fees, but the legal system is not designed for people to represent themselves, and judges may look upon you in a very dim light because you won't know what the procedure is. There are many areas where you can trip up – people are frequently thrown out of court before they even begin for procedural reasons, such as not getting a form stamped in the correct way. It can take a long time to familiarize yourself with the legal process.

We're lucky that there are lots of resources available online, but a lot of people who want to litigate things or bring a bill to parliament believe it's going to be straightforward and satisfying. The reality is sitting in most courts is steeped in indeterminable legal speak. It's very dry. It's very procedural.

You listen to lawyers debate minutiae for hours on end, often with little to no humour, drama or excitement.

To maximize your chances of success with litigation you need to build the right team around you. A successful legal campaign requires a range of talents and perspectives – finding the right legal support is a critical early step. Top lawyers are expensive, but if a cause is important enough you may be able to get services for free, as **Bill Browder** points out:

> You don't have to be a lawyer to change the law. You just need a basic concept. You don't need a law degree to understand or come up with the concept behind the Magnitsky Act. The idea is simple: when people kill for money, we should freeze their assets. Once you have your basic concept, you should find lawyers who share your passion and will hopefully work with you on a pro-bono basis. It's always uncomfortable to ask people to do stuff for free, but you need to ask in order to get that critical help.

Be smart and humble: ask for help. You mustn't be afraid to ask people to work on the campaign for free. It can be good for a law firm's reputation to work towards changing a law. Law firms are as competitive as any other businesses, and a law firm that engages in getting a law changed becomes the 'go to' firm for cases in that area. The right law firm can make a significant difference to your case.

Ropes & Gray represented three child sex-trafficking victims against Backpage.com LLC. The website transmitted the vast majority of internet advertisements for illegal commercial sex in the United States, including online child sex advertising. Ropes & Gray sued Backpage.com for creating an online marketplace with the intentions of facilitating the sexual exploitation of children in violation of federal and state criminal statutes. Backpage.com kept on appealing and kept on winning, because of the right to publish in America. But eventually, on 6 April 2018, the Federal Bureau of Investigation shut down the platform for sex trafficking. The credit of course goes to the seventeen brave Jane Does, anonymous victims of child sex trafficking, and their families, who became the test cases, but the might of a prestigious firm like Ropes & Gray relentlessly working on behalf of victims was critical to this success.

Each cause has to decide what they're going to spend money on. You may have a big organization that is willing to spend lots of money on litigation and paying expensive lawyers. If you're on your own, then you're going to need to work out how you're going to fund your campaign or how you will get things done for free. Quality lawyers charge expensive fees. Even if they are willing to do some work for free, they may not be willing to put in all of their time for free. In that case, the research and sifting through documents may need to be done by you, by other volunteers or by people at a cheaper law firm. When trying to identify a law firm that is likely to help you, **Gina Miller** recommends that you try and find firms who are known for their pro–bono practice:

> To find a law firm that will be sympathetic and open to considering possibly offering pro-bono services, I think you need to consider the culture of organizations, you need to have a look at the DNA that runs through that organization, the cultural DNA. If the firm cares about giving back to society rather than just making profit, has active networks and events on diversity, social justice, schools engagement - their doors tend to be easier to push open.
>
> Also look at the previous work / track record. I was aware of the work of James Libson and Mishcon de Reya on David Irving v Penguin Books and Deborah Lipstadt - the case that is profiled in the film *Denial* which takes on Holocaust denial - and their history of activism made me confident that they would be strong partners.
>
> Many of my senior legal team either worked pro bono or at cost, but I was insistent we pay the juniors because that was fair and they were working late into the night. It also meant they felt valued, motivated and emotionally invested in the case.

What's good about trying to change the law is that people can see that you're going to make real change. Legislative change is clearly material change, and that's appealing to a lot of people. If you're crowdfunding you will be able to show the public where their money is being directly spent.

A broadly funded legal campaign can be very powerful because not everyone can appear in court every day. Not everyone can be doing the graft of the work, but showing that many people supported your legal effort and paid for you to have the very best lawyers is compelling.

There are some excellent tools available to help you fund your campaign, one of the most effective being crowdjustice.com. Campaigns on behalf of child refugees, people caught up in Trump's 2017 travel ban and junior doctors in the UK's National Health Service have been successfully funded through this platform. Actress and activist **Emma Watson** sees the establishment of the Justice and Equality Fund, which she has personally donated to, as being one of the most important concrete outcomes of the #MeToo movement so far:

> The launch of the Justice and Equality Fund in the UK (TIME'S UP UK's version of the Legal Defense Fund) was a particularly memorable moment for me. It was developed in consultation with UK women's rights and equalities organizations who told us what was needed in the current climate. Through this work we aim to support women who had experienced harassment and abuse, improve accountability and prevent future abuses from occurring. The Justice and Equality Fund (JEF) is managed by Rosa, the only UK-wide fund for women and girls, and is powered by donations from the public. The JEF offers much-needed funds to existing expert services and projects alongside financially supporting developing organizations and grassroots activism. Many people don't realize that very basic services which protect and care for women are under threat, and it's incredible the difference the fund has made in a short space of time.
>
> We haven't reached the fundraising levels of our colleagues in the USA yet, but we hope that more people will be inspired to give at home here in the UK. The JEF has already resourced the vital work of organizations like London Black Women's Project, who provide

specialist advice and support to women of colour and migrant survivors of abuse, and Rights of Women, who will provide a free and confidential helpline led by women lawyers offering specialist legal advice to women experiencing sexual harassment. The fund has also supported keeping the Rape and Sexual Abuse Support Centre for England and Wales helpline open every day and is resourcing the first rape crisis service provision in Northern Ireland in 12 years.

Financial support is a really practical act of solidarity and I hope we can reach even more under-resourced organizations and campaign groups in the future.

This is an example of different areas of activism combining to create substantive societal change: the #MeToo social media movement and the Women's March have created the general awareness required to encourage people to donate. The donations in turn provide funding for lawyers so that people can make changes through the courts. Activism is a long-term game.

Whether you are paying lawyers or asking them to work for free, you still need to convince them to take up your case. It's critical to be able to have clear evidence to show them – if your case is complex or hard to verify, consider partnering with NGOs or investigative journalists to bolster your credibility. If your case involves a personal experience, you must also be prepared to be entirely truthful. **Lisa Bloom**, founder of civil rights law firm Bloom Firm, and who has represented many women who were victims of sexual harassment by men such as Bill O'Reilly from Fox News, advises her clients:

My clients have to be very honest. I tell them, there is no fact as bad as a lie. If you tell a lie, your case, it's going to be over. The judge is going to find out and you're going to lose. There have been times where I found out that a client was lying to me. I conduct an investigation, we're very thorough, and if it turns out that she was lying, we withdraw our support. It's very upsetting to learn that, especially for somebody you're fighting for. You throw your heart and soul into a case, and you find out she's been lying about the central issues in the case the whole time. It's discouraging, but you have to get out and move on and stay focused on all of the other cases.

So, how does Lisa determine which cases she takes on and which she rejects?

I probably reject 98 per cent of the people who come to me with cases. We are very, very selective. I want to represent people who I believe in, who have a credible story that's corroborative. When I represent a client and win their case, it not only helps them but others as well. That's how we view it. For example, I represented a female police detective recently, she's a victim of domestic violence and revenge porn from another police officer who she had a relationship with. He posted explicit pictures of her, sending them to other police officers, and it was devastating to her.

We went into court and we won. We won a five-year restraining order and the judge admonished him. He's not allowed to carry firearms, which means he, probably, can't be a police officer any more. That got a lot of news coverage, and other female police officers have reached out to me thanking me and saying they too were victims of police misconduct.

I always want to take a case that's going to make a difference not only for a client but for others as well, so that they can see it as an inspiration. They can see what is possible.

Remember, your case is unlikely to affect you alone; from gay marriage in the USA to the case of Ella Kissi-Debrah in the UK, whose death has been linked to illegal levels of pollution, litigation on behalf of individuals can have significant ramifications for the rest of society. A lot of change is made through filing lawsuits and litigation. That's how the American civil rights movement got rid of the Jim Crow laws. Supreme Court Justice Ruth Bader Ginsburg is famous for getting women's rights through the courts.

Reach out to civil rights attorneys in your community and look into your issue and see whether litigation is possible. Many countries have constitutions that guarantee equal rights. Are those promises a reality or are they just words on a page? Civil rights lawyers can help you go about making those words mean something.

Storytelling is the most powerful way to put ideas into the world

The law by its very nature is precise, dry and technical, or as Aristotle said, 'reason free from passion'. It is not an emotional tool or weapon. Legal systems are hundreds and sometimes thousands of years old. Even when you are very well versed in your subject matter – well versed enough to litigate something – that doesn't mean that your audience will be informed enough to understand what it is that you're litigating. The art of legalese is not the same as being a great rhetorician.

To accompany the legal campaign you're pursuing, you need a communications campaign that brings people with you, because public pressure undeniably matters. Public protests, marches or rallies in favour of your legal campaign often attract media attention, which can help spread the word about your cause and help garner more support. This support may be financial and enable you to continue to pursue your case, and appeal if necessary. Public pressure itself can demonstrate to judges that times have changed, which requires the law to reflect it. On a purely emotional level, witnessing people taking time out of their lives to support a campaign with passion and commitment may play on the heartstrings of certain judges and put a human face to your legal campaign. We would hope that most judges manage to be entirely impartial and unmoved by external affairs, but bringing out supporters in your favour will help.

Alfie Evans was a British infant boy with a neurodegenerative disorder whose life support was set to be withdrawn. His parents wanted to transfer him to a hospital in Italy but were threatened with legal penalties. After taking the case to the press, the family received mass amounts of public support from people who referred to themselves as Alfie's Army and even appeared outside court every day in support – they became impossible to ignore. The parents lost their case, as did the parents of Charlie Gard who experienced similar tragic circumstances, but the public outcry has ignited a vigorous debate about parents' rights which may yet spark reform.

Ultimately, the law is there to represent the will of the people, and when you can show that the will of the people has changed or diverges significantly from the letter of the law, you are demonstrating to judges that the law must be amended. Storytelling – showing why a certain law will help people know the moral thing to do – is crucial, because the wording of the act or the legislation is likely to be very technical and unemotional. You need appeal to the heart of the public and the minds of the judges.

The impartiality of judges should never be presumed – judges can be political beings. There are judges who will view a case through a personal or political lens no matter how strong your arguments are. The notion that all judges are going to be the best people to decide whether a law is passed may not be true, but on the whole judges will weigh up the extent to which something is legal or of legal merit within the constitution and/or laws of your country.

Your narrative needs to be comprehensive yet easy to understand. Journalists are on deadlines – they don't usually have time to wade through intricate legal and constitutional amendments. They need a story that's going to pack a punch and sell papers if they're going to cover your campaign.

The campaign to legalize gay marriage in Australia resulted in 61 per cent of people voting to allow same sex-marriage in 2017. **Andrew Bragg** was the national director of the Liberals & Nationals for Yes campaign. He describes the importance of public advocacy in that historic result:

> Changing the law requires a good understanding of people's hopes and aspirations, but also a sense of literacy levels [an understanding of the issue] the general public holds on your issue. Undertaking research is the first step. Once you have a sense of what people are looking for, I recommend setting short and long-term goals. You need to build literacy and pressure in that order.

Our biggest problem was keeping people on message, and that was overcome by having almost daily phone calls with our key spokesmen and women. Our central message was voting yes was about fairness and families, which resonated.

Australia has a history of losing similar mass public votes (only 8 out of 44 referenda have passed since 1901). Our campaign helped deliver 71 out of 76 coalition seats. Public advocacy maintained the pressure on the government and the parliament which eventually yielded the result. Without balanced public advocacy, the vote could have been lost.

Consistency and commitment are critical in maintaining your campaign's momentum. You need to develop a communications strategy which takes a long-term view, as a legal campaign can last years. Changing the law is something that by its very nature takes a long time, which is a good thing in many ways because laws should be robust and difficult to dismantle.

You'll need to be prepared to slug it out in court for a long time and to plan for a public opinion battle that may last even longer. This can be especially true in conservative societies or on controversial issues. Getting the public involved in your campaign can demonstrate to legislators and the establishment, who may be resistant to change, that your cause is a social concern. Often, the public will share your outrage at horrific crimes or abuses – but you may need to familiarize them with the facts if they have been deliberately obscured or covered up for a long time.

Satta F Sheriff is the founder of Youth in Action for Peace and Empowerment in Liberia, a children and youth-driven NGO founded to advocate, promote, empower and defend the rights of Liberian children and vulnerable groups. She found that public support was critical in passing the Liberian Children's Law:

Public advocacy plays a major role in a law-changing process. The more the people are involved, the louder the message can become. In turn that makes channelling the message to lawmakers easier. Moreover, advocacy that is driven by people is more likely

127

to be accepted by people. Inclusion of the public in campaigns to change laws is critical in the law's effective implementation.

The Liberian Children's Parliament was actively involved in the passage of the Liberian Children's Law. I remember how we knocked on the doors of almost every stakeholder and lawmaker, and on many occasions paraded the streets of Liberia. We used different channels to convince policymakers to internally implement the United Nations Convention on the Rights of Children through the Liberian Children's Law. We presented the cases of over 12,000 child soldiers who had been resettled, babies and girls who were raped, trafficked, beaten, mistreated, deprived of education and the right to a nationality and an identity. After a few years, the Liberian Children's Law was finally passed and signed in to law by the President of the Republic of Liberia.

In getting the media on your side, you need to be judicious in how you foster relationships with journalists. Civil rights attorney **Lisa Bloom** uses press conferences carefully. You shouldn't feel that you need to have a press conference, however, Lisa points out that there are three key benefits:

1. When everybody is telling your story, it's better to seize control of the narrative and tell it yourself. Imagine if you're in the news and everybody is talking about you. They're interviewing your neighbours, coworkers, friends, family and they're getting it wrong to a large extent, while you just have to remain quiet. It's very frustrating to be in that position. I encourage my clients to write out their stories, we go over it, and we make sure that it's exactly the way that they want to say it. Then they stand up and tell their story. It's very empowering.

2. We want the other side to know that we are fearless. We have the right to speak out publicly and we're going to. Secrecy usually helps the other side in my cases. Whether it's the government or a company, a celebrity, whoever it is, if they're accused of

wrongdoing, secrecy helps them. The media teams are there to investigate facts, this means they may discover information which is very helpful to our case.

3. Press coverage brings out witnesses. I had a case in 2018 against a city council member accused of sexually harassing my client. We tried to get it resolved but the city was not cooperative. Finally, we had a press conference. My client was nine months pregnant at the time. She was very brave. She was very nervous, like everybody is before a press conference, but she stood up and did it anyway. I looked right into the camera and said, 'If you have a similar story about Council Member Fernandez please contact me.' A couple of days later a woman called me and she said, 'Lisa, were you talking right to me when you said that?' I said, 'Well, I don't know. I guess I was.' She also had a similar story and I represented her as well – together we ended up bringing down this council member. He's now off the city council. We got a very substantial settlement for my first client and my second client ran for city council and she is now in his seat. It's a wonderful outcome.

Media relations can be immensely challenging, especially if you haven't worked with the press before. There is little room for nuance in reporting, you need to present your story in a way that is as black and white and attention-grabbing as possible – make it easy for people to see who is right and who is wrong. You have to be able to tell a story and sell it to people, so that they're interested in championing that story. As you make progress in the campaign, ensure you are keeping everything in the public sphere. Everything that you do should be on the record. If there isn't an article, a blog or a social media post documenting your work, it may as well not have happened. If the media isn't interested yet, record every meeting and moment online so that, when interest does pick up, people are able to go back and see all the work that has gone into the campaign.

Creating a culture of accountability, not blame

Just because something bad is happening does not mean it is being done legally. Often we don't need to change the law to solve a problem, we need to make sure existing laws are enforced. These days there's a brilliant place to start – the internet. These are the questions you need to ask:

- Is it illegal to commit a certain action in your country?
- If yes – what does the law say exactly? Are there legal cases in which this law has been used?
- If no – in which country is it illegal and what does that law say?
- Has anyone tried to get a law like this passed?
- If yes – who? And why was it not enacted?
- Who are the people of influence who might support such a law being enacted?
- Who are the legal experts in this particular field?

In countries with an established legal system, a lot of the wrongful incidents will be illegal. Corruption and bribe taking is illegal in most countries, but that doesn't mean that it doesn't happen. In these cases, you are looking to enforce the law against certain entities or individuals which can be incredibly difficult, especially if those are powerful companies or people. The crucial thing is to work with experts and people with legal knowledge to discern what the law is and whether it applies in your instance. Is there a loophole which your case is falling through, or is there a very clear law that is being broken?

Holding people to account when they're breaking the law – especially if they're a police officer, a judge or a politician – is very difficult. But it is still one of the most important aspects of preventing wrongdoing and it's not impossible. Cardinal George Pell is going to jail for sexually assaulting children. He is to date the most senior Catholic cleric to be convicted of sexual assault – yet only a few years ago people were too scared to bring cases against parish priests, let alone cardinals. The law enables us to speak truth to power. If you're able to prove in court that someone has broken the law, you can ensure more people are held to account. Successful prosecutions will deter other wrongdoers.

Emma Watson points out that the most positive change from legal action is an overall change in culture which creates genuine accountability:

> Accountability may take many forms, depending on who is the abuser, who is the survivor, what the abuse consisted of and the context in which the abuse takes place. It's important to separate the concepts of punishment and accountability. For me, punishment is often too focused on individuals ('a few bad apples', etc.) and lets institutions, systems and cultures off the hook.
>
> There are many forms of accountability relevant to abuses of power – legal consequences, institutional accountability, cultural accountability, personal accountability . . . in my mind, accountability involves some kind of acceptance of responsibility, acknowledgment of wrongdoing and learning towards change.
>
> The ultimate goal of accountability should not be punishment but prevention in the first place. Abusers are more likely to be deterred from offending behaviour if they know they'll be held accountable. People experiencing abuse are more likely to come forward if there are transparent, robust and proactive accountability procedures in place.
>
> Accountability also involves creating a preventive culture in institutions, companies and teams that protects against abuses of power. People who enable abusers or perpetuate a culture permissive of abuse also need to be held accountable. The revelations and debates over the past two years have shown us time and again that sexual harassment and abuse is not just a problem at the level of individuals, it's a systemic problem.
>
> Speaking from within my own industry, I think accountability would imply a context where national legal processes, industry

standards and the harassment and abuse policies and procedures of companies can be effectively implemented without a person's power and influence prejudicing or hindering the process. I believe accountability would mean a climate where people from all backgrounds, and in all types of roles, feel able to raise their voices and be taken seriously, without fear of reprisals, and are aware of and trust the processes in place to protect them and hold abusers accountable.

Often, it is not the law that is preventing people from being held accountable – it is the culture of impunity. While there are laws that state sexual harassment and assault are illegal in all contexts including the workplace, victims were continually not believed or were shamed for coming forward with a case.

This is particularly true of the 2015 Brock Turner case, when Turner, a former Stanford University student, was caught sexually assaulting an unconscious female student. Turner was sentenced to just six months in jail and three years of probation, although he ultimately served just three months in jail. The prosecution had requested a sentence of six years in prison while the maximum sentence was fourteen years. The law was in place to give Turner a more severe punishment, but the judge called for a minimal sentence. There was speculation that as a white male Stanford student Turner received preferential treatment which was heightened when Judge Aaron Persky, who oversaw the case, stated, 'I take him at his word.' Fortunately now, in the #MeToo era, victims of sexual assault and harassment are beginning to feel comfortable sharing their experiences in the pursuit of justice.

There are also often too many loopholes in the law. Given that many of our laws were written by men many centuries ago, they may be flawed. The US Constitution famously states, 'All men are created equal' – and that was only supposed to apply to white men at the time. The people have reinterpreted this to say 'all men' means mankind, and so includes women, but that was not the original intention.

Their antiquated nature means that the laws may not cater for minorities, especially emerging minorities such as migrant groups or people with conditions such as autism, which wasn't scientifically understood a century ago. These people may be inadequately protected by the law because they weren't taken into consideration at the time of the law's drafting. One Young World Ambassador and former Ms Wheelchair USA, **Dr Josie Badger**, has been instrumental in bringing about a new law in Pennsylvania:

A vast majority of infrastructures were created without people with disabilities in mind. At best, these infrastructures must be retroactively fitted to allow for the mere presence of people with disabilities in the community. In the United States a majority of the inaccessibility is due to a lack of understanding. This void of knowledge provides a space for the disability community to provide education and ultimately recognize the worth of people with disabilities. Physically, structurally and conceptually, communities struggle to support individuals with disabilities to a level that allows them to be self-determined, active citizens. This is really apparent when it comes to employment.

The #IWantToWork campaign started through a selfie campaign in which young self-advocates with disabilities met with their local legislators and told them why employment mattered to them and explained the barriers to employment that they were currently experiencing. Each of the meetings was finished by the self-advocate and the legislator taking a selfie together, holding up a sign that displayed the campaign hashtag #IWantToWork. The campaign became popular among Pennsylvania legislators, with many reaching out to the campaign's staff to ask when they would have their meeting, and their selfie.

So far, the campaign has assisted in the passing of two pieces of legislation. The first was Pennsylvania Act 26 of 2016 Work Opportunities For High School Students With Disabilities Act, which encouraged the state to support students with disabilities in obtaining paid employment while still in high school and ultimately increased funding to assist in employment transition services for young adults with disabilities. The second bill was Pennsylvania Act 36 of 2018, Employment First Pennsylvania. This act stated that the primary goal for an individual with a disability who has graduated from high school is to obtain competitive, integrated employment. The campaign is currently working on additional legislation to allow workers with disabilities to continue to receive medical assistance.

For Josie and her team, finding a campaign which benefitted the legislators and provided them with positive publicity (always a benefit for government officials!) helped build the support they needed to get the bill through.

Creating cooperation and collaboration can be done by individuals, as in Josie's case, but often the best approach is to identify organizations who can form a broad alliance. Recognizing where your power lies and how you can yield it to change the law is also incredibly important.

Mina Tolu is part of the executive board of IGLYO – the International Lesbian, Gay, Bisexual, Transgender, Queer & Intersex (LGBTQI) Youth and Student Organisation, and also works for Transgender Europe, a European human rights network that strives for the human rights and equality for all trans people in Europe. She explains how forming a broad alliance was used in the legalization of gay marriage in Malta:

I founded an LGBTQI youth organization together with other students at the University of Malta and we started to collaborate with MGRM, the Malta LGBTQI Rights Movement, which worked on the policy elements of marriage equality and legal gender recognition. We focused on public advocacy. We organized poster exhibitions and human library events at colleges, allowing students to get the opportunity to come ask members of the LGBTQI community anything they wanted to.

We also met with politicians such as Joseph Muscat, who was the leader of the opposition at the time and later Prime Minister of Malta. Four members of my organization accompanied me to the meeting. We wanted to ensure that we were presenting a range of LGBTQI stories and experiences to Muscat to show him there

is no 'one size fits all' narrative. We were able to be very direct
and honest with him and other politicians we also met with. Being
part of a youth organization allows you to be more radical than a
traditional organisation which is expected to be professional and
moderate. If politicians disagreed with us, they could not trash us
in the press as we were students and they would have surely been
met with a public backlash. This is in part why the student climate
strikes have been so effective. Politicians can't criticize children
and young people without seeming petty and overly aggressive.
Recognize where you hold power and use that in your advocacy to
change the law. It can be difficult to get a seat at the table or even
be let in the room, but when you do - use it to your best advantage.

When it comes to changing the law, your appeal has to be first and foremost
to the lawmakers. Is there something in it for them? You should examine
what a change in the law would mean for elected representatives and for
lawmakers. Does it keep them in power? Does it give them profile? There's
no harm in looking at who gains what from this change in the law.

One Young World ambassador Jaha Dukureh had a very clear
understanding that only an executive order from the president could outlaw
female genital mutilation in The Gambia. She followed him from village
to village on the campaign trail until he eventually met with her; two days
later, on 23 November 2015, FGM was banned in The Gambia.

Be aware of who you have to convince in order to change the law. If
your law directly threatens them, it is unlikely that it will pass and you
should consider alternative routes. For example, if you want to pass an anti-
corruption bill and there is corruption in government, you may need to find
an alternative route to pressure for change rather than directly working with
government agencies. Reaching out to international forces to stimulate
external pressure may be an effective way to deal with this issue.

Kevin Mendez is president and a founding member of Belize Youth
Empowerment for Change (BYEC). He is also an HIV & TB adherence
counsellor with the Belize Ministry of Health. Until recently homosexuality
was constitutionally illegal in Belize, and Kevin witnessed the role that
coalitions can play in changing the law:

Same-sex sexual activity was illegal in Belize until 2016, when the Supreme Court declared Belize's anti-sodomy law unconstitutional. There were several LGBTQ+ organizations working on this court case. As the president of Belize Youth Empowerment for Change I was asked to partner with the organization that led the constitutional change – the key to the constitution being amended was a network of advocacy groups who were doing research on the ground to provide as much information as possible to the legal team.

We engaged with focus groups of LGTBQ people and allies. Many people didn't understand why changing the constitution was necessary. There were LGBTQ people who said that they had never been arrested so didn't understand why the law had to change. We patiently explained that no one should have to live with the risk of incarceration over this issue. We had to change people's perception of what human rights were, we had to inform them that this was a violation. It was important to engage with these people and create a community that would support the bill. If the LGBTQ community was apathetic there was no way we could generate enough pressure on lawmakers to take this issue seriously. Working with communities across Belize was a critical part of this campaign. We had to ensure people were on our side.

We even had discussions with faith-based leaders. Some did not respond well while others surprisingly did. We brought the issue to the Council of Churches, of which the Anglican church is a part. Not only did we receive its support but the Anglican church opened its doors to LGBTQ people and publicly welcomed them. We talked to priests about the importance of their leadership. We tried to get them to acknowledge their power and responsibility. Putting a human face to the issue was incredibly effective. We asked them to imagine what it would be like if their friend or relative was being abused because of their sexual orientation. We used statistics about abuse and the spread of HIV to back up these claims and drive the message home. By engaging with these groups of people we were able to identify important stakeholders and allies who would support the bill. As a result, the cause received much publicity.

Creating broad-based support requires patience – you need to methodically engage with all of your stakeholders and take time to explain the issues to them. As Kevin points out, even the people who are most going to benefit from the law being changed may not understand its importance immediately. Similarly, victims living in fear may be the most resistant to campaigning or sharing their experiences. It is only by building alliances and developing networks that we can create the groundswell that is necessary to turn the tide.

Without struggle, there is no protest

While alliances are effective and create bridges across communities that can contribute to effective activism, you ultimately don't try to change the law to make friends. The mind-set of an activist has to be one that focuses on the result you need above anything else.

You have to maintain your persistence because changing the law is going to take a long time and it is going to eat up energy, patience and attention. You may have to appeal or go through multiple processes, so you need to be aware that the system itself is almost designed to knock you back. In a contentious legal system, you have to argue against people. There are very few circumstances where there won't be somebody who doesn't believe the law should be changed or someone who will want to scrutinize your case, argument and evidence to a granular degree.

When people argue against your issue it can feel like a personal attack and can be incredibly demoralizing. But when you are setting out to change the status quo and you're rocking the ancient boat, you are bound to experience some pain while doing so. Persistence is key.

If you have to relitigate, it can feel incredibly tedious. It can feel demoralizing and exhausting, and it can be costly. Often you are presenting the same facts over and over again, as they're not going to change materially within a couple of years. Not everyone has the attention span or the persistence to see this through. **Bill Browder** shares his recommendations for the mind-set that is needed to change the law:

> Any human rights activist is effectively at odds not just with their enemies, but with the governments they're trying to get support from. People think if they go in and act nice, governments are going to do what is right, but then they often get frustrated when that is not the case.
>
> Governments can be your toughest adversary and one should go in with no intentions of making friends. You should approach them with the intention of forcing them to do things they are uncomfortable doing. However politicians, elected representatives, can be your allies - elected people generally run for office to do the right thing.
>
> You have to be tough, you have to be ready to ruffle feathers. You have to be ready to offend people because otherwise you won't get anything done. One of the problems I've encountered with human rights activists is that everyone wants to get along with each other. You should not be so abrasive that no one wants to work with you, but you should be ready to fight for your ultimate cause - you have to be charming and annoying at the same time. You have to be ready to make a lot of people uncomfortable. You don't need to be liked. You need to be respected.

Some people feel that, in order to change the law, civil disobedience is necessary. We, on the whole, think that breaking the law will set your cause back in many ways. You may lose your personal liberty. The public may denigrate your cause because people will see you as a lawbreaker, and therefore an untrustworthy criminal. You will also lose the respect of the legal establishment. We mostly live in societies that discriminate heavily against people with criminal records. We're not saying that that's right or wrong, but it's certainly fact. You should want to build the strongest case possible with no footholes for anyone to trample over you.

However, when the law is wrong, sometimes we need to break the law to show how absurd it is, or how immoral. Sometimes civil disobedience is the only way of demonstrating that. However, if you're trying to appeal to judges, politicians or the legal establishment, that can be more difficult to do from a jail cell or with a criminal record.

One issue that many activists face is that the legal establishment is the very issue they are trying to solve. For example, human rights advocate **Valeria Gomez Palacios** lived with fear for her family and friends as a result of her activism against the brutal Ortega regime in Nicaragua. In the end, she had to look outside of the country to hold the regime to account, using **Bill Browder**'s Magnitsky Act. The Magnitsky Act is a hugely powerful tool because it doesn't require prosecution. It is one of many examples of how the international community can support activists in countries who have limited accountability for the government and its entities. Valeria explains how it is working:

> On 19 April 2018, the Nicaraguan police, directed by President Ortega, opened fire on groups of peaceful demonstrators protesting unjust social security reforms. The months since then have been mired by State-sponsored violence and repression, resulting in over 300 extrajudicial killings and 600 political prisoners. Nicaraguans can't go to the police because it is the police that are killing us. It is because of this that I knew we had to ask for international help.

> I met with various US senators to enact sanctions on the Nicaraguan government for human rights violations. Advocating for sanctions was hard. No one wants their country to be sanctioned, but the government had already destabilized the country and the sanctions were not meant to affect the people – we specifically advocated for targeted sanctions and the application of the global Magnitsky Act. Working with the US Senate, we had to get senators to care, so we created various Twitter campaigns

asking US senators and Congress to vote in favour of the sanctions and to stand in solidarity with the Nicaraguan people. At the UN I publicly asked member states of the Security Council what they were doing to support peace and security in Nicaragua. These public meetings also led to private meetings to discuss the situation and how we could work together.

As a result of the sanctions President Ortega's party members broke with him and started denouncing the human rights violations in order to avoid being sanctioned by the US government. Because the sanctions include a provision that they will be lifted as soon as a democratic process is restored and Nicaraguans get the right to elect their own leader, it puts the onus of ensuring democracy in the hands of the Nicaraguan government. The pressure is now on Ortega to resign, given that we are under a dictatorship and he has been illegitimately running the country for the last 12 years.

Ultimately, which ever means you choose to pursue legal change, within your own country or externally, you need to ensure that you have the stamina and resolve to see your battle through. This means taking care of yourself and ensuring that you don't become overwhelmed or burn out.

In the face of human rights abuses or sexual assault, it can seem trivial to make time for rest and self-care, especially if you are extremely motivated and find that your cause takes up headspace every hour of the day. But as **Gina Miller** points out:

If you don't look after yourself, how are you going to fight tomorrow? If Martin Luther King didn't go to bed, he wouldn't have had a dream.

How to change the law checklist

- Don't be deterred by the absence of any law – just because there is no law doesn't mean there shouldn't be one.

- Know that there are many different ways to achieve the change you want – educate yourself as best you can on the legal framework in which you are operating. You don't have to be a lawyer but you must develop your understanding as much as you can.

- If you have to go to court, make sure you have the right team around you – pro-bono legal support is often available; otherwise, consider crowd-funding to ensure you have adequate representation.

- Dealing with the press is challenging – foster relationships with journalists and record everything you do even when the press show no interest.

- Forming as broad as possible an alliance of organizations and influential figures who support the change you want is powerful – look for these allies and involve them methodically, but don't get distracted from your aim.

- If the law you need already exists you must focus on accountability. Check if what you're dealing with is a culture of impunity – you may need to change that rather than the law.

- Understand who will stand to gain from the change you want, and who will stand to lose, and tailor the way you handle both of these.

- Focus on the result you want and accept you may have to alienate some people – don't take it personally when people resist you.

- Be prepared to look for support or enforcement internationally if your national legal system needs to be held to account.

- Develop your stamina and look after yourself – the road may be long but it will be worth it.

Chapter Six
How to end a problem forever

This chapter is about the people who reach for eradication or completion. It's about perfect ambition – perfect in the linguistic sense of the completed action. It's about finding an end and a new beginning.

The key is to identify what your problem is, whether it's human trafficking or carbon emissions, and believe that there can be a perfect future where your problem doesn't exist.

The most inspiring forms of activism are the ones which work towards a perfect ambition. While all actions to make a difference are important, we need to be more concerted, organized and strategic in our efforts if we're going to really move the needle in a meaningful way on any social cause. Ultimately, we should strive for generational change, so that our children will not have to experience the same struggles that we did; our grandchildren will not die of the same diseases that killed our children; the injustices that our grandparents faced won't be faced by us. That is what real, lasting, meaningful change should look like.

Meaningful change is visionary. Whether it's putting a man on the moon or Martin Luther King's dream – to solve a problem forever requires the same awe-inspiring vision that helps people imagine beyond their current reality. It's about tapping into peoples' imaginations and allowing them to believe in the impossible dream they hadn't dared envisage.

Of course, not every individual feels able to be a part of this type of visionary change, and only a few people are able to take on the huge and often life-consuming responsibility for driving it forward. But, every person is able to choose how they can spend their time and money, and if more people acted with thoughtful purpose, all the small actions could be directed into something much more impactful. The story of President Kennedy's visit to NASA is a great example. When he asked the janitor mopping the floor at NASA what he did there, the janitor responded, 'I'm putting a man on the moon.' Whoever you are, your actions can play a part in a bigger movement.

To enable people to feel purposeful about the role they are playing, you need to make big ideas tangible, concrete and inspiring. Imagining a world without AIDS is much more inspiring than imagining a world with less AIDS. It's much better for humanity if we all work towards a world *without* AIDS.

The more systematic and purpose-driven this kind of activism is, the stronger the outcome will be. All the people in this chapter are incredibly methodical about what they do. They also all started somewhere. You're not going to solve a problem forever by just sitting in the library. Similarly, you don't solve a problem forever by rushing in – planning and research have to go hand in hand with action in the field.

Vision is the art of seeing what is invisible to others.

All the UN's Sustainable Development Goals are about completeness: zero hunger, education for all, zero poverty – either getting to 0 per cent or getting to 100 per cent. For most people, 75 per cent feels like enough: 75 per cent of children getting an excellent education sounds fantastic. But what about the other 25 per cent? Who is that statistic leaving behind?

It becomes very easy to allow people to slip through the cracks. It becomes easy to accept that some sex workers will always have HIV or some children are never going to get into college. We shouldn't accept these things as a given. We have to keep on challenging the accepted norms and question their validity, morality and preventability. You have to be very ambitious to not be satisfied with an 80 per cent positive statistic. Never let the statistics make you complacent. Even if poverty is decreasing, you should be asking yourself: Why is *anyone* living in poverty? When you look at it from that perspective you can see past the statistic and begin to identify the people who need your help.

It's also important to see past successful events. The election of Barack Obama as President of the United States would have exceeded what many civil rights activists would have expected when they heard Dr King speak and explain his dream of equality years before. It was so far beyond the imagination of most people living in the Jim Crow era. But racial inequality is not a problem that has been solved. American society does not live in a country of complete racial harmony and equal opportunity. Of course, the election of Barack Obama was an important and meaningful moment in civil rights history, but it meant a lot of people felt that issues of African–American equality were no longer as urgent and were brushed off.

President Obama stated in an interview with Marc Maron, 'The legacy of slavery, Jim Crow, discrimination in almost every institution of our lives, that casts a long shadow and that's still part of our DNA that's passed on. Racism, we are not cured of.'

It's important to celebrate victories such as the election of the first African–American president without obscuring the perfect ambition, in this case of true equality.

At the time of writing, a perfect ambition has been achieved in sub-Saharan Africa. Trachoma has just been eradicated in Malawi. Eight million people in Malawi risked losing their sight because they suffered from trachoma – an infection which causes a roughening of the inner surface of the eyelids. This roughening can lead to pain in the eyes, the breakdown of the outer surface of the cornea of the eyes, and can eventually lead to blindness. As a result of the Trachoma Initiative, in 2019 people are no longer at risk of losing their vision. The ITI team trained 12,524 people to locate and diagnose people with the disease. This significantly reduced the time surgeons needed to spend on screening patients. The initiative also supported the installation of 1,617 hand and face washing stations at 147 schools to help stop the spread of the disease. After four years of tireless work the team successfully treated over 12.9 million people.

The word 'tireless' here is important – the road to solving a problem forever is long and the work relentless. Each one of the people involved in the ITI played a crucial role; just like the NASA janitor, everyone has their part, however seemingly small, to push the ball that much further.

Pioneering physician **Larry Brilliant** was on the UN team that led the successful World Health Organization smallpox eradication programme in 1980. He describes how his team eradicated smallpox, one of history's deadliest diseases, by directing individual actions towards this perfect ambition:

> We went door to door in India. Our 150,000 people made almost
> 2 billion house calls to find every single virus, every case. Then
> we had to rapidly vaccinate everyone within one kilometre, two

kilometres, three kilometres and all of their contacts. We did see that the number of secondary or tertiary cases was going down, so we had a lot of confidence. That's not the way it looked to the newspapers. Our strategy was to find every case. Before, cases were not being reported. India went from reporting almost no smallpox to having 188,000 cases of smallpox. It scared everybody. It made it look like our programme was not only not stopping smallpox, but must be in some way creating smallpox, which, of course, we weren't. Those were pseudo-epidemics caused by our strategy.

There was a moment in time when our success in finding every case terrified people. Government officials wanted to close down the programme. We had to be confident and hold out a little longer, and instead of finding more cases, we ultimately started to find fewer and fewer smallpox cases because the programme was working. In fact, the duration between the peak of the outbreak and the last case of smallpox took just under a year.

If the volume of work undertaken by Larry and his team wasn't daunting enough, the onslaught of criticism and resistance they faced must have seemed overwhelming. Only you can know what keeps you going in terms of your own cause – you have to keep reminding yourself why you're doing the work:

We continued to be optimistic and pressed on with our work, despite strong resistance, because we had seen so many babies die. Many times I'd go into a village and I'd have a WHO jeep with me, I would open the door and a mother would come up to me and hand me her baby because I was a United Nations doctor. She would say, 'Heal my baby', and most of the time that baby was already dead. When you've seen thousands of children with smallpox, many of them who die from the disease, you want to conquer that more than you would want to sleep, more than you want to eat, more than you care about how tired you are. Relentlessness and perseverance were key, but so was the meticulousness. However hard it got, it was exhilarating - I have never felt as alive. How you feel about yourself is a very small percentage of the issue, nonetheless, it contributes to joyfulness and we worked with real joy.

Let the perfect ambition drive you – it wasn't enough for Larry Brilliant that fewer babies died of smallpox – he wanted to ensure that not a single baby died of smallpox ever again. By focusing on one baby at a time, he was able to eradicate a disease which killed 300 million people in the 20th-century alone. This is the type of activism than can truly solve a problem forever. Tasks always seem impossible until they're done.

Start somewhere but not anywhere

You can't set out to solve a problem forever unless you know a lot about your problem and have a meaningful strategy that is based on evidence, knowledge, research and field work. You need to know your enemy and choose what battles you're going to fight first and last. You need to think carefully about how best to approach it and who you will have to engage first. **Reshma Saujani**, founder of Girls Who Code, explains how she first encountered the lack of women in the tech industry:

> When I ran for Congress in 2010, I visited schools and classrooms along the campaign trail. And when I lost, something about my time visiting those schools stuck with me: the lack of girls in computer science classrooms. After doing more research, I realized that no one was even talking about the lack of women and girls in computer science. So I pulled together some funding and a team, and together we taught 20 girls how to code in a tiny bit of borrowed office space. And now, six years later, we've reached 90,000 girls, and we're not slowing down. We're well on our way to reaching gender parity in entry-level tech jobs by 2027. I never could have imagined seeing this kind of success so soon - our

college-aged alumni are choosing to major in computer science or related fields at 15 times the national rate – and I'm so excited to see what's next.

You can't be what you can't see. Our girls don't imagine themselves as coders because they don't see women coding. They see men coding. They see images of boys in hoodies sitting alone in front of computers. They see Mark Zuckerberg and they see Steve Jobs. So it shouldn't come as a surprise that women make up less than 25 per cent of the computing workforce - despite making up a majority of college graduates and a near majority of family breadwinners.

At Girls Who Code, we aren't just equipping our girls with computer science skills - we are teaching them to be brave, to be confident, to know that they have the power to be anything they want to be.

When approaching a problem for the first time it is important to be bold and driven as Reshma points out:

There have been so many moments in my life where I wanted to take the easy way out, to back down when failure seems imminent. But then I remember to be brave - not perfect. And when I take the chance to be bold and to exercise my bravery muscle, failure doesn't hurt nearly so much as I expected it would – and sometimes, things even go right. We'll never be able to make a difference and change the world unless we're brave – so I practise bravery every single day.

One of the likely reasons the problem hasn't been solved yet is because not enough is widely available or known on the topic. When you're starting to solve a problem, you should always be learning right up until the last minute. That last case might be the one that you need to learn most about. When you set out to solve a problem, you are setting out to learn as much about the problem as you can. Just because something is technical, medical or scientific, doesn't mean you can't understand it. If you don't understand what you're trying to cure, you will never know how to fully eradicate it from the planet.

To make a meaningful contribution, you should set out to educate yourself to a high standard, immersing yourself in the subject. **James Chen** is on a mission to improve the world's ability to see – his global campaign Clearly was launched in 2016 to enable access to glasses for everyone in the world. James has made it his personal mission that if a human is to set foot on Mars in the years ahead, everyone should be able to see it happen. He had to begin somewhere and he chose Rwanda:

> We chose Rwanda because it's a small enough country that we could test on a national scale and have results within a reasonable timeframe. We were initially extremely sceptical of partnering with the government, but the Health Minister Agnes Binagwaho really got it and ended up being the optimal partner, proving that you have to be open-minded in your approach and be willing to change tack as you learn. In 2010, only 15 per cent of the population had access to local eye care services. Fast forward to today and every single person in Rwanda can benefit from local, affordable vision correction and treatment. Working in partnership with the Ministry of Health, 2,700 nurses were trained and over 2.5 million Rwandans received a vision screening either at their local health centre or as part of a nationwide outreach programme reaching all 15,000 villages.

> Well-meaning philanthropists often go into negotiations with an arrogant mind-set. They may have been highly effective experts in their chosen business for their whole lives and have decided suddenly to write massive cheques to solve social problems they know nothing about. In the business world, the assessment of efficacy is made by the stock market, which allocates capital to winning ideas and starves the bad ones. But in the social arena, where there isn't an easy profit-and-loss metric,

engaged philanthropists need to help channel information and resources to the right kind of initiatives to have impact. Engaged philanthropists, donors and investors provide information where there is a lack of information. Our initial project in Rwanda has provided many very valuable lessons and plenty of data. There may be NGOs or not-for-profits with good marketing pitches, but do they really have what it takes to move the needle? Engagement and focus are critical if we are going to cut through the BS you often find in the social arena.

A successful initiative in Rwanda is giving Clearly the fuel to expand to other countries.

You have to start small in a way that's manageable that you can improve on. So many pilots and demonstrations are stopped halfway through because they weren't achievable in the amount of time that was allocated to them. At the same time, you need to be able to show the scalability of your idea. One of the big problems of renewable energy at the moment is that a lot of smart technology just can't be produced fast enough. Even Tesla cars aren't made as fast as people want them and as a result people will buy an alternative product because they can't get what they want.

Even if you can't scale immediately, you have to show how you could in the future. If you can only show how your model works in one specific village your idea won't catch on in other parts of the world. One of the organizations that demonstrates this best is Lumos, which seeks to end the harm that the institutionalization of children in orphanages has on their development. The word orphan is often a misnomer as 80 per cent of the 8 million children living in institutions have a living parent. Children need constant care, physical contact and attention which is rare in even the most equipped orphanages. In some of the worst circumstances disabled children have been locked up in cages due to a shortage of resources and staff. Even in the best circumstances, staff often struggle to cope with the needs of children, leaving them isolated for hours.

Orphans are more likely to suffer from anxiety and depressive disorders. The longer children stay in these institutions the worse their mental health becomes. Every three months spent in an orphanage before the age of three years old can stunt a child's cognitive development by one month. After six months, the children may never fully recover. Short-term volunteering in orphanages makes the situation worse and can often lead to attachment disorders amongst children who get accustomed to volunteers who then leave them to return home. It is a saddening fact that children who are given up due to poor economic circumstances are worse off in orphanages where they are subject to more abuse and neglect than they would have been at home. Thirty-seven out of every hundred children may suffer from violence or sexual abuse in an orphanage. However, due to the popularity of international adoption, orphanages have become hotspots for human trafficking. 'Child finders' travel to impoverished regions, promising parents a good life for their children. These children are then taken, and in some cases are stolen, from their parents, are put up for adoption and sold for a hefty price to foreign parents. This is the work that Lumos focuses on in its goal to end the existence of orphanages.

Georgette Mulheir, the chief executive, advises activists to demonstrate that their work can withstand even the most challenging circumstances:

> Demonstration work is exactly where you need to start because you cannot solve the problem immediately all at once. Be careful of the word 'pilot' – too many countries have been the guinea pigs for schemes that aren't seen through – but you do need to prove your concept in order to persuade everybody to come on board and agree to contribute. The commitment will require more time than you might initially think is necessary: my experience is that things do not really change much in two years but things can change a lot in five. If you get donors committed to the project for five years you can do a lot of good. When that time is up, governments, donors and other partners will likely continue the work independently.

> In terms of choosing where you conduct a demonstration, I think a small area is best. Try to achieve something small and contained. In Moldova, we have helped the government get nearly 90 per cent of the children out of the institutions and into family care over the last ten years. They're now committed to getting the rest out over

the next three years. A politically stable region would be wonderful, but it's not a prerequisite. Moldova is the poorest country in Europe and, in the time we have been working there, there have been ten or eleven changes of government, which shows that it's not impossible to do this work in politically unstable environments.

We try and prove that our methodology works in a range of settings – from the straightforward to the complex. When we started working in the Americas we picked two demonstration countries: Colombia and Haiti. Colombia was the more straightforward because the social services there are at the more sophisticated end of the spectrum and there is significant money being invested as part of the peace process. Haiti, on the other hand, is one of the most challenging countries, especially as the earthquake and natural disasters have created a high number of 'emergency' orphanages. By showing that the Lumos approach works at both ends of the spectrum, we can encourage everyone in between to get involved.

Start with what is manageable, but don't only start with the easy wins. Easy wins are great, but easy wins are always going to be just that: easy. In order to convince people to come on board and support your idea you will need to prove your work can be resilient and deal with the tough issues. That is how you prove strength and longevity.

Lumos exemplifies this kind of thinking and has not shied away from doing meaningful work in challenging circumstances. In Ethiopia, a country that has suffered from conflict, famine and poverty, Lumos has set up a programme to find Eritrean families in Ethiopia who will foster Eritrean refugee children when they arrive there. Unaccompanied refugee minors are often cited as a group who necessitate institutions – Lumos's scheme means that instead they can live with Eritrean families who speak their language, who have their culture and who understand why they fled Eritrea. Lumos managed to implement that system, cutting out the need for orphanages, in one of the most complex refugee situations in the world. This proved that if they could make it work there, it could work anywhere.

You need to show people that your idea can then be implemented even in the most difficult of places, because that proves to be a hugely inspirational framework that can be quickly adopted and transposed to other environments.

Power from partnerships

If you want a problem to be solved forever, you're never going to solve it on your own. One charity, no matter how large or influential, is not going to solve hunger by itself. To be really effective, every group that has a stake in the issue has to be brought together with clear, regular communication. Ideas need to be explained and shared. Progress needs to be celebrated together. Each stakeholder has to sense the progress towards the solution and the role they are playing in it. Ideally they would collaborate and work together – that is when you can have a coalition that delivers for everyone.

That might mean you don't get the credit for creating a solution, but ultimately you're not working to grow your organizations or gain prestige, you're there to solve the problem. That means you should celebrate when someone can take your best practice and implement it effectively themselves. Accept and embrace the fact that you don't have to do everything yourself.

On the whole, solving a problem forever means solving it globally, and that means exporting your knowledge to other countries, customs and values. Sometimes those places will be less progressive or have a lower level of overall education, or a less complex understanding of the issue. You may have to inform a lot of people about the problems in that country. And this is where things can get incredibly tricky, because you won't know as much about another country as you do of your own – what problems mean for them and how their social and political ecosystem is woven. Or, indeed, whether this is the biggest problem they need to be concentrating their energy on. Any presumption by a foreigner will not only be challenged but can be completely wrong.

Careful harnessing of local knowledge and the people who are directly affected by a problem is critical. Having the right partners on the ground is crucial to your project's sustainability. One Young World Ambassador

Nicolle Fagan cofounded the Palau Legacy Project, an initiative to make tourism more sustainable to protect the natural wildlife and environment in Palau, Micronesia. She discovered:

> When we started working on the Palau Pledge we knew that we had to move quickly. The permanent damage to the environment was happening so fast that we knew we had to take immediate action. This meant operating and activating quickly and nimbly on the fringes of government to support existing policy but also to move things forward at a rapid pace. This often put us in a compromising position. We were an unproven team in this space trying to enact a world-first concept. When you are doing something new and untested it's hard to find funding and support.
>
> In the end, we were able to partner with both government and non-government agencies to gain the necessary support we needed in order to launch the Palau Pledge, but it took a lot of time to establish the trust to make that happen. Tommy Remengesau Jr, the President of the Republic of Palau, has a phrase that he often says when he's making public remarks. 'There are three keys to success. Partnership. Partnership. Partnership.'
>
> Our team has really come to embrace this concept. It's through inclusion and partnerships that we have been able to mobilize support without ostracizing other groups. On such a small island, we can't afford to ostracize any members of the community, so we often had to spend extra time listening, sharing and answering questions, making sure we were really earning the trust of the community before we attempted to launch our 'crazy idea'.

If, like Nicolle, you're not from the place in which you are working, you should prioritize identifying good local partners. Being humble and ensuring that you are doing everything you can for the project to be presented through a local prism is critical, because local people are going to have to keep the programme going once you've left. Identify stakeholders who could be local champions, because ideas that are proposed from within a community are more likely to be accepted than those coming from an external source. The more inclusive your activism is, the more sustainable and successful we believe it is likely to be.

Larry Brilliant points out that a perfect ambition – a genuinely ambitious and inspiring plan – can, in itself, be a uniting factor:

> Our doctors came from over a hundred countries, they spoke hundreds of languages. There were Jews, Christians, Buddhists, Hindus, Jains, Shinto and Muslims. There were men and women of all ages and races, and we worked together and loved each other. The Russians and Americans buried the hatchets that divided them at the time. That's proof that if you have a noble enough calling, and a grand enough challenge, everyone will understand that they're all in it together.

> You cannot solve a global problem with provincialism. Albert Einstein once said, 'You cannot solve a problem with the same level of consciousness that created it in the first place.' You have to go to a higher level of consciousness. To be able to solve a global problem, you have to be able to think of a global world. That, to me, is the abiding lesson of smallpox.

To embrace this global mind-set, you need to appreciate there's much you don't know, there's a lot you don't understand and you can never walk a mile in someone else's shoes. If you come from a place of humility, the psychology of being in that mind-set will help guide you towards not being overbearing, or overly critical of a culture you may not understand. People will be able to sense whether you're faking that or not. Authenticity is invaluable and every activist has to proceed from a point of genuine care.

Sometimes, of course, this will mean partnering with people who seem to be directly opposed to your mission. If you're going to get stuff done sometimes you have to deal with, even work with, the 'other' side, or people who see things very differently from you and may even oppose what you're trying to do. You will encounter some really bad people on your journey.

Are you going to let your personal morals get in the way of helping people who are in need? Maybe you will – even if that means the people in this village don't get the medication they need. That's a decision you have to make. Chances are, if you've set out to give everyone a certain medication, you're going to make the deal because that's what will help you do what you set out to accomplish. You didn't set out to pose moral objections to those in power, no matter how problematic they may be.

Compromise is not a dirty word. When you have a perfect ambition, it's easier to compromise because you know what your end goal is. Even if you feel uncomfortable making deals with people you disagree with, you will know what you're doing it for. **Grace Forrest** is the founding director of the Walk Free Foundation, an international human rights group with an objective to end slavery, in all its forms, in our lifetime. She explains:

> For any issue, the sense of urgency has to be balanced with our ability to be effective and create long-term systematic change. We must look at the big picture. Walmart is the largest supply chain in the world outside of government. It has approximately 400,000 suppliers. If it can create, from the top down, an ethos that is based on empowerment and zero exploitation, that could fundamentally change the lives of thousands of people throughout the world, and alter perceptions of the acceptability of forced labour across countless other supply chains.

> But that's not going to happen if we're attacking them on every issue we find. If you look at any major supply chain, you will likely find slavery, and that company probably isn't alone. If your message is too black and white it leaves no room for nuance, conversation, negotiation or steady improvement of transparency. We have to collaborate through the grey.

> I do believe that there can be a time and a place to call companies out publicly when they are doing the wrong thing but we use that as a last resort. We need to change the game, not shoot down one

player. Attacking the source of the problem could result in burning a bridge that you need to cross to make change.

If we're going to end global slavery, we need to work together. At Walk Free, we work with all sorts of groups because we know that if that end goal can be achieved, it will have been worth it.

Diplomacy and extending empathy are key to tackling a problem. Allies can sometimes be found in the most unlikely of places as **Thuli Madonsela**, who helped draft the South African constitution and served as Public Protector from 2009 until 2016, explains:

Seeking to gain support for social justice has taught me to engage influencers whose views I found problematic, with as much empathy as possible. In this regard, I found Nelson Mandela's emphasis on seeking first to understand and using your understanding as a basis for engaging to be understood, helpful. This was my experience recently when I engaged a top politician on the legacy of past legalized injustice.

As we talk to business and other privileged groups about the need for a Marshall Plan-like project to catalyse the elimination of poverty and achievement of visible progress on socio-economic inclusion of left-behind groups and communities, we find that seeking first to understand the world view and concerns of those who disagree provides a basis for establishing some common ground and better clarity on points of divergence. We increasingly find that many of those that were genuinely on the other side because of limited knowledge become formidable partners for change once convinced.

There are of course moral absolutes, where you don't need to comprise. Whether you're working on LGBT rights or eliminating female genital mutilation, you will always have red lines you aren't prepared to cross. Knowing where you're ready to draw that line is really important at the start of your activism, because you will be confronted with uncomfortable realities and you need to prepare how you will respond before you are on the ground. **Thuli Madonsela** reminds us of the importance of being purpose driven:

> Whatever your quest or cause may be, remember to remain ethical in your approach regardless of the fact that those on the other side may be unethical. To remain ethical you have to lead yourself. That means influencing and inspiring yourself to do what you know is right and not giving in to mob psychology.
>
> Purpose is the glue that binds a team. It helps us not to worry about who gets the glory and enables you to lead when you should and follow when you must. This I learned during my term as Public Protector. Transactional thinking is dangerous as the long-term impact may be counterproductive. A single expedient act may seed a culture that is destructive to your ultimate cause or organization. Ultimately, a commitment to serve helps carry you through turbulence. Above everything, commitment to a cause you love gives you hope in possibility and faith in your ability to do it and others to follow.

When deciding on where your red lines are, focus on your beneficiaries. Who will or won't receive help depending on your course of action? This is a challenge multinational NGOs like Save the Children face on an everyday basis. CEO of Save the Children UK, **Kevin Watkins**, has to weigh up the benefits of working in countries whose governments are, in some cases, morally very dubious:

> There are countries we operate in where we're delivering life-saving services for children with local health authorities. These are often countries which may have war criminals heading the government with the most appalling records on public expenditure, on human rights protection. You have to make really tough decisions. Ultimately you ask yourself: 'Is the benefit of what

I'm doing here outweighed by the cost of turning a blind eye or not speaking out publicly about an injustice?'

We have to find ways without getting trapped in the quicksand of complexity. The development sector transforms the lives of millions of people around the world. What we have to do is to combine the best elements of professionalism with the reality of what we find on the ground. Ultimately our role is helping and building relationships with people who have been deliberately excluded. If we refuse to work in certain places, it's usually going to be the vulnerable and the innocent who suffer most.

The work you do will inevitably encounter complications. Keeping your end goal in mind is critical, as it will enable you to be more decisive and reactive when faced with tough decisions about what you need to do and how you will achieve it. Not every project will have elements of emergency response in the same way that natural disasters or pandemics do, but we can all be challenged to make quick decisions. **Grace Forrest**'s mind-set of being prepared to 'lose skin off your knees' is helpful and will prevent time being wasted agonizing on the direction your mission will take. You may fall and lose skin off your knees but you have to get back up again and be prepared to face small injuries along the way to achieving your cause.

When working globally, you may encounter cultural differences which seem near impossible to overcome, but the more you partner with people on the ground to do things in a way that's natural and appropriate to them, the more likely there is to be sustained uptake of your work. You will also need to build local and regional networks who can cross-share information to create a more sustainable ecosystem that isn't reliant on outside help. **Georgette Mulheir** advises to identify local champions to help you succeed:

Your first move should be to identify and find the best local experts. They're already working on these issues in some way. They may have gaps in their knowledge, so we make them part of our international team. Find those amazing local people and really empower and support them. Have them lead.

Even in the most challenging environments you can find champions for your cause. In Sudan, when the Bashir government was committing genocide in Darfur, there were incredible people in the ministry of labour and social welfare in Khartoum State who were doing amazing things in a very challenging environment for some extremely vulnerable children. Identifying those champions in government and then giving them opportunities to learn is crucial.

The more you can do the sharing from country to country, the better. For example, we've got lots of Russian and Ukrainian organizations who are learning from our Moldova team. These countries were all part of the Soviet Union, so it doesn't feel like an external organization forcing change when our regional branches work with their neighbours to educate and share best practice.

In terms of building coalitions, don't take the credit. It's not about you, it's not about your organization. The only way that this will work is if we all genuinely work together. We are just an equal partner in that coalition with everyone else because that's the way you really make change happen. For me, the great thing is when you get to a stage where people forget that Lumos was even involved and they're just doing the work. That's success.

Ego and the desire for glory can be the death of so many projects. When you set out to solve a problem forever you need to ensure you care more about solving it than you do about taking the credit. This mind-set will help you empower partners because you have removed your own importance from the work. When you get this right it incentivizes your partners to take action, because they can get political or financial accolades for themselves which may encourage them to keep going.

Planting seeds of trees under which you will never sit

Self-sufficiency is a core pillar in sustainability. People doing things for themselves in their own way is what will ensure your project adapts to the context it's being implemented in. The practicality of this is critical, but the psychology of self-sustainability is more important because that gives people a sense of pride and dignity.

When people can see what it is exactly that they can contribute to your campaign, themselves, they can adopt your project. But they won't necessarily want to, or be able to do, exactly what you've done. They may have another way of approaching action to achieve the same end – so you, and your campaign, need to be flexible and adaptable.

One of the issues with much of the charitable and aid work going on at the moment is that it robs its recipients of their dignity when it makes them subjects of charity. Nobel Peace Prize recipient **Professor Muhammad Yunus** is a Bangladeshi banker and economist who developed the concept of microcredit. He was one of the first to identify this:

> Governments give foreign aid and churches are devoted to charity. The problem is not that there is not enough attention or resources, but rather that it is not given in the right direction. Charity does not solve the problem, charity only maintains the problem of poverty; it doesn't let it get worse. Elimination of poverty is about more than keeping people alive. You have to make them active so they can take care for themselves.

> One of the flaws of capitalism is that it is based on the wrong interpretation of the human being: that the Capitalist Man is driven by self-interest. That is a profit-maximization principle. It finds greed in everybody. The correct interpretation is that human beings are not only selfish but also selfless. The question becomes, how do you promote the selfless part in the business world?

The second flaw is that everybody is encouraged to become a job seeker. That does not fit into human nature. Human beings are creative. We are go-getters. We are problem solvers. So we are encouraging every young person to become an entrepreneur instead. If an illiterate woman living in a remote village in Bangladesh can turn herself into an entrepreneur, why is a literate person with a university degree sitting around because no one will give him a job? We have equipped him with the wrong mental lens. That is where we went wrong. Unemployment is an artificial state and it doesn't belong to human beings. We are not born to sit around and watch, doing nothing. Today, our education system produces job seekers ending up with a job application when it should prepare job creators armed with a business plan. This is a very different mind-set and it leads to a happier life and more stable economy.

Over the past 20 years, global poverty has been cut in half with extreme poverty declining in every region of the developing world. The current generation has been called 'the first generation in history that can end extreme poverty' by the World Bank. The largest source of charitable giving comes from individuals, who donated $410 billion in 2017 in the United States alone. However, as Professor Yunus points out, this money is not always spent wisely. In 2008, the UN said that we could end world hunger completely with $30 billion. Yet this seems such a remote possibility even though the finances are there. Every year, Americans throw away more $165 billion worth of food in unwanted snacks and meals. Our problem is not desire or resources but strategy and direction. We don't work closely enough with the recipients of aid to make our efforts sustainable.

Matt Damon and **Gary White** cofounded Water.org. Inspired by **Professor Yunus**, they used microcredit to replace traditional charitable models to help people get clean access to water:

Gary: More than 800 million people around the world lack access to safe drinking water; nearly three times that number lack access to a managed sanitation. There is never going to be enough charity in the world for everybody to get access to a tap and a toilet.

Matt: In many cases people who live in these conditions pay up to 25 per cent of their income in order to secure water. That means they are paying ten to fifteen times more per gallon than the middle class in their own countries are paying. It is expensive to be poor.

Gary: We help people living in poverty tap into their intrinsic power as customers and as citizens. And what that means is basically helping them get access to microloans so that they can get a water connection at their home. The problem contains its own solution. It is a very simple concept.

Matt: Our partners have disbursed more than 4.5 million loans, and the repayment rate is 99 per cent; 88 per cent of the recipients are women. Through this model we have reached more than 21 million people with safe water and sanitation. WaterCredit is a remarkable programme. It's been successful beyond anything we could have really hoped. And so, as we keep running these numbers up, and keep proving and reproving the model, that's really our best argument going forward to engage the capital markets.

Enabling people to create their own cost-effective, sustainable solutions shouldn't involve doing things *for* them. Preserving recipients' agency and dignity enables them to become active participants in your solution and energizes communities: hence the emergence of microcredit as being one of the most esteemed forms of development over the last two decades. It's important to remember that microfinance is not a quick fix; it's a long-term, sustainable solution that requires ongoing support.

You can't manage what you can't measure

Be meticulous with your data. If your aim is to have zero cases of an illness, you need to measure every case. If you want to ensure every child aged ten is able to read and write, giving out school books at random is not going to help you achieve that goal even if it is a lovely thing to do.

There appears to have been progress since 2000, when the UN's Millennium Development Goals were announced. In 1990 more than a third of people in the world lived in extreme poverty. By 2015 the number was only 10 per cent. The UN estimated that over the last three decades more than one billion people no longer lived in extreme poverty.

Every year millions are donated to end poverty, but because there is an insufficient measure with which we can apply these funds, track them and ensure their effective delivery, 736 million people still live in extreme poverty and a further 3.4 billion people still struggle to meet their basic needs.

The UN itself relies on multiple sources of data, among which the Gates Foundation is one. The Foundation tracks diseases such as malaria, polio and HIV in order to eradicate them. It is not easy to collect data in villages with no internet or electricity, but it can and has been done. Data is critical.

Basic benchmarking has a profound psychological impact: if someone says you've got 85 per cent in a test, next time you want to get at least 86 per cent. It's only human nature to want to improve the previous benchmark that has been set. If you don't set benchmarks, you can't improve on them.

To achieve a perfect ambition, accurate data is even more important. If you don't know when you're at 50 per cent, how will you even know when you're at 100 per cent? Your funders and supporters also need to know how you're doing, and these days you can report online really easily. You need to define what and how you are measuring, and report meticulously, regularly and transparently.

But measurement is not something that you may find inspiring initially. Let's face it, it doesn't ignite passion in most people. But, in fact, it is something Bill Gates loves to do. His passion for data analysis provides the bedrock of the reputation he has built for the Gates Foundation.

Think through how you're going to measure your own efforts. If you aren't able to include certain aspects or account for certain things, it's better to explain your methodology and improve it over time rather than wait to publish any figures. This can be contentious but regular reporting and sharing of data will help.

Grace Forrest's work in modern-day slavery required beginning to research and report on something that had never previously been globally measured:

> When we started, the data collection of modern slavery was zero because that term wasn't really recognized. Defining what you are measuring can be very difficult. We define modern slavery as a systematic removal of a person's freedom for personal or financial gain. Our measurement includes forced labour (state-imposed forced labour, forced labour exploitation and forced sexual exploitation of adults and commercial sexual exploitation of children) and forced marriage .

> Our research is now the world's leading data set on slavery, galvanized through the joint Global Estimates on Modern Slavery published by Walk Free, and UN agencies the ILO and IOM. Together we have estimated that on any given day in 2016, 40.3 million people were living in modern slavery, and over the last 5 years 89 million people have experienced some form of slavery. As shocking as these figures are, they should be considered as baseline estimates. For example, we still can't accurately measure and include the number of forced child soldiers or people trafficked for organs because the research has been too difficult and dangerous. Equally there are regions of the world with low estimates due to the limited access we have to these areas due to war and conflict, or because the sub-populations of interest are very hard to reach. Because of these challenges we know our figures are strong but conservative.

The ability to devise a way of measuring a situation allows us to fully understand the extent of the problem. In this case, it allows the world to see and understand the issue of modern-day slavery and uncover previously hidden aspects of slavery in our supply chains. If we don't count the numbers of slaves, we won't know exactly how many need to be freed. The data is always our most helpful tool in achieving a perfect ambition.

Measuring impact can be an overwhelming task as there isn't one set way of accounting for a problem and ensuring that your data is truly representative. Many people try and detail as accurately as possible, but they make their data technical and complicated which ends up making it off-putting and, at worst, inaccessible to the masses. There are plenty of tools – apps and websites – available online which can help you, although choosing one tool over another can be difficult too. At One Young World we use the social return on investment methodology which helps us calculate the social return on every dollar invested into a One Young World Ambassador initiative. This is an appealing end result because it gives donors confidence that their money is being spent in a considered and impactful way.

Kevin Watkins, CEO of Save the Children UK, acknowledges that impact measurement can seem too daunting or something that doesn't need to happen from day one, but argues that it's always best to be showing some measurement even if it isn't perfect:

> Impact measurement is really, really critical, and it has also become a mini-industry. Part of that industry is very high end with complicated randomized control trials, building big baseline surveys, tracking them over many years, often in environments where it's incredibly difficult to do. It can be immensely difficult and costly, meaning that you can't do it in every single situation.

> But there are things that you can do in every situation. What you can always do is the basic cost-benefit analysis. You can say we put $100,000 into these clinics, as a result of which another 50,000 children were immunized, as a result of which we were able to treat another 15,000 cases of diarrhoea. We know from the simple

correlation data that one in every forty of those cases would have resulted in a fatality which has been avoided.

Even though this is common sense we don't always do it, and it's something that we've recognized in the organization that we need to be way better at. People are often afraid to be honest about how far donations do or don't go. I think more transparency will give donors more confidence, but it will require more in-depth explanation.

For example, I was in South Sudan, in a place called Abyei, which is up on the border with Sudan. It's in the middle of a conflict. We're running health programmes there. We have six clinics that we're operating and are expanding into ten. This is in a country which has a total of 30 clinics, 15 of which are closed, serving the whole country. It's an incredibly difficult environment to operate in as there is no functioning government up there, you have to create everything from scratch. On the basis of some back-of-the-envelope calculations we worked out that it costs roughly $18 for every child who attends one of our clinics. It actually seems like a lot of money, $18. It's not cheap, and if you're doing the same thing in Accra in Ghana, which is much safer and more developed, you could do it for $5. But in South Sudan, you've got to build the clinics, import a lot of the staff and provide security, and you've got to find people who are willing to work there. That's not easy.

With an in-depth explanation like this, the public can then decide if they would rather put their $18 into South Sudan for a lower but harder won social return or whether they'd rather spend their money in Ghana where they could help more people who are in less dire need.

Setting out to capture and communicate your data will enable you to work smarter as well as harder. You will be able to target your efforts in a strategic way, which can be incredibly motivating. There are so many misconceptions about making a difference that are critical to break down if we are to solve problems. An example of truly understanding the data is through One Young World's work with Lumos, where we have learned that only one in eight children in orphanages are actually orphans. The rest all have a living parent and are usually living in institutions because of poverty or health reasons. Donating to and volunteering with orphanages is not the best way to help children in need, but Lumos have a significant challenge in convincing well-meaning donors that they should spend their money on family-based solutions rather than orphanages, where children are at significant risk of exploitation.

Georgette Mulheir and the team at Lumos are able to use data to convince people that solving a problem forever is possible: their mission is to remove all children from institutions by 2050 and Georgette's confidence in this mission is all based on things they have learned from rigorous impact measurement:

My first reason I know that it's possible is that orphanages and institutions, while very harmful, are completely unnecessary, in the sense that all children can be cared for in a family or in a family-life environment. Even children with the most complex needs can be cared for and have happy lives, either in a family environment or in a small scale but very high quality residential home. Countries we are working in have proven that this is possible, so we know that it's unnecessary to keep kids in institutions.

The second reason I know that it's possible is because it's really serious and harmful to keep children in institutions. Brain imaging has shown the level of harm done to the brains of children living in orphanages. The damage is devastating and people are beginning to understand that orphanages are harmful rather than a social good. Put simply, children do not flourish outside of families.

The third reason is because orphanages are actually much more expensive than family-based care. Once we start looking at the money that's being spent on orphanage care in most countries, it's so much more expensive than supporting those children in families. We know that the resources exist to solve this problem.

As in many cases, following the money allows Lumos to work on solving a problem forever. So much of our world is shaped by the impact of resource distribution, so if you can prove that money is going to waste or is causing harm, you are making the most compelling case to many people that their resources, money or time should be used effectively to deliver the best possible outcomes. Money talks – capitalist systems demand a return on investment – and so if you set out to prove your case from a financial perspective you can make it clear why you need to change the way things have been set up.

Data can also help us see problems in a new light. So often – as with the example of food waste – the issue is not resources but distribution. **Matt Damon** and **Gary White**'s take on water distribution helps us appreciate that the threat of water wars in the future is real but entirely avoidable:

Matt: It would take less than 1 per cent of the drinkable water to give every single person – the 844 million who currently lack access – 40 to 50 litres of water a day, the amount to meet basic needs. There is a misunderstanding that there's just not going to be enough for everybody to survive, but that certainly is not true.

Gary: If you just look at increasing the efficiency of agricultural use of water by only 2 per cent, that would be enough to give people basic water, all 844 million that lack it right now. So it's not a matter of, 'Is there enough water to go around for people living in poverty?' because they are showing up with a sipping straw while the rest of us are drinking through a fire hose.

Matt: It's not a supply problem; it's a distribution problem. I get the sense that, because we're going to go from 7 billion to 8 billion to 9 billion people living on the planet, everybody's focused about water scarcity and water security. We need to dispel the notion that there's not going to be enough water for the people we serve, because it's simply not true.

This applies not just at a global but at a community level too. A local food bank may well receive excess donations of a certain item, let's say canned goods, but very few of other high-demand items such as hygiene products. Better communication with donors would help divert resources more efficiently and serve the community better. For this hypothetical food bank, data measurement would be critical to help make sure that resources were being donated to the people who most need them – for example, disposable nappies will be invaluable to young mothers who can't afford to buy them, but not that useful in an old-age home.

Quite often the solution lies in the problem itself. The resources to solve the problem may already be available to you, and with the right innovation or communication you could put them to better use. In Lumos's case, the orphanages which they are transforming into family support centres already have the staff and the facilities, but they require retraining. Only good data can tell you these things. Your project is never too small and it's never too early to measure data.

Finish the fight

So much of activism makes a difference but doesn't solve the problem forever. The tenacity and dedication to ensure that the problem is solved forever is quite a rarity, and things happen well beyond the activist's control – extreme weather, seismic activity, new highly infectious diseases. Changing leadership in government and business can also result in drastic priority shifts, which mean projects are too often abandoned before they are completed. Similarly, the media is a fickle friend, and a highly visible issue can suddenly disappear from public consciousness very quickly because it is no longer the flavour of the day.

The metaphor of a marathon versus a sprint doesn't really apply to solving a problem forever – it is many marathons being run in a relay or at the same time by many people. Your own journey can only ever be a small part of the story because you will need so many partners and teammates to achieve your perfect ambition.

The obstacles which stand in the way often become the way – the impediment to action can advance action. The ways in which we adapt to adversity and setbacks can make us stronger and smarter. As Benjamin Franklin said, 'The things that hurt, instruct.' **Georgette Mulheir** has found that preparing for the setbacks mentally helps her overcome them:

> It's a long journey. The journey will be two steps forward, one back I would love to say it isn't and that it will always be plain sailing but that's not my experience. When you're making those two steps forward, you feel great. You feel absolutely wonderful, the world's your oyster . . . and then something hits you like a train and you can be devastated by it. Now I embrace the step back. When I make a leap forward, I'm waiting for the thing to hit me. Then, once it has, I think great, that's out of the way, so now I can take another step forward.

Often the setbacks come because some areas of the problem are harder to solve than others. At the beginning, the problem looms so large it is almost amorphous, but by the end there will be small tranches that seem irredeemable or too complex to solve. The final mile is often the hardest, but it is crucial that, when you set out to solve a problem forever, you plan for the final 1 per cent as well as the 99. In the case of disease, unless it is completely irradicated it could spread again; similarly with social ills such as racism – just because they only exist in a tiny pocket of society does not mean that they can't multiply very quickly. Unless a problem is solved completely, it is not solved at all.

As daunting as this prospect might be, the reward is worth the struggle. As fraught with difficulties and dilemmas as your work might be, there is so much joy to be had in the accomplishment, as **Larry Brilliant** knows:

> The idea of American football is you have got to take a ball and run it a hundred yards. The last yard is the hardest. We used to say that the last yard had another 100 yards hidden inside of it.

One of the happiest days of my life was the day that I drove to the airport with a Land Rover tyre and a huge shipping crate to be sent to the head of communicable diseases in WHO in Geneva. We were sending the car tyre because this fellow said that we were on a fool's errand, that the people who were trying to eradicate smallpox were idiots. He said that we would never succeed, that we would fail, that we would fail legendarily. And that if ever we did eradicate smallpox he would promise to eat a Land Rover tyre.

I sent him a tyre and attached a note in which my boss Dr Nicole Grasset had written:

'Dear Doctor, as we agreed, we have eradicated smallpox, now you must eat this tire. We look forward to your reply – please let us know if you require any ketchup or mustard to consume the tire. Would you kindly give us your report as to the texture and flavor?'

How to end a problem forever checklist

- Believe that there is a perfect future in which this problem doesn't exist. See past the statistic you are confronting and start identifying the people you need to work with.

- Set out to become an expert in this field, immerse yourself in information and intelligence.

- Remember that the solution may lie within the problem – you don't have to dismantle systems in order to change them.

- Be systematic in your approach – planning and research are the essential elements. Plan for the hardest scenarios as well as the easier wins.

- Bring together representatives of every stakeholder group and take them with you – celebrate progress together.

- Start small in a way that's manageable – but shows scalability – and use this as your demonstration and proof of concept. Remember that scale and sustainability go hand in hand.

- Export your knowledge across borders where the problem also exists and ensure you work with local stakeholders and local knowledge by identifying the right local partners.

- Compromise where and when you need to – it's easier when you can see a clear end goal.

- Care more about solving the problem than taking the credit – and you will get there faster.

- You must set benchmarks – then you can improve on them. Report meticulously, regularly and transparently.

Chapter Seven
How to change a big organization

Changing large organizations is the activist's task

'Big' is regularly placed in opposition to the activist: big business, big oil, big pharma. But with the term 'big' also comes the possibility of 'big difference'.

Even if an activist is a lone wolf, the involvement of a large company, NGO or government organization is often needed in order to make a difference. Whether it's climate change or the gender-based pay gap, when large organizations become a first adopter or alter their course, they can be the driving force behind meaningful change.

Organizations have significant influence over such large swathes of society. The UK's National Health Service has 1.3 million staff, McDonald's 1.5 million, and that's not to mention their patients/customers and suppliers. Volunteers for the world's largest charity, United Way, stand at 2.8 million people, and 1.7 million people volunteer for the Salvation Army.

The spending power of large organizations can rival many nation states. For example, in 2017 Walmart earned more than the whole of Belgium, and there are only 16 countries with a GDP equal to or greater than Apple's current market valuation. Newer companies are also beginning to command the fiscal power of nation states – Spotify's annual revenue is greater than that of Mauritania, and Netflix's is greater than Malta's.

This amount of influence can be seen both as intimidating and inspiring. As difficult as these organizations are to take on, by getting them to change, even by a degree, you can make a difference to so many people very efficiently, effectively and, often, permanently. However, the sheer size and scale of these industries can make change seem impossible. There will often be numerous systems and processes you will have to penetrate and change will usually be slower than you would like. But activists don't exist to protect or abide by the status quo – our job is to *challenge* it in order to make a difference. If you are the initiator of change within an organization or the outsider demanding change, you will need to be prepared to convince a multitude of people that your vision will benefit the organization in the long term.

All of these things come into stark relief in organizations that have operations in many countries. This is where the role of leadership is absolutely critical. The C-suite (the CEO, CFO, COO, etc.) have to set out their mission, objectives, strategy and executional tactics with absolute clarity and then ensure that national and local leadership does the same. Even so, everyone in a leadership or management position needs to be convinced on all points – otherwise parts of the mission will never be achieved.

Our work at One Young World has proved that organizational change is possible and it *can* be instigated by one individual. We have seen time and time again that young leaders with bright ideas can make enormous changes to big companies. We've also seen people make a series of small changes that have led to a real shift in culture and impact.

While this chapter may not apply to every activist – not everyone works in a large company after all – we can all benefit from understanding the machinations of large concerns and be inspired by how radical transformation can come about. Whether it's local government, a school or factory, everyone will encounter a large organization that they would like to change at some point. Whether you're on the inside or the outside, having a sense of how the levers of power work is important to activists everywhere.

By nature, humans often avoid or are afraid of change. Many who work for large organizations are likely to thrive from routine and process. While people are happy to complain around the water cooler or on a break among their colleagues, not many turn their talk into real, solid action.

Most organizations have an element of 'that's the way it's done around here' embedded in their culture. It can be difficult to determine whether a practice has come about through default or design: we so often fall into habits by accident. However, often organizations have put a lot of time and thought into the way things are done, and numerous people are invested in keeping them that way.

Naturally, staff members will be nervous about putting their heads above the parapet as they rely on their jobs for security and income. Don't be frustrated by this self-interest, it is perfectly understandable and you must accept it as part of the reality of a big organization. You may also be fearful for your job or position within the organization yourself – even if you are a volunteer rather than an employee, you will care about your affiliation with the organization, but this is also why you care enough to want to bring about change.

When suggesting change, communicating your commitment to the organization is of utmost importance. Pointing out problems can appear confrontational, and there will be some who perceive your actions to be destructive to their roles and methodology, so it is critically important that you make it abundantly clear that you want to help the organization succeed. The key is doing this respectfully: change from the inside rarely comes from revolt or revolution. People need to see the change as a win–win negotiation – both for themselves and for the organization.

Hold the vision, trust the process

Not long ago, all orders flowed from the top of a company or a charity. As the world has evolved, leaders understand the importance of feedback loops from people on the assembly lines or in the frontline of customer service. Companies usually have formal feedback processes – be that through human resources, management or a trade union.

This is a critical tool to harness, and your first step should be to take full advantage of formal processes. This offers your organization an opportunity to address the problem and can be the most straightforward way to enact change. However, even if your proposal is brushed aside, this process will give you the benefit of feedback. Our ideas can often seem like masterstrokes in our mind, but they have to look as good on paper too. Ask why the organization didn't think your idea was feasible, and then either adapt your plan or begin to prepare your counterargument to the issues they raise, building an even stronger case for change.

Is your organization genuinely interested in change? Truth be told, you won't know until you've tried to raise your issue – nothing will change unless you try. **Blake Mycoskie** is the founder and chief shoe giver of TOMS, and the person behind the idea of One for One, a business model that helps a person in need with every product purchase. TOMS credits feedback as being the reason the company has been successful, demonstrating that by providing feedback you can change an organization's strategy or practices, even if you're in a country far away from its head office:

> We are constantly challenging ourselves to do better. We have learned so much since TOMS launched in 2006 and we continue to listen to our Giving Partners and consumers to hear feedback and figure out how we can improve. We heard them and challenged ourselves with an original goal to produce one third of our Giving shoes in the regions where we give. We have since exceeded this goal with local factories in India, Vietnam and China. This decision was made so that we can ensure we are sustainably supporting the regions we serve.
>
> Additionally, we learned that the Giving shoes we originally created weren't always appropriate for some of the regions we give in, so we developed a variety of shoe silhouettes to meet the needs of specific terrain, school uniform requirements and youth development programmes. We also provide a 'Last Mile Contribution' to our partners so they don't incur expenses associated with receiving, storing and distributing shoes. Our giving today is so much more impactful because we listened to our partners and were willing to change how we'd historically done things.

You may be relatively senior in an organization, in which case you need to remember to proactively engage with these feedback loops yourself. You can always benefit from new ideas, and the most valuable ones often come from those who are on the lowest rungs of the ladder. Blake urges everyone, no matter how senior or junior, to take feedback seriously:

Listening is hard – no one wants to open themselves or their company up to criticism. But it's vital to hear those you serve, try not to get defensive and reflect on how to improve. At TOMS, we work very closely with our Giving Partners who are on the ground in the regions we serve. They are an important sounding board for us and provide regular feedback so that we can address the most pressing issues in the communities we serve. It's humbling and essential to know when we are not the experts and then to surround ourselves with trusted advisors to guide us as we continue to grow.

Ultimately, the best organizations understand that good ideas can come from any stakeholder, be it a manager, an employee or customer, and should cultivate these relationships so that they can capitalize on the collective power of ideas.

Of course, some feedback may not improve your idea, indeed it may dilute it and impact its potency. On the other hand, watering down your proposal may make it more palatable to others in the organization or easier to implement and, therefore, more feasible. Your job as an activist is to weigh up the pros and cons of compromise and decide if your concept will lose its integrity if it is changed, either subtly or radically. Ideas in and of themselves only count for so much: success depends upon those who not only think innovatively, but have the skills to put their ideas into action.

Olu Odubajo is a One Young World Ambassador from KPMG who took advantage of the formal processes his company had in place to offer feedback and helped their expansion by making them more inclusive to people from BAME backgrounds. He took part in the firm's pilot reverse mentoring scheme, where junior and senior members of staff are paired up. The senior member of staff is coached by the junior member, turning the traditional power and experience dynamic of mentoring on its head. Through this, Olu had access to senior leadership in the company and was able to pitch his initiative:

At One Young World I heard stories of young leaders who used their organizations to create change. I learned you don't need all the answers at the beginning, you just have to start. I came across a UK government report showing how black heritage employees are increasingly choosing to become self-employed and launch start-ups after experiencing barriers in the job market, only to find that they then struggle to get the right support and opportunities to grow their business. Another UK government report indicated that ethnic minority businesses can potentially contribute £24 billion to the UK economy – yet they also indicated that it's more difficult for ethnic minorities to obtain funding to actually grow their businesses. These findings struck a nerve with me, and the seeds of helping to create a level playing field for black entrepreneurs were sown.

Before attending One Young World, I had senior leadership exposure and a positive impact through taking part in and expanding KPMG's reverse mentoring programme, where I had been paired with UK managing partner Philip Davidson. This gave me the platform to discuss how KPMG could play an important role in championing black heritage talent. Coming back from One Young World 2017 in Bogotá, I wanted my idea of creating a Black Entrepreneurs Award to get noticed, fast. So, rather than pinging off an email, I recorded a video explaining why a social mobility programme was critical to what we do at KPMG and sent it to Philip Davidson.

I must have done something right, because after an invitation to pitch this idea, my suggestion was approved within a few weeks and, six months later, the KPMG Black Entrepreneurs Award officially launched. KPMG Black Entrepreneurs Award is a bespoke 12-month business acceleration programme designed to support black heritage entrepreneurs and their start-ups to become investment-ready. The aim is to accelerate, recognize and celebrate their success. Winners receive business workshops, mentorship, publicity and a cash prize.

Olu didn't take the efficacy of a formal process for granted – he made sure he stood out from the dozens of suggestions that senior people within organizations receive by creating a video. Ask yourself how can you make your suggestion stand out? Take time to think about presenting your ideas in creative and memorable ways that can be easily shared throughout the organization. Use as much innovation as you can, and enhance your communication with multimedia technology, so that more people can find out about what you are proposing and be inspired to lend their support.

Hone your idea and your pitch

Ultimately, in a big organization, not every idea will be realized and implemented. To make change, having a good idea is not enough. Your idea needs to be right for the organization. Even then, not every organization will immediately see the benefit in your idea or have the culture or desire to implement the changes you seek. It is so important that you are truly passionate about your cause because you need to care enough to make it successful.

Whatever you propose for your company, take time to show how it complements the company's strategic direction and be sensitive to timing. For example, if a company's ambition is to cut costs, you may need to wait for that to be achieved before you start campaigning to pay outsourced staff a living wage. On the other hand, this may be a helpful time to plant the seeds for your campaign, as your company will need to have one eye to being prepared for the eventual upturn in business. Build the business case by showing how your idea does not conflict with current priorities and can support them in the future. Showing that you have planned for five or ten years ahead gives your idea more credibility and indicates your commitment to the organization.

A loss-making case will rarely be successful. You will waste time by being commercially naive. However, profits aren't the only thing that contribute to commercial success. **Dame Vivian Hunt** is managing partner of global consultancy giant McKinsey & Company, and is a leader in the firm on leadership and diversity. She points out:

You must find the business argument behind the issue you want to solve. Once you have an issue that's important to you and to the company, it is crucial that you can explain your mission in business performance terms, as well as capability building or ethical terms.

When pitching your idea, frame the benefits around the goals of the company. These might include the commercial benefit it brings, but also the quality of jobs it provides, the licence it might give the company to operate, or how it will make the company more sustainable. For example, localizing parts of your supply chain might not make your pricing more competitive, but it will give you a more powerful story to tell your customers and the stakeholders. It may also help you with your branding, partnerships or your geopolitical position.

As a hypothetical example, let's imagine you are working towards a large contract. If you can explain how you can meet goals around performance, capabilities and ESG, you may stand out versus the alternatives.

Luckily for today's activists, we live in an era where morality and a company's ethics are becoming increasingly important in terms of commercial success. While 'bad' organizations still perform well, more and more investors and shareholders are motivated by, or at least take into consideration, the way in which companies handle environmental, social and governance (ESG) issues. There is increased scrutiny around these issues, and a scandal can cause huge reputational damage. In 2015 the Environmental Protection Agency discovered that Volkswagen diesel cars sold in the US had a 'defeat device', software which changed the performance of the car during emissions tests, with the result that the engines emitted nitrogen oxide pollutants up to 40 times above what is allowed in the USA. The scandal not only hit public trust in the company and resulted in a series of multibillion-dollar fines, but also knocked 25 per cent off VW's share price.

As a result, there are now serious commercial penalties for companies who don't take ESG seriously. This should give you confidence when thinking about how you present your idea. It may be that it requires investment or money, but if you can show the commercial benefit further down the line the initial cost becomes less off-putting. **Paul Polman**, former CEO of Unilever and one of the world's most prominent sustainable business leaders, believes that CEOs are much more likely to listen to customer and employee concerns about social issues than we might imagine:

> Too many people, in my opinion, are of the belief that banks are too big to fail, but people are too small to matter. This isn't actually the case – every corporate movement was actually a people's movement that businesses understood. For example, when it comes to plastics, consumers are way ahead of any company in the world in terms of identifying the issue and demanding action. Similarly, the pressure from customers for companies such as Delta and Hertz to terminate special discounts and benefits for NRA members following the Marjory Stoneman Douglas high school shooting meant that they severed ties with the NRA at a remarkable speed. Even the decarbonization movement in finance stems from university endowments demanding ESG investments. People don't want to buy from companies that don't have souls, and if a company doesn't actively participate in societal issues, people don't want to work for them any more.
>
> But then, there are also too many issues where consumers are still under the impression that they cannot make a difference or that companies are taking action when, in reality, nothing's happening. At the end of the day, income inequality is still going up and climate change is still going in the wrong direction. What is important now is that consumers or citizens channel energy towards the right behaviour, rather than trying to punish the wrong behaviour. A race to the top is always far more effective than a race to the bottom. Politicians are in the punishing game because they're in it for the short term – they can only think ahead to the next election cycle. If it's a race to the top, you actually get system change. A boycott movement on coal is not going to be

as successful as rewarding the energy companies that are more serious about the transition to green energy.

For systems change to occur, you need to look at the company from an outside-in perspective rather than inside-out. Don't just aim to fight for your company – fight for all of the people that your company needs in order to succeed long term in business; that includes employees, consumers, suppliers. If we think about all of our stakeholders – starting from the people working in the farms right through to the people buying in the supermarket – we can make sure that society at large wins, not just shareholders.

Success comes from finding win–win solutions. Make your case boldly. Show that the organization will benefit in the long term from the changes you are suggesting and remember that most people who work for your organization care about more than just the bottom line. That doesn't mean you can ignore productivity or profits, but you shouldn't be shy about pointing out that softer factors, such as morale and reputation, are absolutely essential to your organization's success. This type of activism requires a granular understanding of your organization and its component parts and a desire to show that you are thinking beyond the next quarterly report.

Ultimately, issues such as transparency and environmental consciousness can be viewed as future proofing – preventing future legislation or climate shocks from impacting the organization. Making the case that your activism today will benefit the organization in the medium to long term will encourage decision makers to think that you're not simply rocking the boat – you are looking out for their interests.

Of course, the issue you champion may not seem obviously relevant to your company at first. **Luke Davies** is a One Young World Ambassador who works for Barclays. He became passionate about addressing the issue of climate refugees after attending the One Young World Summit in 2015 and took his activism to work, innovating a way for the bank to contribute to climate action:

I was inspired by the One Young World Summit in Bangkok and in particular the speech given by Bryant Zebedy – a One Young World Ambassador from the Marshall Islands. During his address to the delegates, Bryant explained that the Marshall Islands will be under water by 2050 because of climate change. I couldn't believe it, and wanted to take action. Bryant then raised an idea I hadn't encountered before – the idea of 'climate refugees' which refers to those who are displaced by the negative consequences of client change. Following the summit and after extensive research, this idea of climate refugees became urgent to me – how could I not act?

It was not easy – I had to create a commercially viable solution to a massive global issue. Creating a product/solution required senior sponsorship, which meant that I had to be commercially minded when trying to win over senior management. It took weeks to generate a business plan for the bank – which would return some profit, but also help achieve change in our lending criteria. I wanted our lending teams to understand that an environmentally friendly credit facility would be a safer bet than a poorly governed company when it came to the environment. I carried out countless hours of data analysis in order to convince the decision makers in the organization that this was the right thing to do.

The Green Deposit is essentially a savings account but for large, monetary values. Traditionally, our clients were never aware of the assets their deposits were funding, however with this product we can only use the money for Green purposes – it's a fundamental step change in how we allocate our balance sheet. The bottom line is that the product will allow and require Barclays to invest and lend to Green companies and buy only Green Assets.

This product is a first to market solution and is driving behavioural change, not just across Barclays but the entire financial system.

Only then will we see a true step change in the way we approach the mission to a low carbon economy.

Luke's activism shows that not all activists are in the streets with a placard. Many are sitting behind desks in suits. The change he made within such a large and arguably traditional organization is really significant and will help shift the entire industry which, as Luke points out, is absolutely essential if we are going to see the step change on climate action that is required to achieve the Paris Agreement by 2030. Could the company you work for be doing more to help accelerate the transition to a green economy?

Talent wins games, teamwork wins championships

Luke was a fairly junior member of staff at Barclays when he decided he was going to take action on his area of passion – climate refugees – through making a change in the organization he worked for. One of the ways he managed to achieve success was to build a coalition and get sponsorship and support from others in the organization.

First of all, you should try and get the backing of your direct superior. Whether that's a line manager or the regional coordinator, don't be tempted to circumvent them. Get your superior's feedback and ideas, and try to find ways for them to get some credit too. Sadly, some managers are too insecure to be led by someone junior to them and feel that creativity and innovation coming from below is a threat to their power. This can happen at any level in a company: your direct boss may be supportive but their manager may feel threatened by your use of initiative. Sharing the credit and developing the narrative of mutual success will help counteract these tendencies. It may be that your activism is repeatedly shot down by your superior, in which case you will have to go around them, but trying to bring everyone with you is the most sustainable and powerful way to achieve change.

Above all, change only happens in organizations because people pull together to get the work done. Alliance-building is a delicate process that can easily go astray. It takes time, effort, commitment and sometimes not getting what you want. But, if you want to accomplish your personal mission, you must have allies within the organization. **Dame Vivian Hunt** reflects that this is one of the most important steps in terms of creating long-term change:

Remember that changing an organization requires a team of people. We place too much emphasis on this notion of individual advocacy – one person against the system. When you're working in a company, you're in a system. Once you've identified your improvement idea, most of the time is going to be spent on changing the mind-sets of leaders and scaling-up the implementation. You're going to have to do more than simply tolerate your colleagues if you want to change things. You have to engage with them and build relationships. If you have a really ambitious idea, that journey will require a network and capabilities that are beyond what you as one individual employee or one team have. Change is going to come from all parts of the organization. Most companies learn a huge amount from their customers, employees and partners in their supply chains and partnerships. Great ideas to improve the business can come from anywhere.

You need to think of yourself as a network, not just a pioneering person or a tiger team within a company and recognize that change will take time and it's going to come with trade-offs. This is especially true of larger companies with big systems which are under immense financial, operational and social pressures. Changing these companies is different to working in a start-up because these are large institutions and will take time to change properly.

This doesn't mean you need to be impatient or give up. The case for change and the demonstration of a quantifiable impact for investors and many other good attributes can be proven quite quickly. That said, proving the case alone is not what delivers the change. It's much more about the intervention point, the operating model, the capability system including incentives and implementation discipline that builds and embeds real change.

As **Dame Vivian Hunt** points out, you need a certain amount of support to have senior people agree to your idea, but you also need support to implement the idea. If your initiative requires everyone in an organization to change the way they do something, you will need multiple champions at all levels of the organization, reinforcing the positive message and the benefits of your idea. This will help people to overcome the hurdle of the inconvenience of change.

Alliances are built from individual allies

Big organizations are often described as 'faceless' because they seem impersonal and unapproachable. One of your jobs as an activist is to try and be a visible face within the organization that people recognize and associate with your cause. As with all activism, making a difference within a big organization comes down to making enough individual people care about your issue and feel compelled to do something. You'll need to take the time to seek out individuals, foster relationships with them and hear them out.

Simon Rodgers is a One Young World Ambassador who was responsible for transforming Aviva's LGBT network and making the company not only tolerate difference, but celebrate it as well. His work has real impact, Aviva went from being the UK's 91st most LGBT-friendly employer in 2014 to the 15th in 2015. Simon has learned that investing time in a truly personal approach pays off:

> One of the main challenges we faced from the beginning and over time was getting people involved; getting people to step up and do things out of their comfort zone, to visibly 'out' themselves, and to help us change hearts, minds and perceptions to make our workplace more inclusive. Two of the greatest tools I had for this

were coffee and wine. And while it may seem I say this in good humour, I am being entirely serious!

An invitation to coffee is less formal than a meeting, and frames the time commitment expected. It's more personable, and can be more flexible. It keeps the subject open without a fixed agenda. It puts people at ease, and gives the busiest of people a break during the monotony of days filled with meetings. And who can turn down the kind offer of being bought a coffee? As for a glass of wine, this is even more generous an offer (particularly at London prices!), more sociable (thus giving the opportunity to build a more personal relationship), and who wouldn't be glad to have the excuse to escape the office for something lighter than another meeting.

Some of the strongest relationships I formed, and some of the boldest allies I brought on our journey, were the result of a coffee or a glass of wine. And I advocated this to the others working with me. I was always very clear that if someone expressed an interest in getting involved in our movement we had to meet them in person. We could never be a mailbox, or the custodians of a mailing list to which we threw a newsletter at every now and then. We had to make everything relatable and personable so that we could really engage people.

Over the years I built networks far and wide, and was ultimately appointed as the chair of Aviva Pride, which I had expanded across the UK and also reached out to other locations. Of course this was a result of the hard-working, passionate and determined colleagues who share the same vision as me for making change and believing that we had a golden opportunity to make things better for our LGBT colleagues at work, and also to impact the lives of LGBT people outside of work. We were all very aware that while our work reached LGBT colleagues, we were also reaching colleagues who have LGBT children, or who have LGBT friends and family. And we extended our reach to community and charity engagement, having enormous impact in our local and national communities.

One of the things that can prevent us from building an effective network is the mind-set that networking is self-serving and that establishing relationships is only, or mainly, for our own benefit. A strong network is built of mutually beneficial relationships, with both parties reaping rewards. Be respectful of your colleagues' time by working out how you can help them – you need to prove that you aren't only seeking to work more closely with them to further your cause, but that you also genuinely care about their success and truly value your relationship with them. In the process of getting to know someone, you understand how you can add value and help them, and they are then willing to help you and further your cause. We can all learn from Simon's discipline in ensuring that every single person who was added to the network had a personal one-on-one meeting to make them feel welcome and seen. Everyone wants to be recognized as an individual and you can personally contribute to making a big organization seem less 'faceless'.

Strong and mutually beneficial alliances can help each colleague survive and thrive, and to get things done more quickly and smoothly than if you were to go it alone. A strong network supports and advocates for you. It helps you sell your ideas across the organization and brings more people to your cause. Once you make connections and offer to help others achieve their goals, your contacts will respond in kind when you have a need. Knowing that there are people who have got your back can reduce stress and boost your confidence.

Who could your allies be? Your list of potential allies goes much further than your direct superior and your peers. We always believe that the best coalitions are the most diverse – as ever, ask yourself who isn't at the table yet and be the one to invite them to contribute. Envision your end goal – who is affected by the change you are proposing? Make sure you include them in the early stages of the discussions so that they can become champions – if the people who are most inconvenienced or negatively affected see the overall benefits in the reforms, you are halfway there. Similarly, they will be best placed to help identify pitfalls and suggest better alternatives.

In building an alliance at work, you must be accountable for what you promise people. **Carole Stone CBE** has been called Britain's best connected woman. She was for many years the producer on BBC Radio 4's current affairs programme *Any Questions?*. She is now the managing director of YouGovStone, where she established a think tank with a global panel of over 5,000 leaders from a range of fields. She points out:

> Connecting people, exchanging ideas and building friendships are essential for making effective change in our world. It is important that we deliver on any promise we make, however big or small: if we do not follow-up we are likely to be thought of as sloppy. Our reputations are after all partly made by word of mouth.

> Be generous with your contacts and keep in touch with those you want to see again perhaps by sending a message if you know they have an important landmark coming up.

> I hold regular gatherings of friends and colleagues – I call them 'salons' – always at the same venue, on the same day of the week, at the same time. An hour and a half is ideal. I hold mine from 6pm to 7.30pm on a Monday at my office. You could begin by sending three dates inviting people to join you on one of the dates for coffee or drinks.

> I have a database of over 50,000 people which takes time to maintain and expand. It's essential to make sure you update people's titles and job roles and indeed to ensure they are still alive!

> And do remember it is often the things we don't do in life that we regret more than those things we do that fail. Do have a go.

> Stretch your potential, make a difference.

Being reliable is important in all aspects of professional life and it's incredibly important in activism. Just because it's your passion project does not mean you shouldn't be as professional as you are in other areas of your working life. If people view you as proactive and accountable, they are more likely to recommend your initiative or speak well of you. Your reputation is ultimately all about word of mouth.

One Young World Trustee **Elio Leoni Sceti** has been the CEO of numerous large corporations, including frozen food giant Iglo and record company EMI. He reflects that bringing your 'true' self to work is an important part of being a successful activist there. By embarking on a cause-driven activity in a large company you are already blurring the lines between personal and professional – Elio believes this is critical to creating a more authentic and personal organization:

> There came a time when I thought, 'Why am I at work a different person than I am at home? Why am I more hard-nosed in business?' In business, there is an expectation to prioritize profit above all else, but that didn't seem natural to me. I was lucky enough to be in a position where I questioned myself and that's when I realized I wanted to make a difference. I realized I could make a difference simply by being who I am. That then led me to make different decisions, to create different teams, to promote different people, and so on and so forth.
>
> I think that the difference between real change and green-washing is real belief. There are many people who generate sparks, but the person that makes the flame is the one that feels inside that something needs to be done and lives it in their own personal life, in their business life and in their social life.
>
> If you don't let your purpose permeate every aspect of your life then you won't make a difference. There'll be a moment when you'll be in the position to make a decision at work and you will either stand by your beliefs or you won't. You are much more likely to make a truly moral decision if your principles and behaviour

are the same in all areas of your life. Your one moral decision will then have a ripple effect - as you model moral behaviour in a big organization, you promote your values and open up channels of communication so that other people feel like they can take personal values into account when it comes to business decisions.

Don't raise your voice, improve your argument

Framing your idea in a way which shows that your organization will benefit and building a meaningful alliance of supporters will mean that you may not encounter too much resistance when it comes to proposing and implementing your idea. However, when change doesn't happen most of the time it's because someone doesn't want it to.

Some people enjoy change – it can provide them with an opportunity or enable them to learn new things and grow personally and professionally. Others find it uncomfortable and prefer a set routine. These are usually the people you will find suspicious of change and more likely to resist.

Even if someone doesn't seem convinced or isn't a likely ally, you may be able to win them round by building a personal relationship with them. Winning over naysayers is largely about communication. If they understand your idea correctly and don't misinterpret your intentions or misconstrue the outcomes, many people will eventually come around to supporting you. However, good communication is also about listening, so it's important to establish a feedback loop with the naysayers as well as with your supporters.

Let them see the authenticity and sincerity that Elio spoke about – make them feel heard but also be honest about your motivations. Set out to earn people's trust as well as their endorsement and respect. Showing that you have good intentions and genuinely care about making a difference may be all you need to win them over. Change is never painless, but it can be a lot less painful for everyone when it is done with good, clear communication.

All too often when activists encounter resistance to change, they can't find the persistence they need. We often encounter young activists at the bottom of a company or enthusiastic CEOs who become frustrated with what gets called the 'sticky middle' – i.e. middle management. **Paul Polman** reminds us that developing an understanding of their priorities is key to successful change within a big organization:

> There is a group inside the company which we always conveniently call the middle management, but they are a group of real workers that don't have the time to construct all these plans, nor do they have the luxury that workers at the bottom have to shout for all the things they need. These are the people that are the backbone of the organization. You need to spend a lot of time with them. They have to deal with a lot of conflicting pressures.
>
> You have to respect pressure points and the dichotomies in business that people have to deal with. You have to respect middle management. They are just trying to do their jobs. They might not always be aligned with the objectives that you hope to achieve. Businesses are under enormous pressure to deliver. It's hard for middle management sometimes to see how they can make these trade-offs to become more sustainable. We discovered in order for us to move much faster than our overall ambitions that we needed to spend more time on driving the broader systems change.

The lesson here is be analytical and understand *why* people are resisting change – with the case of middle management it may be because they are under pressure to cut costs and so investing can seem counterintuitive. In order to be a successful activist you must interrogate the situation and find the answer. If you get to the heart of why people are resisting change and, as Paul points out, you are respectful of these people and their conflicting pressures, you can adapt your proposition and make it more acceptable to them. By working with a resistant group instead of against it, you give your cause a better chance of acceptance.

Change doesn't happen in isolation

The organizations this chapter has dealt with have, on the whole, been large companies, but the lessons can be extrapolated and applied to any large organization that requires change, including a government, educational systems, charities and community.

We asked CEO of Reckitt Benckiser **Rakesh Kapoor** how he applies lessons from his large organization to some of the large social initiatives the company works on. One of the largest initiatives is around health and hygiene in India, Pakistan and Nigeria, to end the deaths of children under five from diarrhoea. This involves engaging with local communities to change cultural practices:

> With any social impact initiative the key challenge to overcome is changing deeply embedded behaviours to create sustainable change. Building infrastructure alone will not solve cultural practices, and build understanding as to why people should, for example, have toilets in their village as opposed to practising open defecation. We worked with an NGO to deliver a mass behaviour change programme to address the issue of eliminating deaths from diarrhoea, which is completely preventable.

> We ensured that the activities covered 80 per cent of the community – so we 'wrap our arms' around an entire village. We engage with key groups of the community – e.g. healthcare professionals, schools, faith leaders – as it is they that drive the behaviour change. Children are also a very key part of driving change – they go home and tell their parents they must wash their hands, for example. They put pressure around having a toilet in the family and not defecating in the open.

> We also created a social enterprise model. Women were provided a livelihood by selling hygiene products, e.g. soap, etc. As trusted members of their community (i.e. a friend and neighbour), other women were happy to regularly buy the products from them and,

very importantly, listen to the seller about key hygiene advice. Dettol (for example) is the most popular product in the basket of goods.

It's not difficult to identify the similarities in changing a village and changing an organization: communicate your idea well and show how it will benefit people; create an alliance between the people who buy into your idea; reinforce the idea until it becomes accepted. What is important, too, is that this has been sensitively adapted to the village setting. Context and appreciation for cultural settings is always going to be key – things may not be *that* different in your neighbouring team or nearest town, but there will be enough differentiation that you will need to adjust your approach accordingly.

Ultimately, whether you are creating change from the bottom up or top down, changing a big organization takes time. Nothing happens immediately when so many people are involved; the often unwieldly mechanism needs to reassemble before it changes. You are a shepherd, who must mobilize your flock before you move it to new more modern pastures.

Paul Polman reminded us of the proverb 'if you want to go fast you go alone but if you want to go far you go together'. Many of the changes activists are passionate about, such as women's empowerment or climate action, are changes they wish to be sustained for good. For changes to last in any organization, big or small, they have to become part of the culture and all the members need to be bearers of that culture.

Realizing that a big organization needs to change can feel isolating and intimidating but, as activists, we have to remember that in order to make a difference we must start somewhere. The advantage of making change within a big organization is that you are already surrounded by people with whom you have things in common – you have all chosen to be associated with that organization and all are, to varying degrees, invested in its success. If you didn't want the organization to be successful, you would probably leave.

Hold this close as you try to change an organization – all of your colleagues or fellow volunteers will have some kind of stake in building the future you have in mind and with the right alliances and communication, you can all make a difference together.

How to change a big organization checklist

- Recognize that 'big' is to your advantage – you have the power to influence more people and make a bigger difference.

- The leadership of the organization has to be completely convinced about your aims – then they will lead the change themselves.

- Respect 'middle management' and have a thorough understanding of the pressures they face from above and below and be prepared to spend time convincing them and giving them credit.

- Make it clear that your activism embraces the success of the organization – you are a positive force.

- Ideally your idea must be right for the organization, clearly in line with its mission and strategy; timing is key to ensuring that your aim is appropriate to its current financial objectives.

- Take full advantage of the existing formal processes – they can and do work. Understand the means to get feedback right across the organization – take the feedback into account and keep improving.

- Be bold in setting out your idea – and ground it in detailed knowledge of how it benefits the organization.

- Think of yourself as a network and not only as an individual – it will take many people at many levels to achieve what you want. Build alliances, invest time in personal approaches wherever you can.

- Be patient – you're turning around a huge tanker. A big organization can't be changed by one person or one team alone, you need to bring everyone with you over time.

- Be your true, authentic self – it's too hard to manage yourself as a split person, one in private and one in the workplace.

Chapter Eight
How to fix something that isn't right

In an age where information is tightly controlled by publicists and marketing agencies, real scandal is often only revealed with the help of whistle-blowers, and the abundant courage of whistle-blowers in the face of the great risks they take is often astounding and moving. Once whistles are blown, however, the problems need to be addressed and steps taken to ensure that violence, unfairness or criminal activity does not continue. In this chapter, we examine how various activists have responded to crises, investigated historical wrongdoings and empowered individuals to create a better and more accountable culture.

Fixing something that has been going wrong is about taking meaningful steps towards reform and permanent erasure. To make changes on serious issues – such as the 52-year conflict in Colombia or sex trafficking that occurs in the UK – there's no room for activists who simply wish to engage in moral grandstanding or virtue signalling. Anyone can criticize from the outside, but this chapter is for people who are prepared to take risks and those who are prepared to compromise and concede in order to make lasting change.

Swedish chemist Svante Arrhenius expressed fears about fossil fuels and man-made climate change as far back as the 1890s, yet it is only within the last few years that we have witnessed global protests and strikes for change. Politicians in 2019 are taking the issue more seriously – it was the number-one issue for the elections in Australia – and it is finally becoming a mainstream topic of public conversation. In fact, many issues that deserve attention have been around for centuries. Some of these problems, such as racial discrimination and inequality, are deep-rooted and stem from geopolitical phenomena such as colonialism and the transatlantic slave trade which began in the sixteenth century.

Many of the people we have spoken to in this chapter have had to respond to scandal or historic wrongdoing that wasn't their fault: they have decided to help fix a problem in society or within a large organization.

However, just because something isn't your *fault*, doesn't mean it isn't your *responsibility* to fix it. Correcting something that's been done wrong is about shouldering responsibility because, often, if you're not part of the solution you are part of – even the embodiment of – the ongoing problem.

Facing up to historic problems requires honesty and bravery, and deciding on a course of action requires careful analytical judgement. And addressing crises amid scandal and scrutiny is one of the greatest tests of leadership.

Never shrink from speaking truth to power

In the last chapter we discussed how to make change from within to achieve our vision of a better future, but sometimes distancing yourself from the situation and refusing to be a part of a system any longer is actually what is needed. Sometimes, despite best efforts, issues can't be changed from within, and by staying in your position you inevitably remain part of the problem. At that point, it can be better to step away and speak out.

So many issues that have hit the headlines in recent years have only come to light as a result of whistle-blowers, who have taken great personal risk to expose everything from war crimes to tax dodging and sexual abuse. Whistle-blowing requires a tremendous amount of clarity of thinking and bravery to be done well. You need to have a very clear and distinct reason for why you are calling out what's going wrong rather than working within the existing system to change it. As we argue in chapter four, sometimes to solve a problem disruption is necessary – when gentle ripple effects don't work, you have to throw a big rock into the disquieted waters. Only transformational leadership can cause the type of change that you need to uncover what's going on.

Whistle-blowers can attract press attention and increase scrutiny from government, and sometimes you need these external pressures in order to push internal stakeholders to shoulder responsibilities that are otherwise too easy to ignore or neglect. Whistle-blowing, boldly confronting things that have gone wrong, is not about personal responsibility as an activist – at some point you have to say *not in my name* as a human. We need people to summon the utmost bravery in order to step out of the shadows and uncover the truth. We also need those few courageous people to feel supported so that they can go to the point of no return in the name of moral progress.

By blowing the whistle, you may lose your job, and other companies may not want to hire you because they don't trust you to keep their secrets. Like all activism, undoing something that's going wrong or has gone wrong can come with personal sacrifice, but there is hopefully something greater to be gained – a common good that is unmeasurable.

During the course of her work as a detective constable in the serious crime division of Greater Manchester Police, **Maggie Oliver** had interviewed many victims at length over many months, uncovering harrowing stories of the systematic abuse of girls as young as 11. In 2012, nine members of a paedophile ring had been sentenced for grooming and sexually abusing young girls in Rochdale. However, she knew that was only scratching the surface, and she was continually shocked by the repeated failure of senior officers to record many allegations, to prosecute serial offenders or most importantly to protect the young victims. She was ultimately forced to choose between her conscience and her career, and felt morally bound to resign and speak out publicly to expose this long-standing neglect. As the first police officer ever to do this, she had to face up to the very real possibility that she might go to prison, but she now reflects that standing by her principles was the best practical solution:

> My own conscience would never have allowed me to turn a blind eye, but the personal consequences for me were horrific and far-reaching. It is no exaggeration to say my life will never be the same again, as it has changed in almost every way. I lost my career, my income, my home, my health, my colleagues, my full pension, my sanity at one point, and many years of my life fighting this battle. It is still a part of my life every single day. Eventually I was heard and the public reaction has been phenomenal, they have supported me and restored my faith in the decency of humanity. The public all feel the same way as I did and I am approached on almost a daily basis by people who recognize me and come along to say they agree with what I have said, which is immensely moving.

I would encourage anyone who sees injustice and neglect to think carefully before they embark on the journey I did, and to be prepared for a long, hard fight ahead . . . but for me it was not really a choice. I could not ignore what I saw, and I guess I now see myself as a campaigner and an activist fighting for justice, for basic human rights, and for the rights of women and children everywhere.

Would I do the same again if faced with the same choices? Absolutely. Because despite what I have been through, I am proud that I ultimately found the strength to stand up for what was *right*, despite what I was forced to endure. I can look at myself in the mirror and know truly that I have done my best, my conscience is clear and even today I still continue to support some of the girls in Rochdale who were failed so badly.

Speaking up is not an easy thing to do. Deciding that you are going to come forward can be immensely daunting. It takes a lot of courage to take action. It can also be intimidating to begin to question whether an organization or group of people is actually doing something wrong – especially when it involves people who are senior to you. Becoming a whistle-blower is one way to make authorities aware of practices that violate the codes of conduct, steal taxpayer money, endanger lives or break the law. While it may feel disloyal, remember that whistle-blowing ultimately protects people and the organization itself by identifying harm and forcing them to take action.

The ultimate excuse for any problem is that 'everyone else does it', but we all know this just isn't good enough. Unfortunately this rationale is found in government, in business and in civil society – there can be many vested interests surrounding a wrongdoing. If it's possible to get away with doing things the wrong way, many people will do it. Once it becomes routine or starts making money, people will always find ways to justify it to themselves. This is where activists are crucial – speaking out for what is right is your duty as an activist, even if it might cause uncomfortable disruption. If you are threatened or intimidated by people who benefit from the wrongdoing, don't let it deter you – instead, make it increase your determination to come forward.

If you are considering being a whistle-blower, do contact an attorney who has experience in handling whistle-blower cases before you take any action. Many governments and charities also offer specialist advice you can request. Each case will vary depending on its circumstances and it is essential to get legal counsel on what steps suit yours. It may benefit your cause to take your issue to the press and increase publicity but that course of action may also limit legal rights you are entitled to. Surround yourself with as much of a support network as you can – whether that be family, friends or peers. The messenger of bad news is often targeted so be prepared to be receive criticism. In these moments, it is of the utmost importance to remember your cause and focus on why you are taking action. There will be days when fear takes hold and you question your actions. But, like Maggie, ultimately coming forward may well be the best decision of your life, as you can play your part in changing the way things are done and stopping the wrongdoing.

Maggie Oliver has these top tips for those considering blowing the whistle:

1. Gather your facts so you can prove what you are saying is true. This will also serve to protect you should your actions lead to arrest or, even worse, prosecution.

2. Audio record every official conversation you have - as my path has shown me, when evidence needed (such as my grievance meeting minutes, and other records) was conveniently 'lost' by the organization.

3. Take a witness you trust along to every official meeting you attend.

4. Document everything you do, and send an email confirmation of every meeting you have and details of what was discussed and agreed.

5. Lodge an official grievance to prove you have highlighted all your concerns.

6. Seek independent legal advice.

7. Protect yourself as much as you possibly can. Speak to your own doctor. Seek support at work, wherever possible. My nurse in HR was phenomenal and was a great support to me, and knew everything that was going on.

8. Finally, when you have exhausted all internal routes, seek other bodies such as (for me) the IPCC, my MP, the children's commissioner and then the Home Office. Although none were any help at all, at least I could say I had tried and exhausted every road possible. The only way left to me in the end was via the media. And they were my salvation.

Be the one to whom people can turn

On the flipside, a whistle-blower or complainant may have made you aware of something that has gone wrong or is going wrong in your organization. They may have flagged corruption, malpractice or bullying that you weren't aware of – perhaps it was almost in your peripheral vision, but now it has fully come to light you have to handle it and address it. Are you going to be brave and root out all wrongdoing and do your best to ensure it doesn't happen again?

Yes. You are.

Addressing historical wrongdoings, especially if they're still going on, is always incredibly complex. There is a reason why things have stayed secret. As well as addressing the wrongdoing, you have to address the climate of silence which will by its nature be hard to break. Secrets are burdens. Collective secrets are pre-imposed and often forceful and oppressive binds.

When a conspiracy or culture of silence has developed, activists need to think carefully and sensitively about how they can go about giving people a voice. Fear can bring out the worst in people: we all avoid discussing important things because we are afraid of being ridiculed, criticized or punished.

The way you deal with people and make them feel is already part of the solution. You need to try and develop trust and create an environment in which people can name problems and address them without fear of retribution. It's important to be patient and tolerant because many of the people who will be sharing their experiences will be doing so from a place of pain, uncertainty and mistrust. If they are going to be open about their experiences, which they may have kept hidden for a long time, the way in which they are treated and the seriousness with which their complaints are dealt with is critical in allowing them dignity and helping them not only to move on but be freed from fear.

The way the investigation is conducted will set the tone for how effective the solutions can be. If the survivors, whistle-blowers or complainants have faith in the process of the investigation and feel that they are treated with respect, they may be more willing to engage in constructive solutions further down the line as you are doing the most critical thing: rebuilding trust.

Often investigations of historic wrongdoings, such as the inquiries into abuse in the Catholic Church or the Truth and Reconciliation Commission of post-apartheid South Africa, require deep and thorough examination of a painful past. For example, the last residential school in Canada was closed down in 1996, and eventually the sickening stories about the methods used to sever indigenous children from the influence of their families and assimilate them into the dominant 'Canadian' culture were brought to light. Over more than a century, tens of thousands of families were torn apart as children were kidnapped or forcibly removed from their homes and sent to boarding schools where they often faced the most horrifying abuse and mistreatment.

The Indian Residential Schools Settlement Agreement, the largest class action settlement in Canadian history, began to be implemented in 2007. One element of the agreement was the establishment of the Truth and Reconciliation Commission of Canada to facilitate reconciliation among former students, their families, their communities and the rest of Canadian society.

Senator Murray Sinclair served the justice system in Manitoba for over 25 years. He was the first Aboriginal judge appointed in Manitoba and Canada's second. He served as chief commissioner of the Truth and Reconciliation Commission, participating in hundreds of hearings across Canada, culminating in the issuance of the TRC's Final Report in 2015. He also oversaw an active multimillion–dollar fundraising programme to ensure that survivors were able to travel to events and hearings and play a central role in the process, and reflects on how the TRC process itself was able to become the basis for healing:

> The Truth and Reconciliation Commission's Final Report is a testament to the courage of each and every survivor and family member who shared their story. Probably the most important part of the truth and reconciliation process was to talk to the victims and to talk with the victims in a realistic way. That meant that they had to be given the means by which they could talk freely, they could talk openly, and they could talk accurately about what it was that they have been through and gone through. That sense of truth determination was important to the whole process because it's the foundation for what you do going forward.
>
> Our intention at the Truth and Reconciliation Commission of Canada was to establish the history of Canada vis-à-vis indigenous people as a part of Canada's national memory and to ensure that it stayed as a part of Canada's national memory forever into the future. So long as Canada existed, it would have this as part of its memory and it would not be able to forget.
>
> It has concerned me from the outset that there was a belief from the beginning among some parties to the process that all we had to do was let the survivors talk, and then we could forget about it and go forward, because the survivors would have had the chance to whine and complain, and that was enough. The reality is that the truth determination process teaches us that not only were the indigenous people the victims of this history because they were

the ones who were told that they were inferior, but that non-indigenous kids and society as well grew up believing in the myth of superiority of European nations. They believe in the justice of their privilege. They believe that indigenous people are inherently inferior in terms of their rights, in terms of their belief systems, in terms of their existence. Those people in those privileged positions are not yet ready to condone a new relationship in which those who they have oppressed for so long are actually going to be their equals. That's a very difficult part of the conversation of reconciliation.

As **Senator Sinclair** demonstrates, allowing people to express their truth is an important and difficult step which may often take a lot of time and care. That is really only the start, however, as once people have come forward they will expect action to be taken. In order to maintain the fragile trust you have built, you need to manage expectations about what concrete steps are possible and what will come next.

Many of the things that have been done wrong have been cyclical, ongoing, repetitive issues. Breaking the cycle of abuse or violence can't always be achieved if you insist on punishing all of the perpetrators, because again this would create resentment in the community which could prevent the creation of a lasting peaceful solution. Often issues are too complicated to point the finger at a single perpetrator and so trying to apportion blame is reductive. Senator Sinclair reflects on the role of atonement in creating a positive way forward for indigenous communities:

In Canada today, I remind all Canadians when I talk to them that this is not an Indigenous problem. We should not look at residential schools as having been only a process by which indigenous people were victimized, but we have to see this as a Canadian problem – that this process of oppression has had a damaging impact upon Canadian society as well.

The ultimate purpose of righting an injustice would be for us to be able to move on together or to move forward together.

The element of punishment is not going to result in a continued relationship or establishment of the relationship of peaceful coexistence. Atonement is different from punishment. When it's a forced punishment or a coerced punishment, then the relationship of violence continues with a different perpetrator and a different victim.

The truth and reconciliation process is really to allow for peoples to be able to come to terms with their past in a way that recognizes that they do have to continue to live side by side, that they do have to continue to coexist. Therefore, the best way to do that is to find a way to establish a process of atonement, a process of reconciliation whereby they can literally put the past behind them but still learn from it and benefit from those teachings.

The word 'reconcile' derives from the Latin *reconciliare* – to bring together again. Creating unity between communities in which there has been injustice or violence is no easy task. As **Senator Sinclair** points out, truth-telling, in isolation from efforts to punish abusers and to make institutional reforms, can be viewed as nothing more than words.

But without any truth-telling or reparation efforts, punishing a small number of perpetrators can be viewed as a form of political revenge. Even reparations can pose many problems. When not properly linked to prosecutions or truth-telling, reparations are often perceived as 'hush money'– an attempt to buy the silence or acquiescence of victims.

The question of how best to deal with a divisive past of mass violence is not a new one. Dealing with the consequences of war or widespread human rights violations raises large practical difficulties as well as bringing old traumas back to the surface.

You can't take back the past, but you can fight for the future

The many problems that flow from past abuses are often too complex to be solved by any one action. Judicial measures, including trials, are unlikely to suffice. If there are thousands, or hundreds of thousands, of victims and perpetrators, how can they all be dealt with fairly through the courts – especially in cases where those courts are weak and corrupt or, indeed, complicit in the historic crimes? Even if courts were adequate to take on the task of prosecuting everyone who might deserve it, in order to reconstruct a damaged social fabric, other initiatives would be required.

A comprehensive approach to achieving peace and justice is often termed transitional justice. This approach emerged in the late 1980s and early 1990s, mainly in response to political changes in Latin America and Eastern Europe, where there was a clear desire to address systematic abuses by former regimes without endangering the political transformations that were underway. The United Nations has defined transitional justice as 'the full range of processes and mechanisms associated with a society's attempt to come to terms with a legacy of large-scale past abuses, in order to ensure accountability, serve justice and achieve reconciliation'.

One of the most recent applications of transitional justice has been as part of the Colombian peace agreement led by former president **Juan Manuel Santos**. The conflict in Colombia killed as many as 220,000 people with 25,000 still missing, and 5.7 million displaced over the last half-century. A peace process between the government and leaders of the Revolutionary Armed Forces of Colombia (known as the FARC), the country's largest insurgent group, halted the violence in 2016. The process faces many challenges, including being voted down in a referendum because of widespread public concern that the peace deal offered too much leniency to perpetrators of violence. But the deal's architects are hopeful that the approach will lead to a sustainable peace. As Santos explains:

> War and conflict are always manipulated and taken advantage of by people who like to use fear to achieve their objectives. We're seeing this all over the world. It is the way to promote polarization

and extreme positions which are completely contrary to tolerance, compromise and peace.

For many people in Colombia, the application of Transitional Justice to people who committed all kinds of atrocities was and still is unacceptable. People believe the perpetrators ought to go to jail for the rest of their lives and won't accept anything less. However, if we were to respond in that way it would mean the continuation of war. An imperfect peace will always be better than a perfect war. For us in Colombia, this means guerillas are sitting in Congress – ultimately, I think it's better that their views are discussed in Parliament than borne out by bombs, shootings and kidnappings.

There is no such thing as a perfect peace agreement because a peace agreement is a compromise made by human beings. Both sides are giving away a part of what they cherish. The irony is that a good peace agreement leaves everyone somewhat disappointed initially. And if that is the case, it shows the agreement is well balanced and does not favour one side over another.

How we handle conflict within any community is important to the long-term success of that community. Not every conflict can be easily handled or resolved positively. If a conflict is ongoing then you need to decide how to best deal with it in a way that is *appropriate* for the community. When we compromise to settle a conflict or dispute, we have to be realistic that the outcome might be less than we had originally hoped. The final decision may be one that is acceptable but not optimal, which means you may encounter reluctance or resistance as the result seems like a loss.

When you're aiming to solve a problem that has been going on for a long time, particularly where there are drastically opposing sides, presenting a vision of a future which everyone can work towards is critical. You need to inspire in the people who have suffered that if they work with you now there will be a better tomorrow, and that the vicious cycle will be permanently broken for their next generation. Santos breaks this down into Peace-making and Peace-building:

> Peace is divided in two different phases. The first is what we call peace-making. That is sitting down with your enemy, your adversary, and signing a peace agreement that will end the war. The other phase, which is more difficult and takes much more time, is peace-building. That is the reconciliation, teaching and persuading people to forgive, to leave what happened behind, to try to look to the future with a different perspective.

> We went beyond what normal peace agreements do and designed the process in a way that would ensure development plans for regions that were affected by the conflict. At the same time, we introduced a chapter on gender to give women a special place in the reconciliation process because they were victims of this conflict in a plethora of ways.

> During my eight years as president, I also learned how important it is to reconcile also with the environment, to defend one of our most important assets which is our biodiversity, that war had destroyed in many ways.

Whatever issue you are facing, you can apply this approach – the short-term confrontation of the problem and the long-term, sustainable solutions. They have to be constantly weighed against each other in order to achieve your vision of undoing the harm that has been done. Maintaining a long-term view can be difficult, especially when emotions are running high and the desire for short-term wins can feel overwhelming. Be prepared to view the occasional downturns simply as part of a longer journey.

Identifying issues such as the environment, which affects everyone, no matter what side of the conflict they fought on, is an important step in bringing people together. Sport has so often enabled people to come together, whether in no man's land in 1914, where British and German troops left their trenches to play football and take photos with each other on Christmas Day, or in post-apartheid South Africa as a united nation cheered on its rugby team to victory in the 1995 World Cup. Identifying common ground is difficult – common ground is often shaky ground – but you must persevere.

Tragedy gives us the opportunity to rebuild

Often you won't be aware that something is going wrong, whether it be in your business, the organization you work for or your country, until it is brought to your attention in a public and, often, startling manner. Responding to a crisis is hard; responding to a scandal is even harder. It can feel like the world is watching and will expect you to change and find robust means in which you can evidence that you've changed. You may be reeling from negative publicity or criticism, but activists need to be on their guard to effectively manage crises. You can't fall back on denial, excuses or casual dismissal. You can't afford to get defensive or go on the attack. You need to be prepared to feel vulnerable and show that you are taking the criticism and need for change very seriously.

The series of scandals in charities that hit the headlines in 2018 shook public confidence in the sector as a whole, particularly the shocking revelations which rocked the international development sector. *The Times* newspaper revealed that in 2011 four members of Oxfam's staff had been sacked and three members, including the Haiti country director, had resigned after allegations emerged that they had employed local women as sex workers while working in Haiti after the earthquake. There were no guarantees that all the sex workers were above the age of consent.

Although the charity had told the Charity Commission that there had been an incident of serious misconduct at the time, it failed to make clear that it entailed sexual misconduct and the dynamic of the abuse of power. Oxfam is one of the most visible UK charities, with charity shops on most high streets and many prominent campaigns, and the story hit a nerve with the public. **Winnie Byanyima**, Oxfam International's executive director, has been responsible for leading the organization as it has reeled from the impact of the scandal:

You have to change and change is hard. We have been working on changing ourselves internally. Asking ourselves, 'How did this happen, and why was it tolerated? Why is it that we didn't take tougher action at the time?'

We lost the confidence of many of our supporters last year, when the story broke about how some Oxfam staff acted badly in Haiti seven years ago. The story came back to really hurt us, and what hurt me the most was the loss of confidence by so many of our own staff who felt they couldn't identify with the organization they had so loved. Then some of our supporters stopped funding us and expressed themselves very angrily; there was a lot of disappointment and pain.

Rebuilding an organization is not easy, and there are no shortcuts. You have to correct the mistake, whatever it is, but you start by owning up to it. You start by claiming responsibility for your mistake. If you don't own up, if you deny, if you hide, you're not on your journey to rebuilding trust. If you fail your supporters, you must look them in the eye, admit your mistake, be humble, seek to learn from those who know better, and change. Show your supporters the change is happening, and they will come back. Activists are like that. They want to change the world so they don't give up on causes. Most people will come back. Some might not, but many will. You'll carry on with new ones, and those who will give you another chance.

It was a humbling moment for us because we are a very loud organization, we are a campaigning organization, we point out the wrongs of others. Now it was our turn to accept, be humble and take responsibility for our wrongdoings.

As Winnie shows, no matter who you are or how well intentioned you may be, it is important to acknowledge responsibility when you are at fault. Take a moment to reflect before you respond to criticism; acknowledging every mistake provides you with an opportunity to engage with those who have felt wronged in order to rebuild and refocus your work.

Trust starts with truth and ends with truth

Rebuilding lost trust has several elements to it.

First of all, establish the facts with the highest level of integrity and accuracy you can muster. Trust is based in confidence that you are being truthful and transparent with people, so ascertaining the truth is critical. Sometimes establishing what has happened is especially difficult because it's being purposefully concealed – historic misdoings have been covered up, and there may be a culture of secrecy and silence because people have been afraid to speak out. Scour records and paper trails. You may need to convince people that what they have been told to think is actually based on mistruths.

Secondly, you need to communicate your findings. Revealing the truth of what has happened and showing the extent of the work that you've done to get to the bottom of the problem is a crucial step.

When you communicate what's been done wrong, you have to approach it from a place of humility and vulnerability. Defensiveness will only be a disservice. The public can empathize with vulnerability and humility; they are aware of the very human nature of mistakes. If you don't sincerely convey your willingness to change from a point of humility, it will be very difficult to build an alliance that will help you rebuild your mission.

Going forward, you will need to make a concerted effort to maintain a high level of integrity in communications. You will need to put out reports and updates much more frequently than you would have done in the past, both to demonstrate your commitment to transparently address how you're dealing with the issues and to continue to admit your mistakes as you find them. It can feel very difficult if you've said you're going to change to then admit another mistake, but actually genuinely acknowledging setbacks as they occur will restore people's faith, because it will become apparent that you're not trying to whitewash what's happened. People's ultimate fear is that the cover-up will continue and the truth will yet again be concealed.

Cultural change, whether in an organization or in an activist movement, is viewed as a long-term goal, but sometimes the tone can be altered very quickly by correct leadership. Commitment from the top incentivizes others to be the change the leaders want to see. Like all aspects of activism, living and being your message is really important and helps others to follow suit.

Kevin Watkins, CEO of Save the Children UK, reflects on the ways in which the charity has responded to revelations about its handling of sexual misconduct claims against two former executives, leading to a review which found that almost one in five members of staff at Save the Children said that they experienced discrimination or harassment in the three years prior to the inquiry:

Everyone who works in your organization has to be a bearer of the culture. That is the real defence of an organization. We did a big internal review of Save the Children with an external organizational ethicist. Sometimes you have to bring in external help and know how to ask for help. Trust is such an important word because trust is what underpins human relationships at every single level.

In my view, there are two really critical requirements of trust. One of them is honesty. You have to have a sense that the institution that you go to or the person responsible that you go to will be honest – they won't try and sweep your concern under the carpet, they won't lie to you, they won't endanger you.

The second thing is you need a strategy that recognizes what the problem is and comes up with practical solutions. Trust is not an abstract principle. I could sit behind my computer screens in the organization and bang out lots of lovely words about how trust really matters, but trust is a living thing and it's behavioural. People need to live it. I think, as leaders of an organization, the main thing you can do is to create the enabling environment for trust.

If a junior person is being harassed, the first thing they need is somewhere they can go with confidence. That will not always be their immediate supervisor. The organization needs to have a mechanism that says, if you don't feel confident, we will provide you with an external person and it'll be dealt with in the right way. We also need to continuously emphasize the consequences of actions such as harassment very clearly to employees. If you say something offensive about somebody because of their sexuality, or you insult somebody on the basis of their belief system or the way they dress, it will not be accepted in this organization.

As a result of the Oxfam and Save the Children scandals, the UK charity sector is suffering from a crisis of confidence which affects the donations, volunteering hours and ultimately means that the people the donations are supposed to support are being deprived. There are all sorts of roles that legislation and government can play in helping address the issues in the charity sector, but a lot of this has to come from the charities themselves. Oxfam and Save the Children experienced very different scandals. Internal sexual harassment of colleagues is very, very different from aid workers abusing their power over aid recipients. However, the questions that were raised needed to be answered, and it's going to take a long time to rebuild trust. A reputation takes decades to build and seconds to lose, but it will also take decades to build again.

Inspire people to believe they matter

The activist's reputation is even more fragile than the average citizen. People hate hypocrisy, especially when it comes from do-gooders, moralists or peace warriors. For instance, environmental hypocrisy is so much worse when it comes from someone who purports to be a very green person. If you've been telling people to make a difference and to do good, they will be filled with glee when you are the one for whom it goes wrong. When you're experiencing increased scrutiny as a result of a scandal or things going wrong, leading by example is critical. The Oxfam scandal, in particular, caused such fury because the very people who were supposed to be helping vulnerable people were exploiting them in the worst possible way.

Leadership is of course essential, but in order for cultural change to be complete you need to empower everybody to work towards it. International advisor on education **Sir Ken Robinson**'s TED Talk 'Do Schools Kill Creativity?' is one of the most watched on the internet (it has been viewed online over 40 million times and has been seen by 350 million people across 160 countries). His work is about fundamentally reforming our assumptions about the education system. He argues that the best way to make change is for people within the system to feel empowered so that they can be proactive about transformation:

> People often feel that systems are too entrenched for them to be able to make a difference: that there is nothing they can do about them. It's important for people to recognize that they do have agency: that things can and do change.
>
> The reason they can change is that human systems are comprised of the actions of individuals, the way they work together and the way their actions syncopate. There is always more room for innovation and movement in most systems than many people realize. There are habits of mind and habits of practice, which recur often because people come to think there are no alternatives. More often than not there are.
>
> The key is for people to see they do have agency. I always say to teachers and other people who work in education that YOU are the system. If you do something different for your students, you're changing the system for them. If you are a school principal and you reorganize how you do things in your school, you change the system for all the people in it. Recognizing that you are an active part of the system is the key to being able to change it.

As an activist, you need to see yourself as an agent of change and inspire others to realize that quality in themselves. Whether it's in a school, city hall or in a social media group, if people feel they have a stake in the process, and their opinions will be taken seriously and they too can impact people, they will take it upon themselves to make positive changes. You need to create an environment for others in your movement in which behaviour is guided more by values than by rules: so that even when 'nobody is watching' people make responsible decisions and do the right thing.

No system is changed because an activist pulls a lever: you need to ensure that individuals feel that they have agency and ownership in a situation so that they themselves can be accountable and, in turn, hold others to account.

This culture of ownership and agency will only follow a culture of trust. This is especially hard when you are working with vulnerable people or people who have been mistreated. **Senator Sinclair** reflects on the impact that abuse had on First Nation communities in Canada which he had to factor into the Truth and Reconciliation Process:

> There was a deliberate effort on the part of governments for several generations to try to prevent this story from becoming known. There's no question that that effort extended not just throughout government, but it extended throughout society as well. We pointed out in our report that there were several instances where prominent people had been informed of what was going on in the residential schools, the abuses that were occurring and what the schools were really doing to indigenous children, not just in terms of the violence that they experience but also in terms of the indoctrination that they were being put through.
>
> First Nation children were being told that their culture was in process of change. They were told that their belief system was wrong. They were told that they were uncivilized. They were told that they were savages and heathens and pagans and therefore did not have a right to continue to follow their traditions and their practices. Canadian leaders had convinced themselves that this was a good thing, that those savages, those heathens, needed to be civilized through a process of Christianization. Therefore, the

overall benefit outweighed the damage that was being done to them.

When people have been deliberately silenced for years or the authorities have conspired to silence them, building trust is going to be a long mission and will likely to be painful for all involved. Whatever harm has befallen the wronged party with whom you are dealing, you should take into account that their suffering will have reduced their faith in your ability to help them or your sincerity to create real change. A domestic violence victim may have reported abuse many times before they arrive at your shelter. A whistle-blower may have raised numerous concerns with management about fraud before they finally phone the police. You yourself may have lost faith with the system or no longer feel your objectives can be achieved. **Winnie Byanyima** offers the following advice for activists trying to build a more positive culture:

> If people are feeling burdened and are suffering, you are not being successful. You must make it possible for people to fight today, and fight tomorrow, and live to fight another day. So you must make activism a sustainable process in which people give their time, their intellect, their creativity. They must enjoy doing it with others.
>
> Activism is not martyrdom. What I mean is that you may feel very passionate about a cause, but activists are people who build people power, power with others. They shoulder a bit of the struggle, and a bit is shouldered by others and together, they carry a big burden. It is not about sacrificing yourself totally. It's about giving what you can, enjoying the challenge with others and taking the credit with others. Very successful activism is about engaging people in joyous ways. Activism should make them feel fulfilled, and make them feel that they have made a contribution.

Accountability breeds positivity and responsibility

Twitter isn't a historic wrongdoing – it's a fairly new medium. The landscape in which Twitter has been operating within since 2006 has probably changed more than Twitter has in that time. Neutrality used to mean neutrality, but the way in which we view the concept of neutrality when it comes to platforms and publishers has changed completely, partly because discourse has become more aggressive on the internet. For Twitter, neutrality is in itself a partisan stance, because in practice it means you're not moderating speech or interrupting what may be hate speech or threats of violence to others.

Twitter cofounder **Biz Stone** believes that 'everyone has the right to free speech, but not everyone has the right to have their free speech amplified on Twitter.' Twitter was quickly perceived to be synonymous with or to have aligned itself to the American First Amendment. The company leadership had to take a very drastic decision to separate the brand from that.

Working out when your organization needs to ask for help is important, but you also need to consider where the best source of help may be. In Twitter's case there wasn't an authority to turn to, so they had to invest in people who would help them find answers. They called for help not just from their employees and their users, but they also put out requests for proposals from the academic community so that they could take a considered, long-term, evidence-based view on what their role as a public platform should be. Quantitate questions like 'How do you measure the health of online interactions?' hadn't really been posed before in substantive ways and Twitter has invested in finding credible answers to those questions. Thoroughness and the integrity Twitter is bringing to finding credible answers should help people have confidence in the platform and help it continue in a more sustainable way that's less vulnerable to manipulation. **Biz Stone** comments:

> People shy away from taking responsibility, to their detriment. Our employees responded so well to our renewed purpose and it's benefitted every aspect of the company. I think it's going to be absolutely mainstream that companies aren't just in it to make a

profit. They need to provide some societal good on some level, even if it's just a community level. People, especially younger people, won't use your product or service unless they know that your company is standing for something and is taking some responsibility in its role in society.

It's becoming an increasingly important decision-making factor for consumers. On the other side, from my perspective, it's also important in attracting the best talent to our company. The best people, who can command any pay cheque they want, are choosing to work with the company that they know will enable them to be doing societal good in the course of their job. I want to feel good that I'm doing something good.

I make fun of Google's internal mantra of don't be evil. Why don't be evil? Why are they automatically starting on a negative? We can be mean, we could be horrible, we could be terrible, so long as we're not evil. I joked about that and I said, 'Why don't they say be good?' So that's where I want us to be – we're going to be good and we're going to have a positive impact in our community through volunteering, donations and all of those things. It's going to be because it's good business and it feels good and it can attract better people to our company. But one of the things that is so key, you don't just say what you're going to do – you have to do it and then do that over and over again, so people can start to trust you. If you keep saying things and you don't do anything, it just doesn't mean anything.

Confronting the past is difficult – it's hard to know the extent to which we are to blame for the wrongs that are currently happening. Everyone is so quick to apportion blame when things go wrong, which can create a toxic cycle of censure and frustration. As activists, of course, we want to root out what's gone wrong and pursue justice, but creating a culture of accountability is hard, because it means being accountable ourselves. Forever. And with everything that we do.

This may often mean personal sacrifice, like for **Maggie Oliver** – she wasn't responsible for the sexual abuse or the way in which the police and social services disregarded the victims. She wasn't responsible, but she was *accountable*. When you're accountable, you may not have power or control over the situation, but you are not a passive bystander. As the saying goes, the only thing necessary for the triumph of evil is for good men to do nothing.

Whether it was the violence against women and girls who were forced into sexual slavery by the Imperial Japanese Army during WWII or the realization that many countries and families have yet to return Jewish property stolen during the period of Nazi occupation, our era has been in so many ways defined by, or at least informed by, reckoning with aspects of our past that we didn't know about or that we didn't fully understand. Often the privileges people live with in the present are a result of past or ongoing subjugation of other people – this realization can cause awkwardness and shame, which leads to many people trying to avoid the realities of their privilege. To begin to adequately address the issues of the past we need to embrace the true allyship we discussed in chapter four and be honest about how we arrived at the present. Nothing will change unless each person becomes accountable for the part they play in maintaining exploitative power structures.

Fixing things that have been done wrong requires bravery and honesty. You may be at fault. Ultimately, it's better to recognize your fault, to admit with humility where you have gone wrong and what you have to do to change, than to be complicit in something that will often already involve elements of cover-up. Creating a new culture of trust will take time, and it does not have a visible finish line. When things have gone wrong you need to commit yourself to saying and doing the right thing over and over again, until the right thing becomes the new normal.

How to fix something that isn't right checklist

- Prepare for personal sacrifice – while knowing that the greater good you do will outweigh the downside.

- Remember whistle-blowing ultimately protects people and the organization itself by identifying harm and forcing them to take action.

- Get advice from an attorney who has experience in whistle-blowing cases and check out what government protections are available.

- Be aware of a culture of silence – and prepare to tackle this specifically. Create an environment of trust in which people can speak without fear of reprisal. Prepare for it to take time to get people to tell their truth.

- The way the investigation is conducted will set the tone for the implementation of any solution. Make it clear that the truth is being determined – this will make the whole exercise credible and will ultimately affect the solution.

- Bring in external scrutiny or advisors if necessary.

- Understand that people who are part of the problem will not be willing to give up their position even if they know you are right.

- Show that the issue is not confined to the wronged but is an issue for the whole – whether that's a country or a company.

- Identify what will bring people together and create unity going forward.

- Recommit yourself to transparency and honesty – you may continue to make mistakes but you need to be prepared to be vulnerable and admit you need help.

Contributor biographies

Shahidul Alam: Shahidul is a photographer, media activist and director of the award-winning Drik Picture Library in Bangladesh. Shahidul Alam was detained on 5 August 2018 in Dhaka, after demonstrations that began because of the deaths of two school students in a traffic accident before escalating into the widest anti-government protests in years. Shahidul was covering the event as a photojournalist. After more than a hundred days of incarceration, due to intense international pressure, Shahidul was released from prison on 20 November 2018.

Nimco Ali: Nimco is a social activist and co-founder of The Five Foundation and Daughters of Eve, an organization that aims to protect young women at risk in communities that practice female genital mutilation (FGM). Nimco was personally affected by FGM at the age of 7. According to the World Health Organization, more than 200 million girls and women today have been cut in 30 countries. The practice of FGM has also been classified as a human rights violation by WHO.

Josie Badger: Josie founded the I Want to Work campaign in 2016, which advocates for young adults with disabilities in Pennsylvania. The campaign was successful in passing House Bill 400, which provides $18 million in federal funds to enable young people with disabilities to find part-time and summer jobs.

Fatima Bhutto: Fatima is a Pakistani poet and writer. She is the author of several books including *Whispers of the Desert* which she wrote when she was 15 years old. She covered the Israeli invasion and war with Lebanon from within Lebanon during the summer of 2006, reported from within Iran during January 2007 and Cuba during April 2008. Fatima is a long-standing One Young World counsellor.

Lisa Bloom: Lisa is an American civil rights attorney. She is known for representing numerous women who have been victims of sexual harassment and abused by their coworkers and employers. Lisa also founded the Bloom Firm, a civil rights law firm which has represented clients such as Kathy Griffin and Mischa Barton.

Andrew Bragg: Andrew is a Liberal senate candidate for New South Wales, Australia. He is also an author and regularly contributes to the *Australian Financial Review* and the *Daily Telegraph*.

Larry Brilliant: Larry is a pioneering physician and global philanthropist. He is also the Chair of the Skoll Global Threats Fund. The organization aims to confront global threats to human societies – such as climate change, water shortage and disease pandemics. Additionally, Larry is the senior advisor to Jeff Skoll, the founder of the fund. In this role, Larry develops the strategy and approach for the foundation, while also advising Jeff Skoll on ways the organization can drive positive change on urgent social and environmental issues.

Bill Browder: Bill is the founder and CEO of Hermitage Capital Management, an investment fund that was the largest investor in Russia. Bill lobbied for US Congress to pass the Magnitsky Act in 2009. This law punished Russian human rights violators by freezing their assets and bank accounts. The Magnitsky Act was later signed into law in 2012 by President Barack Obama.

Sinéad Burke: Sinéad is a disability activist, educator and a One Young World Ambassador who calls for change in the fashion industry to accommodate for people with disabilities, and greater inclusion for all voices. Sinéad raises awareness through her fashion blog Minnie Melange, amassing more than 15,000 people on Instagram @thesineadburke.

Winnie Byanyima: Winnie is a Ugandan aeronautical engineer, politician and diplomat. She is currently the executive director of Oxfam International. Winnie also co-founded the Global Gender and Climate Alliance, and chaired a UN task force on gender aspects and on climate change. Winnie has also served 11 years in the Ugandan Parliament, served at the African Union Commission, and was the director of the gender team in the Bureau for Development Policy at the United Nations Development Programme (UNDP) in 2006.

Kamolnan Chearavanont: Kamolnan was a delegate speaker for the 2015 Human Rights Plenary Session. Kamolnan started the Voices Organisation in order to help orphans and abused women and children, specifically those who are stateless.

James Chen: James co-founded Clearly in 2016, a global campaign which aims to provide glasses to everyone in the world that needs a pair, regardless of where they live. James founded Vision for a Nation in 2011, an organization with the focus of delivering nationwide eye care across Rwanda. Since the charity was founded, Rwanda has reached nationwide access to eyecare, and over 2 million people have received vision screening.

Cher: Cher is an American singer, actress and the co-founder of Free the Wild. The organization aims to end the suffering of wild animals in captivity and to allow for their release into wildlife sanctuaries. Free the Wild also aims to provide education and support by providing professional carers, handlers and vets to animal captivity establishments. The organization also is working on introducing augmented and virtual reality shows of animals as a replacement for zoos to combat animal trafficking.

Terry Crews: Terry is an American actor, artist, activist and former American football player. He is a public advocate for women's rights and an activist against sexism. He was included among the group of people named as *Time* magazine's Person of the Year 2017 for going public about being sexually assaulted.

Matt Damon, Gary White: Matt and Gary co-founded Water.org, a developmental aid organization which aims to provide aid to regions of developing countries that do not have access to safe drinking water and sanitation. Water.org has transformed more than 17 million lives with access to safe water and sanitation.

Luke Davies: Luke is an office banker with a specialization in fintech, sustainable finance. In 2017, Luke developed and launched the Green Deposit. The Green Deposit allows clients to deposit funds into a Green Account, providing them with the comfort that their balances are being designated towards green projects.

Eh Bee Family: the Eh Bee Family is the funniest family on social media. With Papa Bee and Mama Bee at the helm, they create family-friendly content across all online platforms from Vine to YouTube. The Eh Bee Family has amassed a loyal following of over 18 million followers and over 300 million views per month worldwide. Rossana, or Mama Bee, uses her following and social media influence to promote positive change. Her mission of Love has initiated a foundation, Bee the Change, that funds organizations around the world, promoting the wellbeing and social justice for all people, animals and the environment.

Nicolle Fagan: Nicole co-founded the Palau Legacy Project, an initiative to make tourism more sustainable to protect the natural wildlife and environment in Palau. Part of the campaign has been incorporated into in-flight videos that are shown on every flight that lands in Palau. Through Nicolle's efforts, over 22,000 people have signed the Palau Pledge so far, and the online awareness campaign has reached more than 1.6 billion people globally.

Grace Forrest: Grace is engaged in policy change, activism and dialogue against modern slavery. She co-founded the Walk Free Foundation, an international human rights group with an objective to end slavery, in all its forms, in our lifetime. The foundation successfully campaigned for a national Modern Slavery Act in Australia and in November 2018 Australia passed the world's second federal modern slavery act. That same year Grace won *GQ Australia's* award for Humanitarian of the Year.

Ron Garan: Ron is a former astronaut for NASA, founder of Fragile Oasis, social entrepreneur, humanitarian and author. Fragile Oasis is a grassroots initiative that aims to integrate the shared perspectives of astronauts from different countries and cultures with people on Earth, while promoting space and planetary sciences. Today, Garan bridges his start-up with humanitarian work through his organization Manna Energy Ltd, where the $120 billion carbon market is leveraged to finance humanitarian projects. Ron Garan has served as a counsellor at four different One Young World summits.

David Riveros García: David is the founder of reAcción Paraguay, a grassroots non-profit anti-corruption organization. He is also a founding member of the Global Youth Anti-Corruption Network and is the network development director for the international Youth Ambassadors network. In 2016 David was a consultant at the World Bank documenting the Paraguay component of the Nordic Trust Fund research on citizen participation and human rights. In 2017 David and his NGO led peaceful protests against the former president of Paraguay.

Bob Geldof: Bob is a singer, songwriter, author and political activist. He turned his attention to charity work during the 1984 famine in Ethiopia. Geldof founded the charity Band Aid to raise money for famine relief and, alongside Scottish musician Midge Ure, Bob organized the charity super-concert Live Aid. Today Bob is widely recognized for his activism, particularly his anti-poverty efforts in Africa.

Wael Ghonim: Wael, a marketing manager for Google, shot to international fame in February 2011 as the catalyst behind the anti-government protest movement in Egypt that ultimately led to the resignation of President Hosni Mubarak.

Valeria Gomez Palacios: Valeria is an advocate for refugee and women's rights. Since 2018, she has spoken with officials at the United Nations, UNICEF, the United States Senate Committee on Foreign Relations, the House Committee on Foreign Affairs, and even with the director of Human Rights Watch for the Americas. Through her actions, she was successful in passing both the Nicaraguan Investment Conditionality Act (NICA Act) and the Nicaraguan Human Rights and Anti-Corruption Act of 2018.

Luke Hart: Luke is active in raising awareness and addressing societal issues that lead to domestic abuse and homicide. Luke works heavily with Surrey Police creating materials to raise awareness and deliver training to police officers and the Crown Prosecution Service on coercive control and domestic abuse. Luke is also a White Ribbon Ambassador, in which he speaks out against male violence towards women, and he works closely with many charities such as Refuge and Women's Aid. He is also the co-author, with his brother Ryan Hart, of *Operation Lighthouse*, which details their experience with domestic violence.

Tara Houska: Tara advocates on behalf of the tribal nations, on a range of issues impacting indigenous peoples, at the local and federal levels in the United States. Tara also spent six months living and working in North Dakota fighting the Dakota Access Pipeline. She co-founded Not Your Mascots, a non-profit committed to educating the public about the impacts of stereotyping, and to promoting positive representation of Native Americans. Tara was also on the council of women for the Women's March.

Dame Vivian Hunt: Dame Vivian Hunt is a managing partner for McKinsey & Company's United Kingdom and Ireland offices, and is a senior partner of the firm. She is also a leader within the organization on leadership and diversity. She has spearheaded flagship research connecting diversity to performance. She has also co-authored publications on similar topics such as, 'Women Matter', 'Delivering through Diversity' and 'The Power of Parity: how advancing women's equality can add $12 trillion to global growth'.

Kenny Imafidon: Kenny is the managing director of ClearView Research. He is also the director of Bite The Ballot, an organization with the aim of both developing and executing national campaigns to get young people to register to vote and increase voter turnouts on election days. During the 2014 National Voter Registration Drive in the UK, Kenny helped 2 million millennials register to vote.

Jazz Jennings: Jazz is an American YouTuber, television star and LGBTQ rights activist. Jazz has become one of the leading LGBTQ activists in the United States and has carried the torch for trans children's rights for over a decade.

Colin Kaepernick: Colin is a former football quarterback for the San Francisco 49ers. Colin sparked a wider protest movement, #TakeAKnee, which was intensified after President Donald Trump called for NFL owners to fire players who protest during the National Anthem. Colin was named GQ magazine's Citizen of the Year in 2017. In 2018 he was given the Amnesty International Ambassador of Conscience Award and was awarded the W. E. B. Du Bois Medal by Harvard University.

Rakesh Kapoor: Rakesh is an Indian businessman and CEO of Reckitt Benckiser. The organization is a £10 billion global leader in consumer health and hygiene, including brands such as Dettol, Nurofen, Durex, Vanish and Strepsils. The organization has also taken action along with Save the Children to prevent children dying from diarrhoea, one of the biggest diseases among children under five globally.

Tawakkol Karman: Tawakkol is a Yemeni journalist, politician and human rights activist. Tawakkol co-founded the Woman Journalists Without Chains group in 2005, which aims to promote civil rights and freedom of opinion and expression, as well as democratic rights within Yemen. She also became the international public face of the 2011 Yemeni uprising which was a part of the Arab Spring uprisings.

Cameron Kasky: Cameron is an 18-year-old American activist and a co-founder of the March for Our Lives movement, initiated in 2018 in support of legislation to prevent gun violence. Cameron is also the co-founder of the student-led gun violence prevention advocacy group Never Again.

Doutzen Kroes: Doutzen is a Dutch supermodel, actress and activist. In 2016, she became the global ambassador of #KnotOnMyPlanet, a social media campaign designed to raise awareness and funds for the Elephant Crisis Fund, which uses 100 per cent of all donations to fund over more than 120 programmes to fight poaching and ivory trafficking, while also raising awareness on the African elephant slaughter. Snapchat designed an elephant filter for the launch of the campaign that was used over 300 million times in 24 hours.

Thuli Madonsela: Thuli is a South African advocate and Professor of Law at the University of Stellenbosch. She assisted in drafting the final constitution of South Africa in 1996, and co-developed several laws that aim to strengthen South African democracy. As a strong advocate for gender equality and the advancement of women, Thuli is also co-founder of the South African Women Lawyers Association (SAWLA). She was also a recipient of the Forbes Africa 'Person of the Year 2016' Award, and has been a One Young World Counsellor from 2016-18.

Hussain Manawer: Hussain is a campaigner, social entrepreneur, poet and mental health spokesman. After losing his mother, Hussain began channelling his emotion through poetry, slowly building an online community supporting mental health. Hussain won the Kruger Cowne's Rising Star competition in 2015, after a spoken-word performance surrounding mental health at the One Young World 2015 Bangkok Summit.

DeRay Mckesson: DeRay is an American civil rights activist. He is a supporter of the #blacklivesmatter movement, and he quit his job at Minneapolis Public Schools to commit to the movement full time. In 2015, DeRay and several other activists co-founded and launched Mapping Police Violence, which collected data on people killed by police during 2014. DeRay went on to launch Campaign Zero, a policy plan for police reform.

Bill McKibben: Bill is an American environmentalist, author and journalist who works to counter the impacts of climate change. Bill is the leader of the anti-carbon campaign group, 350.org. Through the organization, Bill has also helped coordinate 5,200 simultaneous demonstrations in over 181 countries.

Kevin Mendez: Kevin is a Belizean social justice activist working on LGBTQ rights and HIV prevention. He is the president and a founding member of the Belize Youth Empowerment for Change (BYEC) organization. Kevin is also an HIV and TB adherence counsellor with the Ministry of Health of Belize.

Gina Miller: Gina is an activist, author and businesswoman who initiated the 2016 R (Miller) v Secretary of State for Exiting the European Union. In June 2016, she challenged the authority of the British Government to invoke Article 50 of the Treaty on European Union. The High Court ruled in her favour.

Jack Monroe: Jack is a British food writer, journalist and activist known for campaigning on poverty issues, particularly hunger relief. Jack rose to fame from her food blog A Girl Called Jack, where she shared cheap recipes she created as a single parent while struggling economically with a young child.

Farai Mubaiwa: Farai is an intersectional African feminist and the founder of the Africa Matters Initiative. Currently the organization has reached over 5,000 people. Farai has also been an analyst for Deloitte South Africa Strategy and Operations Consulting. She was a 2017 Queen's Young Leader for South Africa, and has been a South African ambassador for One Young World since 2017.

Georgette Mulheir: Georgette is the CEO of Lumos, an international children's rights organization founded by J. K. Rowling in 2005. Georgette has over 20 years of experience working with children and families from over 28 countries across the world.

Blake Mycoskie: Blake is an American entrepreneur, author, philanthropist and the founder of Toms Shoes. Toms Shoes have been given to children across 70 countries worldwide, including the United States, Argentina, Ethiopia, Rwanda, Swaziland, Guatemala, Haiti and South Africa. Since founding the organization in 2006, Blake's company currently has extended its product range to include eyewear as well, to provide essential eye care to countries in need. In 2009, Blake and Toms Shoes received the Secretary of State's 2009 Award of Corporate Excellence (ACE).

Kumi Naidoo: Kumi is a South African human rights and environmental activist. He is the acting Secretary General of Amnesty International, and was the first African head of Greenpeace. Kumi was also the founding executive director of the South African National NGO Coalition (SANGOCO), which aims to ensure that the traditions forged during the resistance to apartheid continue to serve the people of South Africa.

Matt O'Connor: Matt is a political activist and the founder of Fathers4Justice. The organization aims to gain public and parliamentary support for changes in UK legislation on fathers' rights. Fathers4Justice does this through using public stunts and protests often done in costume.

Olu Odubajo: Olu is a global consultant striving to achieve social equality for all. Olu was the first mentor selected to be a part of a reverse mentoring programme with the executive committee of KPMG. The programme aims to build an inclusive workforce. Olu is now leading the drive to get black entrepreneurs to apply for the newly founded Black Entrepreneurs Award that he created.

Maggie Oliver: Maggie was one of the key figures in Operation Span, an investigation into the Rochdale sex grooming scandal. Maggie, who was a detective constable, persuaded vulnerable and reluctant girls to give evidence against the paedophiles who had sexually abused them for years.

Yeonmi Park: Yeonmi is an advocate for the human rights of North Koreans oppressed by the North Korean regime. As a defector herself, Yeonmi has co-authored the book *In Order To Live*, recounting her experience. Today, Yeonmi works with multiple refugee organizations and has contributed to the *Washington Post*, *New Focus International* and Freedom Factory. Yeonmi Park was a delegate at the One Young World 2014 Dublin Summit.

Paul Polman: Paul is a Dutch businessman. He was CEO of Unilever, a British-Dutch consumer-goods company, for over ten years. Under his leadership, Unilever has implemented the Sustainable Living Plan, which seeks to double the company's size while reducing its overall environmental footprint and improve its social impact.

Pat Quinn: Pat was diagnosed with amyotrophic lateral sclerosis (ALS) in March 2013. In 2014, Pat co-founded the popular social media campaign known as the ALS Ice Bucket Challenge to raise awareness. The videos were posted on social media and attracted people like Bill Gates, Mark Zuckerberg and Oprah to accept the challenge. The campaign raised 220 million dollars for research. In 2014, *Time* magazine nominated Pat for their Popular Person of the Year Award.

Sir Ken Robinson: Sir Ken is a British author, speaker and international advisor on education to governments and non-profits. Ken is also an advocator for education reform, as he believes that the system has failed students. Ken has led national and international projects on creative and cultural education across the UK, Europe, Asia and the United States. Recently, Ken was also awarded the Nelson Mandela Changemaker Award in 2019 for his 'exemplary work and global impact'.

Mary Robinson: Mary is the former and first female President of Ireland. She subsequently served as UN High Commissioner for Human Rights from 1997 to 2002. Today she is the president of the Mary Robinson Foundation. She is a relentless advocate for climate justice. In 2016, the UN Secretary-General appointed Mary Robinson as a Special Envoy on El Niño and Climate. She has been the recipient of numerous honours including the Presidential Medal of Freedom from President Obama. She has served as a counsellor in One Young World Summits since 2014.

Simon Rodgers: Simon was a delegate speaker for the human rights plenary at One Young World in 2012, where he discussed the plight of the LGBTQ community and received a standing ovation after revealing the slogan on his shirt, 'Some People Are Gay. Get Over It.' He held the position of Chair of Aviva Pride for many years, until being appointed Head of Diversity and Inclusion. Simon now runs his own consultancy, specializing in developing diversity and inclusion strategies and initiatives across a range of workplaces.

Juan Manuel Santos: Juan Manuel was the president of Colombia from 2010 to 2018. In 2016, President Santos was the recipient of the Nobel Peace Prize for his efforts to end the conflict with the Marxist guerrilla organization FARC. During the majority of his career, Santos sought to eliminate terrorism and bring prosperity to Columbia by promoting economic growth. Santos attended One Young World Bogotá 2017, where he opened the summit.

Reshma Saujani: Reshma is the founder of Girls Who Code, an organization that aims to support and increase the number of women in the computer science sector. Girls Who Code is working to close the gender employment gap in technology and reshape the image of what a programmer should looks like. The organization has already reached over 90,000 girls across all 50 states in the US. Reshma has a goal of accruing 1 million woman in the computer science sector by 2020.

Elio Leoni Sceti: Elio is the founder and chief crafter at The Craftory, the first investment house for mission-driven challenger brands. The organization focuses on investing in brands that have re-prioritized their company missions for positive change. Elio is also a trustee and counsellor for One Young World, in addition to being an advisory board member for Room to Read. Room to Read is a global organization that focuses on literacy and gender equality in education across developing nations. Since being founded in 2000, the organization has supported over 16 million children throughout 30,000 communities.

Satta F Sheriff: Satta founded the Youth in Action for Peace and Empowerment (YAPE) in Liberia in 2016. In 2018, YAPE launched a national campaign to fight the Liberian senate's decision to amend the New Rape Law of Liberia, which would weaken the law against rape. In 2019, she initiated the WeSay project, a call centre and online platform which provides information on all sexual gender-based violence across each county in Liberia. Through her efforts Satta has positively impacted over 25,000 adults, children and girls across the country.

Jack Sim: Jack is the founder of the World Toilet Organization (WTO), which aims to grow the global sanitation movement. The WTO founded the World Toilet College in 2005, which has trained four thousand people on safe and clean sanitation since its establishment. Through Sim's initiative, World Toilet Day has been officially established and is endorsed by the United Nations for observance. In 2004, Sim was the winner of the Singapore Green Plan Award 2012 and, in 2018, he was awarded the Luxembourg Peace Prize for Outstanding Peace Activist.

Senator Murray Sinclair: Senator Sinclair was appointed to the Canadian Senate in 2016. He was previously appointed the first Aboriginal judge in Manitoba and

Canada's second from 1988 to 2009. Senator Sinclair is a First Nations lawyer as well, known for his representation of indigenous people and knowledge of Aboriginal law. He also served as chairman of the Indian Residential Schools Truth and Reconciliation Commission (TRC) from 2009 to 2015.

Biz Stone: Biz is an American entrepreneur and co-founder of Twitter. He has been honoured with the International Center for Journalist Innovation Award, and has also been recognized as one of the 100 Most Influential People in the World.

Carole Stone: Carole is the former producer of BBC Radio 4's *Any Questions?* In 2007, Carole became the managing director of YouGovStone, a joint venture with the global market research company YouGov. In her role, Carole established the YouGovStone think tank, a global panel of over 5,000 leaders from a range of fields. Currently Carole works with the YouGov-Cambridge Centre, which brings academic and polling experts together to collaborate on public policy research.

Mark Tewksbury: Mark is a former Canadian competitive swimmer, gold medal Olympian and an LGBTQ advocate. At the forefront of advocacy, Mark spoke at the UN on LGBTQ issues in 2008 and is one of the few openly gay Olympic champions in the world. He is currently the chair of Special Olympics Canada, and sits on the board of the Canadian Olympic Committee.

Hannah Rose Thomas: Hannah is a humanitarian and an artist, who has organized multiple art projects with international agencies within the Middle East, bringing awareness to the refugee crisis. Her most recent project has been with survivors of Boko Haram and Fulani violence in Northern Nigeria. Hannah has been selected for the Forbes 30 Under 30 2019 and is a recipient of the European Women of the Year Award 2019.

Mina Tolu: Mina is a Maltese activist striving to raise awareness for transgender rights and gender equality. Mina has been a part of the executive board of IGLYO, the International LGBTQI Youth and Student Organization. Since 2015, Mina has also worked for Transgender Europe, a European human rights network that strives for the human rights and equality for all trans people in Europe.

Minnijean Brown-Trickey: Minnijean is an African-American civil rights activist. She was one of nine African-American students, later known as the Little Rock Nine. Minnijean has been awarded the Congressional Gold Medal, the Wolf Award and the Spingarn Medal.

Laura Ulloa: Laura has worked for the UNSC in New York, and currently serves as a coordinator for social projects at the Corona Foundation in Colombia. At 11 years old, Ulloa was kidnapped and held captive by FARC rebels for 7 months. Today, Ulloa works with the very people that captured her, to highlight that reformed rebels have trades and talents that can replace weapons and warfare. Laura was a delegate speaker at the One Young World 2018 The Hague Summit.

Kevin Watkins: Kevin has been the CEO of Save the Children UK since 2016. By working with families and their children during early life development stages, Save the Children UK aims to ensure these children can reach their full potential.

Emma Watson: Emma is a British actor, humanitarian and social justice activist. In 2014, she was appointed Global Goodwill Ambassador for UN Women, and became a leading advocate for the #HeforShe movement. The movement calls for men and people of all genders to stand in solidarity with women to create an equal world. Emma has supported international movements against gender-based violence, including #MeToo, which calls for an end to sexual violence and for support for survivors. She is also a part of TIME'S UP, a movement against sexual harassment and inequality which campaigns for safety and equity in the workplace for all genders. In 2018, Emma donated £1million towards the Justice and Equality Fund, a fund developed in partnership with TIME'S UP UK and women's rights organisations. The fund aims to challenge sexual harassment, assault and discrimination across all industries and sections of society by resourcing an expert network of advice and support. At the time, Emma's donation alone brought the organization half way to achieving its initial goal of raising £2million. In 2019 she was invited by President Macron to sit on the G7's advisory Gender Equality Council.

Steve Waugh AO: Steve is Australia's most successful and loved Cricket Test Captain. The Steve Waugh Foundation takes a holistic approach to supporting children and young adults (0–25yrs) with the rarest diseases. In 2003, Steve was awarded the Order of Australia for his services to both cricket and charity.

Joshua Wong: Joshua is a Hong Kong student activist and politician, who serves as secretary-general of the pro-democracy party Demosisto. Joshua gained international recognition at the age of 17, after he played a critical role in the 2014 Umbrella Movement which was in protest of the Chinese government.

Edith Yassin: Edith is the former Chairperson of the Strategic Team of BringBackOurGirls. In 2014 alone the hashtag #BringBackOurGirls was used on Twitter over 3.3 million times. The campaign received much celebrity involvement including Malala Yousafzai, First Lady Michelle Obama and Ellen Degeneres.

Professor Muhammad Yunus: Professor Yunus is a Bangladeshi banker and economist who developed the concept of microcredit. He is also the founder of the Grameen Bank. In 2006, Yunus and the bank were jointly awarded the Nobel Peace Prize. Yunus has received several other national and international honours. Yunus served on the board of directors of the United Nations Foundation and has served as a counsellor at One Young World summits since 2010.

Fatima Zaman: Fatima is a next-generation counter-extremist and advocate for social justice. Fatima was recognized as a 'Future Shaper' at the *Marie Claire* Future Shapers Awards 2017 for her work in countering and preventing violent extremism.

Index

Acknowledgements

The nature of a book such as this means that we owe a debt of gratitude to a whole community who have put in tremendous effort in order to bring together such a diverse range of stories and examples.

The biggest thanks has to go to our researcher Arietta Valmas who became interview scheduler-in-chief, liaising across almost every single time-zone in order to ensure we could make this book a truly global testament to the power of activism. Arietta's dedication to ensuring our footnotes were correct and the transcripts were accurate was the glue that held this book together. Thank you so much Arietta, we couldn't have done it without you.

Our Commissioning Editor, Romilly Morgan at Octopus, has been the driving force behind this book. Her vision for how we could help more people feel empowered to make a difference has allowed the book to take shape. We are so grateful for your support and guidance. A huge thanks also to the incredible team of Megan Brown, Pauline Bache, Jack Storey and especially Sophie Elletson, who have all worked so hard and given us so much help.

We owe a huge debt of gratitude to our incredible agent Zoe King who helped us develop the concept of the book and introduced us to the world of publishing. Zoe is the best agent we could have ever hoped to work with and has been phenomenally kind and creative. It's been such a privilege for us to write our first book with her support.

One Young World Staff

The whole One Young World team has helped in some way with the book, especially Mitchell Antonio Cohen, Kathryn Kirk, Lucy Lu and Anna Taylor.

We are blessed to work with such an incredible team including Sezar Alkassab, Daniel Amazigo, Alex Belotti, Matthew Belshaw, Safoora Bigliari, Megan Blanche Downey, Keith Bremner, Anupama Roy Choudhury, Mitchell Antonio Cohen, Adrien Couderc, Tessa Daling, Chris Day, Claire Dobson, Fiona Doyle, Julien Ferrere, Amy Ford, David Gereda Cardona, Carlota Gomez Tapia, Millicent Emily Hodgkinson, Angélica Huffstot, Fathma Khalid, Stefan Kovacevic, Karen Lacey, Daniel Maunder, Hannah Nagar, Anais Nee, Abigail Parkin, Scott Ralston, Simon Rodgers, Mara Silvestri, Abigail Slade, Stephanie Son, Anna Taylor, Arietta Valmas, Cathy Watts, Tristan Weller.

Thanks also to the One Young World Trustees Jonathan Mitchell and Elio Leoni-Sceti and to Nick Giles and the fabulous team at Seven Hills. We also thank Alan Doss and Mrs Annan of the Kofi Annan foundation for allowing us to share some of Kofi Annan's sage advice and wisdom with our readers.

Kate's Co-Founder, David, Jones has been incredibly supportive of this book and of the two of us – we are very lucky to work with so closely with someone who is himself an activist for women's employment and a brilliant visionary of the nexus in brand marketing and technology.

Contributors in the book:

We have been amazingly blessed to have the opportunity to interview the following people and include their work in the book: Shahidul Alam, Nimco Ali, Josie Badger, Mama and Papa Bee, Fatima Bhutto, Lisa Bloom, Andrew Bragg, Larry Brilliant, Bill Browder, Minnijean Brown Trickey, Sinead Burke, Winnie Byanyima, Kamolnan Chearavanont, James Chen, Cher, Terry Crews, Matt Damon, Luke Davies, Nicolle Fagan, Grace Forrest, Ron Garan, David Riveros Garcia, Bob Geldof, Wael Ghonim, Luke Hart, Tara Houska, Dame Vivian Hunt, Kenny Imafidon, Jazz Jennings, Colin Kaepernick, Rakesh Kapoor, Tawwakol Karman, Cameron Kasky, Doutzen Kroes, Thuli Madonsela , Hussain Manawer, DeRay Mckesson, Bill McKibben, Kevin Mendez, Gina Miller, Jack Monroe, Farai Mubaiwa , Georgette Mulheir, Blake Mycoskie, Kumi Naidoo, Matt O'Connor, Olu Odubajo, Maggie Oliver, Valeria Gomez Palacios, Yeonmi Park, Paul Polman, Pat Quinn, Mary Robinson , Sir Ken Robinson, Simon Rodgers, Juan Manuel Santos, Elio Leoni Sceti, Satta F Sheriff, Jack Sim, Senator Sinclair, Biz Stone, Carole Stone, Reshma Saujani , Mark Tewksbury, Hannah Rose Thomas, Mina Tolu, Laura Ulloa, Kevin Watkins, Emma Watson, Steve Waugh, Gary White, Joshua Wong, Edith Yassin, Professor Muhammad Yunus, Fatima Zaman.

We were unable to include contributions from the following people this time around but are so grateful for their time and wisdom: Cecilia Aransiola, Amir Ashour, Zarli Aye, Ousmane Ba, Aminetou Bilal, Dianne Constantinides, James Da Costa, Madhav Datt, Daniel Duque, Jasminko Hallovic, Vibin Joseph, William Kovacs, Jason Moyer Lee, Jemima Lovatt, Tamika Mallory, Yasmeen Mjiali, Olivier Noel, Hyppolite Ntigurirwa, Spandana Palaypu, Juan Jose Rojas, Anthony Ford Shubrook, Cheick Traore, Thinzar Shunlei Yi, George Zeidan.

Thank you all for meeting us, sharing with us and trusting us with your stories. We had roughly 500,000 words of interview transcripts to weave into a book and we tried to ensure that the quotes that were included were as representative of this incredible community as possible.

To all of the One Young World Ambassadors, counsellors, volunteers and supporters – thank you for enabling us to work on something we care about so deeply. We are so proud to be bringing the stories of the One Young World community to the wider public.

To our friends and family who have cheered us on and tolerated the late nights and deadline frenzies – we couldn't have done it without you. Bruce and Josh, you are our rocks – we are the luckiest women in the world.

About One Young World

Every year One Young World convenes thousands of activists to work together to tackle the globe's most pressing issues, from climate change to conflict resolution.

One Young World is actively supported by a distinguished line-up of counsellors, including Kofi Annan, Bill Clinton, President Mary Robinson, Juan Manuel Santos, Bob Geldof, Archbishop Desmond Tutu, Emma Watson, Meghan Markle and Muhammad Yunus. Counsellors work alongside delegates at the global Summits, sharing their collective experience in creating positive social change.

Since the first Summit in 2010, One Young World has built a network of 10,000+ Ambassadors, whose projects have gone on to benefit more than 20 million people worldwide. Ambassadors include Olympic champion sprinter Kirani James, North Korean defector Yeonmi Park, social media philanthropist Jerome Jarre, Nobel Peace Prize nominees Jaha Dukureh and Amanda Nguyen, mental health activist Hussain Manawer, and Lauren Bush, founder of FEED.

KAMOLNAN CHEARAVANONT

MATT DAMON

RON GARAN

JUAN MANUEL SANTOS

RESHMA SAUJANI

ELIO LEONI SCETI

FATIMA ZAMAN

JOSHUA WONG

SATTA F SHERIFF

JACK MONROE

JAMES CHEN

ANDREW BRAGG

GEORGETTE MULHEIR

WAEL GHONIM

HANNAH ROSE THOMAS

EDITH YASSIN

MAGGIE OLIVER

LAURA ULLOA

BILL MCKIBBEN

HUSSAIN MANAWER

LUKE DAVIES

MARK TEWKSBURY

SENATOR SINCLAIR

RAKESH KAPOOR

VALERIA GOMEZ PALACIOS

PROFESSOR YUNUS

JOSIE BADGER

DAVID RIVEROS GARCÍA

FARAI MUBAIWA

LARRY BRILLIANT

BILL BROWDER

BIZ STONE

GRACE FORREST

MATT O'CONNOR

CHER

GARY WHITE